Controlling Foodservice Costs

Second Edition

PEARSON

Boston   Columbus   Indianapolis   New York   San Francisco   Upper Saddle River
Amsterdam   Cape Town   Dubai   London   Madrid   Milan   Munich   Paris   Montréal   Toronto
Delhi   Mexico City   São Paulo   Sydney   Hong Kong   Seoul   Singapore   Taipei   Tokyo

Pearson

Editorial Director: Vernon R. Anthony
Executive Acquisitions Editor: Alli Gentile
NRA Product Development: Randall Towns and
 Todd Schlender
Senior Managing Editor: JoEllen Gohr
Associate Managing Editor: Alexandrina B. Wolf
Senior Operations Supervisor: Pat Tonneman
Senior Operations Specialist: Deidra Skahill
Cover photo: iStockPhoto/Thinkstock

Cover design: Karen Steinberg, Element LLC
Director of Marketing: David Gesell
Marketing Coordinator: Les Roberts
Full-Service Project Management: Barbara Hawk and
 Kevin J. Gray, Element LLC
Text and Cover Printer/Binder: R.R. Donnelley and
 Sons/Menasha
Text Font: Minion Pro, Myriad Pro Semicondensed

Photography Credits

Front matter: i iStockPhoto/Thinkstock; vii (left) Suhendri Utet/Dreamstime; (right) Meryll/Dreamstime;
viii (top) Mtr/Dreamstime; (bottom) Stratum/Dreamstime; ix (bottom left) Aprescindere/Dreamstime;
xv (bottom left) Petar Neychev/Dreamstime; 85, 113, 201, 280, 281 Nikada/iStockPhoto

All other photographs owned or acquired by the National Restaurant Association Educational Foundation, NRAEF

10 9 8 7 6 5 4 3 2 1

ISBN-10:   0-13-217527-4
ISBN-13: 978-0-13-217527-2

ISBN-10:   0-13-272484-7
ISBN-13: 978-0-13-272484-5

Contents in Brief

Contents

About the National Restaurant Association and the National Restaurant Association Educational Foundation

Founded in 1919, the National Restaurant Association (NRA) is the leading business association for the restaurant and foodservice industry, which comprises 960,000 restaurant and foodservice outlets and a workforce of nearly 13 million employees. We represent the industry in Washington, DC, and advocate on its behalf. We operate the industry's largest trade show (NRA Show, restaurant.org/show); leading food safety training and certification program (ServSafe, servsafe.com); unique career-building high school program (the NRAEF's *ProStart*, prostart.restaurant.org); as well as the *Kids LiveWell* program (restaurant.org/kidslivewell) promoting healthful kids' menu options. For more information, visit www.restaurant.org and find us on Twitter *@WeRRestaurants*, *Facebook*, and *YouTube*.

With the first job experience of one in four U.S. adults occurring in a restaurant or foodservice operation, the industry is uniquely attractive among American industries for entry-level jobs, personal development and growth, employee and manager career paths, and ownership and wealth creation. That is why the National Restaurant Association Educational Foundation (nraef.org), the philanthropic foundation of the NRA, furthers the education of tomorrow's restaurant and foodservice industry professionals and plays a key role in promoting job and career opportunities in the industry by allocating millions of dollars a year toward industry scholarships and educational programs. The NRA works to ensure the most qualified and passionate people enter the industry so that we can better meet the needs of our members and the patrons and clients they serve.

What Is the ManageFirst Program?

The ManageFirst Program is a management training certificate program that exemplifies our commitment to developing materials by the industry, for the industry. The program's

EXAM TOPICS

ManageFirst Core Credential Topics

Hospitality and Restaurant Management
Controlling Foodservice Costs
Hospitality Human Resources Management and Supervision
ServSafe® Food Safety

ManageFirst Foundation Topics

Customer Service
Principles of Food and Beverage Management
Purchasing
Hospitality Accounting
Bar and Beverage Management
Nutrition
Hospitality and Restaurant Marketing
ServSafe Alcohol® Responsible Alcohol Service

most powerful strength is that it is based on a set of competencies defined by the restaurant and foodservice industry as critical for success. The program teaches the skills truly valued by industry professionals.

ManageFirst Program Components

The ManageFirst Program includes a set of books, exams, instructor resources, certificates, a new credential, and support activities and services. By participating in the program, you are demonstrating your commitment to becoming a highly qualified professional either preparing to begin or to advance your career in the restaurant, hospitality, and foodservice industry.

These books cover the range of topics listed in the chart above. You will find the essential content for the topic as defined by industry, as well as learning activities, assessments, case studies, suggested field projects, professional profiles, and testimonials. The exam can be administered either online or in a paper-and-pencil format (see inside front cover for a listing of ISBNs), and it will be proctored. Upon successfully passing the exam, you will be furnished with a customized certificate by the National Restaurant Association. The certificate is a lasting recognition of your accomplishment and a signal to the industry that you have mastered the competencies covered within the particular topic.

To earn this credential, you will be required to pass four core exams and one foundation exam (to be chosen from the remaining program topics) and to document your work experience in the restaurant and foodservice industry. Earning the ManageFirst credential is a significant accomplishment.

We applaud you as you either begin or advance your career in the restaurant, hospitality, and foodservice industry. Visit www.nraef.org to learn about additional career-building resources offered by the NRAEF, including scholarships for college students enrolled in relevant industry programs.

MANAGEFIRST PROGRAM ORDERING INFORMATION

Review copies or support materials

FACULTY FIELD SERVICES
Tel: 800.526.0485

Domestic orders and inquiries

PEARSON CUSTOMER SERVICE
Tel: 800.922.0579
http://www.pearsonhighered.com/

International orders and inquiries

U.S. EXPORT SALES OFFICE
Pearson Education International Customer Service Group
200 Old Tappan Road
Old Tappan, NJ 07675 USA
Tel: 201.767.5021
Fax: 201.767.5625

For corporate, government, and special sales (consultants, corporations, training centers, VARs, and corporate resellers) orders and inquiries

PEARSON CORPORATE SALES
Tel: 317.428.3411
Fax: 317.428.3343
Email: *managefirst@prenhall.com*

For additional information regarding other Pearson publications, instructor and student support materials, locating your sales representative, and much more, please visit *www.pearsonhighered.com/managefirst*.

Acknowledgements

The National Restaurant Association is grateful for the significant contributions made to this book by the following individuals.

Mike Amos
Perkins & Marie Callender's Inc.

Steve Belt
Monical's Pizza

Heather Kane Haberer
Carrols Restaurant Group

Erika Hoover
Monical's Pizza Corp.

Jared Kulka
Red Robin Gourmet Burgers

Tony C. Merritt
Carrols Restaurant Group

H. George Neil
Buffalo Wild Wings

Marci Noguiera
Sodexo—Education Division

Ryan Nowicki
Dave & Busters

Penny Ann Lord Prichard
Wake Tech/NC Community College

Michael Santos
Micatrotto Restaurant Group

Heather Thitoff
Cameron Mitchell Restaurants

Features of the ManageFirst books

We have designed the ManageFirst books to enhance your ability to learn and retain important information that is critical to this restaurant and foodservice industry function. Here are the key features you will find within this book.

BEGINNING EACH BOOK

Real Manager

This is your opportunity to meet a professional who is currently working in the field associated with the book's topic. This person's story will help you gain insight into the responsibilities related to his or her position, as well as the training and educational history linked to it. You will also see the daily and cumulative impact this position has on an operation, and receive advice from a person who has successfully met the challenges of being a manager.

BEGINNING EACH CHAPTER

Inside This Chapter

Chapter content is organized under these major headings.

Learning Objectives

Learning objectives identify what you should be able to do after completing each chapter. These objectives are linked to the required tasks a manager must be able to perform in relation to the function discussed in the book.

Case Study

Each chapter begins with a brief story about the kind of situations that a manager may encounter in the course of his or her work. The story is followed by one or two questions to prompt student discussions about the topics contained within the chapter.

Key Terms

These terms are important for thorough understanding of the chapter's content. They are highlighted throughout the chapter, where they are explicitly defined or their meaning is made clear within the paragraphs in which they appear.

THROUGHOUT EACH CHAPTER

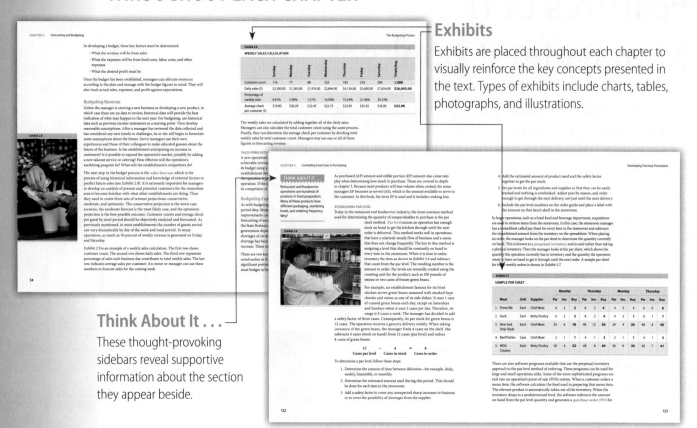

Exhibits

Exhibits are placed throughout each chapter to visually reinforce the key concepts presented in the text. Types of exhibits include charts, tables, photographs, and illustrations.

Think About It . . .

These thought-provoking sidebars reveal supportive information about the section they appear beside.

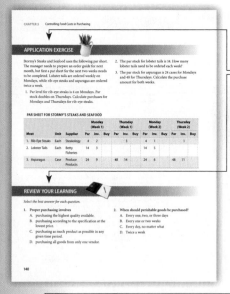

AT THE END OF EACH CHAPTER

Application Exercises and Review Your Learning

These multiple-choice or open- or close-ended questions or problems are designed to test your knowledge of the concepts presented in the chapter. These questions have been aligned with the objectives and should provide you with an opportunity to practice or apply the content that supports these objectives. If you have difficulty answering the Review Your Learning questions, you should review the content further.

AT THE END OF THE BOOK

Field Project

This real-world project gives you the valuable opportunity to apply many of the concepts you will learn in a competency guide. You will interact with industry practitioners, enhance your knowledge, and research, apply, analyze, evaluate, and report on your findings. It will provide you with an in-depth "reality check" of the policies and practices of this management function.

David Ivey-Soto, MBA, CEC, CCA

President

OnSite Culinary Solutions

REAL MANAGER

Philosophy: **Failure—and learning from it—is the best way to create success. Only through risk can one advance. It is important to take risks; it is important to develop relationships; it is important to share. It is from these experiences that one learns and succeeds.**

MY BACKGROUND

I grew up mostly in Los Angeles County, California. Being the son of two academics, we traveled a fair amount while growing up. While I was born in Brooklyn, New York, we had stints in Naperville, Illinois; Cuernavaca, Morelia, Mexico; and San José, Costa Rica in addition to the two times we lived in Southern California. During my high school years, I studied in Spain and France on exchange programs.

I worked as a server-buser during my high school years, but that was a casual job. Then I worked as a server while in college. There I learned that it was about sales. The more sales I made, the more money I made. Overall, I learned that the restaurant and foodservice business was just that—a business. It is important to give the guests a place where they want to go and spend time; additionally, it is important to get them to spend their money there and come back to spend more money again.

After working a few years as a server and then a trainer, I realized that I enjoyed this industry and was good at it. Making a bold move, I ventured off to the Caribbean (not knowing anyone there!) and embraced the opportunity to learn and grow in the industry. I took a chance—bought a one-way ticket to St. Thomas, U.S. Virgin Islands, without a job or a place to live. Within two days, I had three jobs.

The first time I was in St. Thomas, I was there for about two and a half years. I then went back for another year. I also spent time in San Juan, Puerto Rico; Castries, St. Lucia; Georgetown, Guyana (actually in South America but part of CARICOM, the Caribbean Community); and Roseau, Dominica. Altogether, I spent about five or six years in the Caribbean. I came back to the United States for more experience and to go to school at the Culinary Institute of America.

David Ivey-Soto

MY CAREER PATH

As a server, I learned that it was important not to waste time and energy on activities that did not generate more sales and, therefore, tips! As a manager, I realized that I could offer fun promotions and make changes only if I made money from doing them. As a chef, I learned that I could not ask for new equipment and take on new concepts and activities if I did not clear enough money within normal operations.

Something I always think about: **Flexibility is critical. It is important to make changes in the operation to respond to both challenges and opportunities. Modifications to the menu, pricing, scheduling, promotions, and other strategies need to be made accordingly.**

As a server, manager, chef, trainer, and consultant, I have learned the value of controlling costs. Quite frankly, all jobs and roles in the restaurant and foodservice industry must participate in controlling costs. It is an area in which many in the industry do not focus enough attention. I often share this: "It is not hard for someone to give you a kitchen to use; it will be taken away if you cannot make money. You can keep using it as long as you make money."

Remember: **The cost is not the issue if one provides value. By providing value and being able to charge for it, profits will be made. There is a careful balance between cost savings and cost prudence. At the end, perceived value—the price that someone will pay—is the goal to achieve. Taking food, service, ambience, and other components of the experience up a notch allows for charging more. Costs are juxtaposed to the revenue. It is important to focus on the potential revenue and the value-added activities that enhance the overall value.**

WHAT DOES THE FUTURE HOLD?

Controlling restaurant and foodservice costs is the core business aspect of the industry. Without the business aspect, the industry can't survive. The innovations in cuisine, beverage, service, and other aspects of the "entertainment" part of this industry are made possible only through controlling costs.

MY ADVICE TO YOU

My advice to you is threefold:

1. Be willing to make mistakes. The best way to make money is to make mistakes from which you can learn how to make the correct decisions.
2. Controlling costs is about selling for a worthwhile price while purchasing in a manner that is sensible.
3. Higher upfront costs can save money in the long-run if those costs take into account efficiency. This is particularly true with equipment from small wares to heavy equipment.

1

The Importance of Cost Control

INSIDE THIS CHAPTER

- The Relationship between Cost and Profitability
- The Manager's Role in Cost Control
- Types of Costs
- The Importance of Prime Cost
- The Cost Control Process

CHAPTER LEARNING OBJECTIVES

After completing this chapter, you should be able to:

- Explain how restaurant and foodservice costs affect profitability.

- Describe the manager's role in cost control.

- Identify the types of costs incurred by restaurant and foodservice operations.

- Explain the importance of controlling prime cost.

- Explain the basic restaurant or foodservice cost control process.

Part ÷ Whole = %

KEY TERMS

controllable cost, p. 5	line item review, p. 14	quality standard, p. 12
controls, p. 11	loss, p. 4	quantity standard, p. 12
corrective action, p. 15	noncontrollable cost, p. 5	sales, p. 4
cost structure, p. 4	operational standard, p. 10	semivariable cost, p. 5
cover, p. 11	prime cost, p. 9	variable cost, p. 5
fixed cost, p. 5	profit, p. 4	variance, p. 14

CASE STUDY

Susan and her business partner Ryan sat at the kitchen table. They were reviewing a franchise agreement, discussing the pros and cons of opening up a franchise restaurant.

Susan waved at the pile of papers and said, "look, if we open up a franchise, we have to do everything their way. We have to run the front of the house their way. We have to cook only items on THEIR menu exactly the way they tell us to. We won't have any chance to be creative and try out new ideas."

Ryan replied, "But that's the whole point! The guys running the chain have already figured out what works. People go to these restaurants because they know exactly what they're going to get. The whole point behind all of those rules is to make sure that we give the customers a consistent product. Plus, we know what we're getting in to. We have an idea of what our labor and food costs will be going in to this. There's a lot less guessing."

"I hear you," said Susan. "But I'm pretty sure we can figure out how to make a good product and control our costs running an independent operation."

1. How can standardization and consistency help managers control restaurant and foodservice operating expenses?

2. What are the benefits of product consistency for customers and for managers?

THE RELATIONSHIP BETWEEN COST AND PROFITABILITY

Restaurant and foodservice management involves thousands of details, and each of these details can affect the overall performance of the operation. This is especially true in the area of controlling costs. It is not uncommon for busy high-volume operations to have very narrow returns and even losses due to a lack of proper cost controls. Cost control alone, however, is not enough to ensure success in the restaurant and foodservice industry.

It is important for any operation, especially restaurant and foodservice operations, to continuously monitor and control its costs of operations. These costs include production and service costs such as food cost, labor costs, utilities, and marketing. Fierce competition in the restaurant and foodservice industry makes it very difficult to pass increased costs along to the customer.

The average establishment shows a very small profit, and the difference between the bottom line of a financially successful operation and that of a failed business is only around 3 or 4 percent. Considering the rising costs of food and labor, profitability is extremely challenging.

While cost is not the only consideration in profitability, the awareness and focus on costs, together with sound pricing and other operational strategies, helps managers make the connection between costs and profitability. **Profit** is what remains after all expenses are paid. It is figured by subtracting total expenses and food cost from **sales**, the dollar amount the establishment has taken in for food and beverages. Sales must exceed costs for an operation to stay profitable. Conversely, an operation experiences a **loss** when its expenses are greater than its sales.

The basic profit can be expressed as follows:

$$\textbf{Sales} - \textbf{Expenses} = \textbf{Profits}$$

In this equation, the balance of sales and expenses means the difference between profits and losses. If sales are greater than (>) expenses, then a company turns a profit. If sales are less than (<) expenses, then a company experiences a loss. Using resources to generate profits is, after all, the reason for being in business. The resources available to a manager to meet profit goals include employees, food and beverage commodities, and facilities, among others.

As a business grows, managers must continuously evaluate how that growth impacts the **cost structure**, or the proportion or percentage of expense items to sales. Managers must also evaluate whether or not profits are maintained or increased. The expenses that are tracked by managers include items such as labor, food cost, promotion, and rent. Managers need to decide how much of the profits can be invested back into the business for more growth.

THE MANAGER'S ROLE IN COST CONTROL

For any business, particularly restaurant or foodservice operations, the process of cost control has to take place on a day-to-day basis (see *Exhibit 1.1*). The management team must make a commitment to incorporate daily, weekly, and periodic routines to control costs. These involve monitoring and decision making, and represent one of managers' primary responsibilities. Focusing on cost management facilitates profitability, supports development of strategic menu pricing, allows improved financial analysis, and maintains growth.

In most restaurant or foodservice operations, managers take personal charge of an operation's cost control process. However, the size and scope of an operation will determine the extent to which its managers exercise direct control or delegate that responsibility to other staff. Regardless of the type of operation, managers must fully understand all the costs associated with running the business in order to be effective. Cost control is not something that can be done once and followed up only occasionally. Consistency is imperative.

The restaurant and foodservice industry requires managers to plan effectively, manage costs more efficiently, and increase profits. There are many kinds of tools and reports available to help an operation do just that. These include daily sales records, sales forecasts, and expense reports, among other tools. So what numbers should the management team track regularly and consistently? Basically, managers pay the most attention to the three key numbers: generated sales, costs incurred to produce these sales, and profits. As mentioned earlier, profits are the difference between sales and expenses. This book addresses how to manage the numbers and control costs, which should result in increased profits.

TYPES OF COSTS

Many different types of costs are involved when running a restaurant or foodservice operation. Managers can classify these costs in different ways. The most common classifications are as follows:

- **Fixed costs:** Fixed costs are those costs that remain the same regardless of sales volume.

- **Variable costs:** Variable costs are costs that increase and decrease in direct proportion to sales.

- **Semivariable costs:** Semivariable costs are costs that increase and decrease as sales increase and decrease but not in direct proportion.

- **Controllable costs:** Controllable costs are costs that the manager can directly control.

- **Noncontrollable costs:** Noncontrollable costs are costs over which the manager has little or no control.

Exhibit 1.1

OPEN FOR BUSINESS

MANAGER'S MATH

An establishment serves on average 165 meals per day and operates 360 days a year. Although business was brisk, the manager was concerned that the level of profit was very low. Therefore, the manager implemented a waste control program in the kitchen and reduced food cost expenses by $0.15 per customer.

1. What is the total cost savings for this establishment?

2. What would be the total cost savings if the manager was able to find a way to reduce costs by an additional $0.10 per customer?

(Answers: 1. 165 × 360 × $0.15 = $8,910; 2. 165 × 360 × $.25 = $14,850)

WHAT'S THE FOOTPRINT?

At one time, serving water to each guest upon arrival in an establishment was not only customary but also was simply a standard operating procedure (SOP) for many operations. Serving water was just like placing silverware and napkins on a table for guests' use. The rising cost of water and energy has caused many operations to revisit this procedure. As a result, many establishments have implemented a policy of serving water on request.

Is this wise operationally? How can it affect customer satisfaction? How else can an operation conserve water and energy and reduce waste?

Exhibit 1.2

The reason for classifying costs is to differentiate between the costs that managers can control and the ones they cannot control. Identifying and understanding different types of costs helps managers interpret cost-related information and make control-related decisions. For example, does a cost increase or decrease along with sales or does the cost remain the same regardless of volume?

Fixed Costs

Fixed costs are those costs that remain the same regardless of sales volume. Insurance is an example of a fixed cost. Once insurance policies have been negotiated, the cost remains the same throughout the term of the policy. For example, if the cost of insuring the business is $1,000 per month, it will remain at $1,000 every month. Even if the establishment has sales of $10,000 one month, $20,000 the next month, and $15,000 the following month, the insurance cost will always be $1,000 per month. The cost does not change when sales change.

Variable Costs

Variable costs increase and decrease in direct proportion to sales. Food cost is one example. As sales increase, more food is purchased to replenish inventory (*Exhibit 1.2*). Likewise, as sales decrease, less food is purchased. If adequate controls are in place and there is little waste or theft, the amount of food used is in direct proportion to sales.

Semivariable Costs

Semivariable costs increase and decrease as sales increase and decrease but not in direct proportion. They are made up of both fixed costs and variable costs. Labor cost is one example (*Exhibit 1.3*). Managers are normally paid a salary that remains the same regardless of the operation's sales volume. If the manager and chef are collectively paid $120,000 per year, they will receive that amount regardless of whether the operation brings in $1 million or $1.3 million per year. Thus, the management salary is a fixed cost.

On the other hand, employees such as waitstaff and line cooks are paid hourly wages and are scheduled according to anticipated sales. As a result, the cost of hourly staff increases as sales increase and decreases as sales decrease. If proper scheduling is used, the cost will increase and decrease in direct proportion to sales.

Exhibit 1.3

Exhibit 1.4

FIXED, VARIABLE, AND SEMIVARIABLE COSTS IN RELATION TO SALES VOLUME

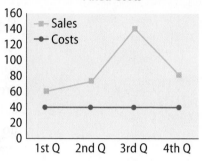

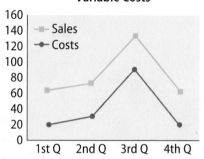

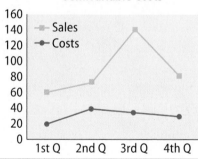

Putting this all together, labor is a semivariable cost because there is a fixed cost component (management salaries) and a variable cost component (hourly staff wages). *Exhibit 1.4* shows how fixed, variable, and semivariable costs behave as sales volume increases.

Controllable Costs

Controllable costs are those costs that managers can directly control. One example of a controllable cost is food cost. Managers can control this cost by using standardized recipes or exercising standard procedures for portion control, menu listing, and pricing, or by one of several other restraints. For example, if the price of chicken increases and no action is taken, the establishment's overall food cost will increase. To respond, managers can either raise the selling price of all chicken entrées, reduce portions, reposition the items on the menu, or eliminate chicken from the menu altogether. By taking action, managers have controlled the increased cost of chicken, resulting in no increase in the establishment's overall food cost.

Another example of a controllable cost is labor cost. By changing the number of hours an employee works, a manager can affect labor costs. For example, if an establishment's sales drop and no action is taken, payroll cost as a percentage of sales increases. By reducing the number of hours worked by hourly employees, this percentage could be brought back into line.

It should be pointed out, however, that in exercising these options, managers must always be careful not to alienate customers. If the selling price of chicken entrées is increased too much, or too many hours are trimmed off the schedule, resulting in poor service, customers could be driven to the competition.

Noncontrollable Costs

Noncontrollable costs are those costs over which managers have little or no control. An example of a noncontrollable cost is insurance. As noted previously, once an insurance policy has been negotiated, managers have no control over the cost of that policy. Another example is license fees. They have no control over the rate charged for bar or occupation licenses. A final example is the operation's lease or mortgage. Once signed, managers have virtually no control over this cost.

CROSSOVER OF COST CLASSIFICATIONS

Clearly, there is some crossover in classifying costs. Variable and semivariable costs are usually controllable costs. Fixed costs are typically noncontrollable costs. While there are some exceptions to this, for the most part it is true.

Another thing to consider is that a particular cost could be classified differently depending on how it is budgeted. For example, if an operation's lease is negotiated at $3,000 per month, rent is a fixed cost. It does not increase or decrease according to sales volume. It will always be $3,000. If, on the other hand, the lease is negotiated at 6 percent of sales, rent is then a variable cost. The amount will increase or decrease in direct proportion to sales volume. From this example, it can be seen that some costs, depending on how they are structured, can be classified as either fixed, variable, or semivariable. This is also a good example of the exception to the rule stated previously—variable and semivariable costs are normally controllable.

Another example is advertising. If managers determine that they will spend 2 percent of sales on advertising, it is then a variable cost. It will increase and decrease in direct proportion to sales. If, on the other hand, managers decide to spend $2,500 per month on advertising, it is then a fixed cost. The cost will not change as sales volume changes.

The only pure variable costs are food and beverage. Most other costs are really semivariable, having both fixed and variable elements. Remember: Expenses that are defined as "fixed" do not vary with sales. Variable expenses, however, will increase and decrease according to sales volume. Managers must use their best judgment to divide expenses into fixed and variable categories. There are no hard and fast rules for the allocations, but this becomes easier as managers gain more knowledge and experience in the restaurant and foodservice business.

THE IMPORTANCE OF PRIME COST

Prime cost is an operation's total food cost, beverage cost, and labor costs for a specific time period, usually a week or a month. In calculating labor costs, include salaries, hourly staff wages, payroll taxes, benefits, workers' compensation, and all other payroll-related expenses (see *Exhibit 1.5*). All three areas (food cost, beverage cost, and labor costs) create opportunities for losses through waste, spoilage, theft, and poor scheduling. Unfortunately, a problem in any of the three areas of prime cost can be very expensive.

There are a number of factors that frequently contribute to the underperformance and often the eventual failure of many operations. These include poor location, undercapitalization, and a poor concept. However, operating with a high prime cost is also one of the main contributing factors. Food, beverage, and labor costs normally represent well over half of the operation's total costs, and nearly 90 percent of the costs that managers have any real control over.

Prime cost is one of the best indicators of restaurant and foodservice profitability and how well the operation is managed day-to-day. Establishments whose prime costs are off target nearly always have challenges with product consistency and food quality, as well as basic poor management practices. How well an operation controls prime cost is very often a good indicator of how well the total operation is being managed.

Because prime cost is such an important number, there should be a line item for prime cost in every operation's income statement. Income statements, which show sales, expenses, and profitability of an operation, will be covered in more detail in chapter 2. For now, see *Exhibit 1.6* for an example of an income statement that includes a line item for prime cost.

Prime Cost as a Percentage of Total Sales

It is an accepted rule of thumb at table service establishments that the prime cost should run no more than 65 percent of the total sales. A prime cost below 65 percent is one measure of whether or not an operation is turning a profit. To calculate prime cost, use the following formula:

Total cost of sales + Total labor costs = Prime cost

Then, to calculate prime cost as a percentage of total sales, use this formula:

$$\frac{\text{Prime}}{\text{cost}} \div \frac{\text{Total}}{\text{sales}} = \frac{\text{Prime cost as a}}{\text{\% of total sales}}$$

Exhibit 1.5
CALCULATING PRIME COST
How to Calculate Prime Cost
Food Cost
+ Beverage Cost
+ Labor Cost
= **Prime Cost**

Exhibit 1.6		
PRIME COST ON THE INCOME STATEMENT		
Income Statement	**October**	
Sales:		
Food	$78,566	
Liquor	4,756	
Beer	6,221	
Wine	8,899	
Total sales	**$98,442**	100.0%
Cost of sales:		
Food	$25,691	
Liquor	951	
Beer	1,369	
Wine	3,115	
Total cost of sales	**$31,126**	31.6%
Labor costs:		
Management salaries	$ 8,171	
Hourly staff wages	19,196	
Payroll taxes	2,855	
Workers' compensation	1,083	
Group medical insurance	591	
Other employee benefits	295	
Total labor costs	**$32,191**	32.7%
PRIME COST	**$63,317**	64.3%

Exhibit 1.6 shows the prime cost for a given establishment in the month of October. In that month, the operation generated $98,442 in total sales. Total prime costs for the month were $63,317:

$$\$31,126 \quad + \quad \$32,191 \quad = \quad \$63,317$$
Total cost of sales   Total labor costs   Prime cost

To calculate prime cost as percentage of sales, a manager needs to use the previous formula and divide $63,317 by $98,442:

$$\$63,317 \quad \div \quad \$98,442 \quad = \quad 64.3\%$$
Prime cost   Total sales   Prime cost as % of total sales

In this example, the prime cost lets the manager know that the establishment achieved a reasonable profit because the prime cost is 64.3 percent of the total sales.

Larger, casual-theme chain operations may be able to keep their prime cost around 60 percent of total sales. Independent managers can achieve a reasonable profit by maintaining a prime cost of 60 to 65 percent of sales, assuming the cost and expense structure in other areas are fairly typical. In quick-service operations, the goal is to keep prime cost at 60 percent of total sales or less. High-volume quick service restaurants (QSRs) that are well managed may achieve a prime cost of 50 percent or less.

It is important to manage food, beverage, and labor costs individually. However, an operation must also consider them in the context of prime cost. If an establishment has a high food cost, it must have a low labor cost to keep the overall prime cost stable. For example, a steakhouse could run a 43 percent food cost and a 20 percent labor cost, while a quick-service operation could run a 25 percent food cost and a 35 percent labor cost. In both examples, the prime cost is below 65 percent.

Operations that are serious about maximizing profitability will want to know their largest and most volatile costs at the end of every week. When prime cost is calculated weekly, managers are aware of challenges quickly and have the opportunity to react quickly. When an area is not meeting the **operational standard**, or the measures established for making comparisons and judgments about the degree of excellence in operations, then weekly prime cost numbers put managers in a much better position to take corrective action before serious financial losses occur or the problem gets out of control.

In fact, weekly prime cost reporting can change the entire operational culture. Managers and staff become more aware and there is an increased accountability. Real-time numbers put managers on notice that they may need to increase their focus or make adjustments.

THE COST CONTROL PROCESS

In every area of a restaurant or foodservice operation, **controls** are an important part of making a profit. Controls are a series of coordinated actions that help keep financial results within an acceptable target range. At every stage of operations, controls need to be established to prevent problems from getting out of hand and to achieve the goals of the organization. Cost controls start with the menu and continue on through purchasing, receiving, storage, production, and finally service. Without controls in place, an operation has no way of evaluating whether the operation is profitable or meeting its budget. Having a control system allows managers to monitor, measure, and adjust many aspects of the operation's performance, including sales, expenses, general efficiencies, and profit. Controlling and reducing costs ensures the ongoing financial health of an operation.

Taking action to reduce operating costs requires understanding which costs might be unnecessary and deciding what can be done to eliminate them. At the same time, any controls implemented must not compromise the operation's standard levels for safety, sanitation, and customer service. With experience, managers learn to quickly spot cost-related concerns in their operations.

The basic cost control process has four steps:

1. **Developing performance standards.** This begins with establishing standards or defining an operation's goals. Remember that standards are measures established to compare levels of attainment for a goal or a measure of adequacy. Standards or goals may be financial, such as targeted profit margin, or they may be a production number, such as covers per workday. A **cover** is one meal served to a customer.

2. **Monitoring actual performance.** Once managers establish the standards or goals, they can measure the actual performance (*Exhibit 1.7*). However, they must remember not to spend the majority of their time tracking numbers or implementing specific controls at the expense of loss of quality of service or food.

3. **Comparing actual performance to performance standards.** Once actual performance numbers are calculated, these figures are compared to budgeted amounts, operational standards, and historical information to identify any variances.

4. **Addressing performance discrepancies.** Managers create a plan to reduce or eliminate the difference between standards and actual performance. However, it is important that the corrective action not create new or larger problems.

Exhibit 1.7

Developing Performance Standards

In the restaurant and foodservice industry, managers, employees, and suppliers are all expected to meet the standards. Standards are levels of excellence against which managers evaluate results. Setting standards is one of the primary responsibilities of managers. Cost control standards guide managers in every aspect of restaurant and foodservice management and operations, from initial menu planning all the way through to purchasing, receiving, storing, production, service, staff scheduling, and cash handling.

Cost standards will vary from one type of operation to another. Consider that for some operations, such as restaurants, catering companies, and hotels, the primary goal is to make a profit. For other foodservice operations, including hospitals, nursing homes, schools, and prisons, the objective is to meet a budget. Even within chain operations, the cost standards might vary from region to region. In general, though, there are several types of standards useful in establishing control over restaurant and foodservice operations: quality standards, quantity standards, and standard costs.

Quality standards set the degree of excellence of raw materials, finished products, and production standards for the employees. Managers must establish a standard of quality for each item the operation purchases using the input from employees (*Exhibit 1.8*). For example, managers might decide that their standard of quality for beef rib-eye steaks is U.S. Grade Choice, cut from a boneless rib-eye roll. Quality and production standards must also be established for the employees. Establishing skills standards required for each position and setting production standards will help managers hire the right person for the right position.

Exhibit 1.8

Quantity standards refer to weight, count, or volume measure. Establishing quantity standards, such as portion sizes for menu foods and beverages, and employee production standards such as one cook per 50 covers, will help control food, beverage, and labor costs.

Besides quality and quantity standards, it is necessary to determine and establish standard costs. A standard cost is the target or goal for the cost of goods or services that is then used to measure other costs. For example, an operation may establish a standard prime cost as 63 percent of total sales. However, actual costs may differ from the standard cost the operation has been targeting. Standard costs may be determined in a variety of ways, each which will be discussed in detail in later chapters.

Monitoring Actual Performance

To understand how an operation is truly performing, managers must collect accurate sales and cost data. Historical sales information is just as important to cost control as it is to other management functions. The relationship between sales and costs is often proportional, and many restaurant and foodservice costs change depending on sales volume. To know whether costs are within an appropriate range, it is imperative to start with accurate sales information.

Sales should be tracked for different periods, including yearly, monthly, weekly, daily, by meal period, and even hourly:

- Yearly and monthly data are used for budgeting and income statement purposes.
- Weekly and daily sales data are used for purchasing and scheduling.
- Daily and meal period data are also used for scheduling and production planning.

Sales information can come from several sources. Yearly and monthly sales information comes from the income statement (see *Exhibit 1.9*). Hourly, daily,

RESTAURANT TECHNOLOGY

OPEN FOR BUSINESS

Several Web sites offer various types of software programs for controlling costs. Use a search engine to locate three different programs that deal with cost control and compare them. Some keywords you can use may be "food cost control software" or "restaurant cost control software." Decide what criteria you will use to compare these software programs. You must have at least four different criteria, examples include price and ease of use. Set up a table on a separate piece of paper to show the data you selected for comparison. If you had to make a choice based on these criteria, which program would you select and why?

Exhibit 1.9

SAMPLE ABBREVIATED INCOME STATEMENT

Abbreviated Income Statement
For the period 10/1/12 to 10/31/12

Sales	$ 1,450,000
Cost of food sold	493,000
Gross profit	**$ 957,000**
Labor expense	$ 420,500
Other controllable expenses	93,000
Noncontrollable expenses	330,000
Total expenses	**$ 843,500**
Profit	**$ 113,500**

ACHIEVING REAL RESULTS

I was the maître d' and sommelier du vin of a restaurant. As part of my responsibilities, I revamped the wine list, changing all of the prices. I rearranged the format and layout. I set parameters for wines that would be allowed to be our house pour wines. I set a policy for how long a wine could remain as a house pour.

Then, I showed this to the chef-owner of the restaurant. He was very upset. He did not understand why I was reducing the prices. I explained that it would force some wines off the list, while also bringing some of the higher-end wines into a closer price-point where they might attract some second looks.

Well, my moves paid off. We increased overall bottles of wine per table from 0.76 to 1.86 bottles of wine per table. Even after lowering prices overall, we increased our average wine bottle selling price from about $28 per bottle to more than $34, as customers purchased more upper-range wines. At the end of the day, we made considerably more money by coupling an increase in sales with a higher price-point for the bottles of wine sold. It was a double win!

and weekly figures are usually generated by point-of-sale (POS) system reports. In operations without POS systems, it is tabulated from guest checks or periodic cash register readings.

In addition to having accurate sales information, it is also necessary to have accurate cost information. Most cost information can be taken from operational records. Many POS systems track inventory, food waste, and employee work hours. Managers can usually run reports of inventory and food costs, payroll costs, and actual labor hours.

Comparing Actual Performance to Performance Standards

So how does a manager know if the cost controls in place are achieving the desired results? The actual results must be checked against the standard. Comparing standard costs with actual costs can help determine how well managers are using the resources available to them. Also, it is important to remember to do the comparison and analysis in the same measurements as the planning, whether they are dollars, labor hours, or some other unit of measure.

Once actual sales and costs are calculated, these figures are compared to budgeted amounts, operational standards, and historical information to identify any variance. A **variance** is the difference between actual results (i.e., sales) and targeted results. Doing this on a regular basis is a good way to check how an operation is running and to prevent future problems by catching them early.

Every item on the budget should be checked against actual figures, and the difference, or variance, should be noted. This is called a **line item review**. When the budget is compared to the actual performance, each item's value should match or be very close to the target or standard. Any difference between the budget and the actual amounts may be expressed as a dollar amount or percentage (see *Exhibit 1.10*).

Remember that managers determine a standard based on many factors, not the least of which is profit. When considering a labor standard, the goal of managers is to produce a quality product and provide quality service. To go below the standard could sacrifice product quality or service excellence. For this reason, it is just as important to come up to the standard as it is to come

Exhibit 1.10				
SAMPLE LINE ITEM REVIEW				
Budget Item	**$ Budgeted**	**$ Actual**	**$ Difference**	**% Difference**
Food sales	$100,000	$90,000	$10,000	−10%

down to the standard. For example, maintaining proper customer service levels requires an operation to have the appropriate level of labor on site at all times. Sufficient hours scheduled for workers in the kitchen will result in an excellent product being served in a prompt manner. Likewise, the correct number of servers in the dining room to take orders and serve efficiently will carry out the company's standards or goals of good food and good service.

In addition to comparing actual costs to standard costs, managers also compare actual costs to historical costs, those costs that have been incurred in the past. By comparing these two figures, managers can see if the operation is improving or regressing. When comparing actual costs to historical costs, it is important to remember that similar periods must be compared. For example, January's labor cost is compared to January's labor cost of the previous year, and Monday's sales this week are compared to Monday's sales of last week.

Special events or unusual circumstances should also be taken into account when comparing historical costs. For example, comparing this Sunday's sales to last Sunday's, which happened to be Mother's Day, would not be a good comparison. A heavy lunchtime rainstorm on Thursday could increase the sales in an employee cafeteria located in an office building, and decrease the sales in an establishment across the street from the building.

Addressing Performance Discrepancies

Over time, even small changes in costs can add up to significant losses. When costs are out of line, the cause should be investigated. Managers must then create a plan to reduce or eliminate the difference between standards and actual performance. This plan will determine the type of **corrective action**, or steps taken to address the problem. The corrective action could be a change in personnel or new product specifications, for example. However, it is important for a manager to not overreact; no one wants the corrective action to create new or larger problems.

Exhibit 1.11

If the budget and actual values do not match, they must be analyzed to see what might have gone wrong. If there is a variance, the manager should identify the source. For example, if food cost is off, then purchasing, preparation, and receiving procedures should be reviewed. If labor cost is off, then scheduling and production standards should be analyzed (*Exhibit 1.11*).

Exhibit 1.12

SAMPLE CORRECTIVE ACTIONS FOR COST CONTROL

To Reduce	Implement These Corrective Actions
Food cost	■ Reduce portion size. ■ Replace food item with a more cost-effective ingredient. ■ Feature items with higher profit margins. ■ Raise menu prices.
Food waste	■ Monitor portion control. ■ Monitor food storage and rotation. ■ Monitor food ordering. ■ Improve communication to reduce production errors.
Inventory cost	■ Order appropriate quantities—avoid having too much or too little in storage.
Labor cost	■ Reduce number of employees on schedule. ■ Ask employees to end their shifts early. ■ Schedule cross-trained staff (for example, server/cashier/hostess).

As soon as the cause of a variance is identified, the manager should take corrective actions. *Exhibit 1.12* lists some examples of corrective actions that can be taken to control various costs. As discussed earlier, managers have more control over some costs than they do over others. Corrective actions can be used only to affect controllable costs.

In addition to taking corrective actions, it may also be necessary to make changes to the operating budget. As circumstances change, some forecasts used to prepare the original budget may no longer be accurate. Reviewing forecasts, at least on a monthly basis, will help managers make realistic adjustments to the budget for upcoming periods. Forecasting will be covered in greater detail in chapter 2.

Managers must develop plans and systems to achieve the established standards. These plans and systems must be capable of producing consistent, predictable, high-quality results. They must provide the necessary structure to implement the plans or programs, as well as provide the necessary resources such as funding, personnel, facilities, equipment, and so on. In any restaurant or foodservice operation, there are many variables and functions that must be consistently executed, every time, with every guest. It is impossible to rely on the employees to create a positive, predictable experience for the guest without a system to guide them.

SUMMARY

1. **Explain how restaurant and foodservice costs affect profitability.**

   If costs get out of line, the profitability of a restaurant or foodservice operation could be seriously jeopardized. Cost controls start with the menu and continue on through purchasing to receiving, storage, production, and finally, service. Without controls in place, an operation has no way of determining and evaluating whether the operation is profitable or meeting its budget. Controlling and reducing costs are both desirable trends for ensuring the ongoing financial health of an operation.

2. **Describe the manager's role in cost control.**

   The size and scope of an operation will determine the extent to which its managers exercise direct control or delegate that responsibility to other staff. Managers, employees, and suppliers are expected to meet the standards set by management. Standards cover the entire spectrum of the restaurant and foodservice business.

3. **Identify the types of costs incurred by restaurant and foodservice operations.**

   Costs can be classified in different ways. The most common classifications are fixed, variable, and semivariable costs. Fixed costs are those costs that remain the same regardless of sales volume, while variable costs increase or decrease in direct proportion to increases or decreases in sales volume. Semivariable costs increase when sales increase and decrease when sales decrease. However, change in semivariable costs is not directly proportional to sales. Costs also can be either controllable or noncontrollable. Controllable costs are those costs that managers can directly control. Noncontrollable costs are those costs over which managers have little or no control.

4. **Explain the importance of controlling prime cost.**

   The major costs that managers have to control are food cost, beverage cost, and labor cost. Together they are known as the prime cost, because they are the highest costs in the operation. For most operations, a prime cost of less than 65 percent is required for that establishment to be profitable.

5. **Explain the basic restaurant or foodservice cost control process.**

   Managers are responsible for developing performance standards for a given operation. The income statement allows managers to monitor actual financial performance. Once actual sales and costs are calculated, these figures are compared to budgeted amounts, operational standards, and historical information in order to identify any variances. When costs are determined to be out of line, the cause should be investigated and managers should take action to correct the problem.

APPLICATION EXERCISE

Julia is reviewing a list of expenses for the operation of her establishment. She notices several jumps in costs compared to the previous month. These are the items that have increased in cost:

• Electricity

• Labor

• Produce delivery fees

• Milk

Given this information, answer the following questions:

1. What can Julia do to reduce these costs in the upcoming months?

2. How might these changes affect the establishment's customers?

3. Are there any costs that Julia cannot reduce?

4. Which of the costs are semivariable, and how can Julia control the variable portion of those costs?

5. What can Julia do to increase profits even if she is not able to cut costs?

REVIEW YOUR LEARNING

Select the best answer for each question.

1. **When an operation's expenses exceed its sales, the establishment is experiencing a**

   A. loss.

   B. profit.

   C. quality standard.

   D. line item review.

2. **What is one benefit of having cost controls?**

   A. It helps keep employees working their hardest.

   B. Managers know if they are meeting their budget.

   C. Managers can make changes whenever they want to.

   D. It makes it simpler for an operation to change the menu.

3. **Who is expected to meet standards set by managers?**

   A. Managers and customers

   B. Employees and suppliers

   C. Managers, employees, and suppliers

   D. Customers, suppliers, and employees

4. **Food cost is an example of what type of cost?**

   A. Fixed cost

   B. Variable cost

   C. Semivariable cost

   D. Noncontrollable cost

5. A type of cost that increases or decreases in direct proportion to sales increase or decrease is known as a
   A. fixed cost.
   B. variable cost.
   C. semivariable cost.
   D. noncontrollable cost.

6. Rent and insurance typically are examples of what type of cost?
   A. Variable costs
   B. Semivariable costs
   C. Controllable costs
   D. Noncontrollable costs

7. What is the restaurant and foodservice industry standard for prime cost?
   A. 45%
   B. 55%
   C. 65%
   D. 75%

8. Which is the most important cost for a restaurant or foodservice manager to control?
   A. Rental expenses
   B. Equipment costs
   C. Marketing costs
   D. Prime cost

9. What is the first step in the cost control process?
   A. Analyze costs
   B. Take corrective action
   C. Collect sales and cost data
   D. Establish standards and define goals

10. Actual costs should be compared against what type of costs?
    A. Fixed costs
    B. Competitors' costs
    C. Controllable costs
    D. Standard costs

2

Forecasting and Budgeting

CHAPTER LEARNING OBJECTIVES

After completing this chapter, you should be able to:

- Explain the purpose of budgets and forecasts.

- List and describe the forecasting methods used by restaurant and foodservice managers.

- Describe types of budgets.

- Identify the purpose of the income statement.

- Describe how to prepare food and labor cost budgets.

- Explain the importance of variance and its use in operations.

KEY TERMS

break-even point, p. 43

budget, p. 22

budgeting process, p. 33

capital expenditure budget, p. 27

controllable profit, p. 32

cost of sales, p. 36

fixed budget, p. 28

flexible budget, p. 28

forecasting, p. 22

income statement, p. 29

long-term budget, p. 27

operating budget, p. 28

percentage of sales method, p. 36

return on investment (ROI), p. 43

sales forecast, p. 34

short-term budget, p. 28

shrinkage, p. 38

simple markup method, p. 37

utilization factor, p. 38

variance, p. 31

CASE STUDY

After working as a technology development manager, Suzanne decided to open her own seafood restaurant called Suzanne's Silver Seas. She thought that her technology skills would be helpful in menu design and restaurant and foodservice forecasting.

In her first year of business, she had help from a consultant to establish her budget. Suzanne felt more comfortable with budgeting and forecasting and decided to prepare the second-year budget on her own. However, in March, the federal minimum wage increased from $6.80 to $7.40. Suzanne also faced labor scheduling issues on weekends, forcing her to have to serve food and seat guests. In addition, lobster prices increased by almost $2 per pound.

By July, Suzanne realized that restaurant sales were down 2 percent and her labor and food costs had increased by 2.5 percent and 6 percent, respectively. She now had to sit down and make a new forecast to save the year. She wondered how she could be better prepared for these surprises during preparation of her budget.

1. What steps might Suzanne take in the future to better predict changes to her costs?

2. What are other potential cost increases that Suzanne might need to consider as she reworks her budget?

THE IMPORTANCE OF BUDGETS AND FORECASTS

A **budget** is a plan that indicates an operation's financial objectives or financial standards. The budget also shows how the operation will use its resources to achieve those objectives in a given budget cycle. A budget cycle is the time period of a budget. The length of a budget cycle varies, but is often a fiscal year. The budget also shows the amount of money the operation will have available to spend. Basically, the budget is a plan that tells a manager how much money should be coming in, and where and how that manager can spend it. Based on the financial standards in the budget, managers make decisions that they believe will achieve the operation's financial objectives. Plus, the budget predicts what will be available at the end of the budget cycle as either a profit or a loss.

Modern budgets were first introduced in the early 20th century as a tool to manage costs and cash flows in large industrial organizations. By the 1980s and 1990s, many operations were hesitant to invest in innovation because they wanted to stay within rigid budgets. Today, budgets have become more than a financial tool. The budget can also be an action plan for managers, making sure that key resources are allocated to activities with the highest revenue and profit potential.

Budgeting requires managers to make predictions about the future. Making future predictions about the budget based on current situations and trends is called **forecasting**. Forecasting is an integral part of the planning process, but also one of the most difficult for managers. For example, it is doubtful that many restaurant and foodservice operations planning for the 2011 budget cycle could have predicted how political challenges in the Middle East would affect world markets or the major price increases in almost all commodities. Such dramatic economic changes may be unexpected, but they are not unique.

To forecast sales, most restaurant and foodservice owners and managers may simply estimate how many customers will eat in the operation over the next week and how much they will spend on food and beverage. They then purchase food and supplies to accommodate that number.

If forecasting is so unpredictable, why is it done? The planning process requires managers to think in advance about opportunities and threats and develop contingency plans that can be quickly and easily initiated. As a result, the cost of responding to adverse circumstances can be reduced significantly. Managers may also be able to take advantage of opportunities to build a competitive advantage in the market.

Advantages of Budgets

So, why spend the time and effort to develop a budget when circumstances are always going to change? The budgeting process does a few very good things for any organization:

1. **Improves interdepartmental communications:** Managers must consider all the aspects of the operation as part of the budget process. Sales, expenses, human resources, facilities, and equipment needs all must be coordinated. If the chef wants a new range and the dining-room manager needs new glassware, there must be discussion and negotiation. An effective budget creates direction and limits the confusion between departments.

2. **Provides a common goal:** Goals can be inspirational and motivating to the entire team if set correctly. During the budget process, realistic goals or standards must be set. However, it is best if management can convert financial goals into process-focused and tangible objectives. For example: increase dessert sales by 15 percent, which will help achieve the forecasted revenue target (*Exhibit 2.1*).

3. **Provides accountability:** A budget provides goals for departments and individuals. It also assigns accountability for generating sales and controlling costs.

Exhibit 2.1

4. **Establishes a measurable target:** Budgets allow managers to plan and measure the results. It is much better, for example, to discover a possible loss situation ahead of time through a budget than to come in to work one morning to find an operation is close to bankruptcy.

5. **Provides a control tool:** If standards have been established in advance, it is possible to compare actual results with targets and clearly see variances.

6. **Requires forward-thinking:** Budgets help avoid surprises. For example, do menu prices need to rise in response to anticipated future increases in food or labor costs? The answers to questions like these help managers plan for growth.

7. **Considers both internal and external influences and factors:** Managers have to identify and acknowledge the influence of internal factors, including menu prices, seating capacity, and seat turnover. External factors may include additional competition, the local and national economic environment, inflation rates, and the local labor market.

THINK ABOUT IT ...

We cannot predict the future, so some people will suggest that we do not need to budget and forecast since the future is uncertain. Why might budgets and forecasts still be useful business tools?

Disadvantages of Budgets

Of course there are more positives than negatives involved with creating budgets, or managers would not go through the process. However, a manager must be aware of the potential disadvantages.

1. **Preparation and implementation time:** Time costs money. The budget process is not a one-person job; it requires cooperation and collaboration. People working on a budget are diverted from their normal responsibilities.

2. **Confidentiality:** Budgets contain sensitive information about salaries and wages. Only a few select people in the organization, sometimes only one or two, can have access to or work on the budget.

3. **Forecasting:** Budgets are based on forecasting, which can be very volatile and unreliable. The best a manager can do is use available data and measure them against the trends that impact the organization—for example, the economy or competition.

4. **Support:** The budget process and the budget itself must have support from the top down including upper management and owners, and the bottom up including chefs, waitstaff, and other nonmanagement employees. Sometimes the allocation of resources can cause friction between departments.

5. **Control:** Budgeted dollars may be difficult to control. Some managers may interpret spending targets as "use it or lose it," if an expense in a given department is overestimated. This is especially true if the following year's budget is based on the current year's expenses. Often the department wants to match the budget forecast and protect the budget from being cut for the next period.

THE FORECASTING PROCESS

Most companies find the budget process challenging even under stable conditions. Managers often spend significant amounts of time developing, refining, and adjusting their budgets. Under volatile conditions, when economic forecasts change from week to week, developing one reliable budget to coordinate operations and track performance for an entire fiscal year is very difficult. While following the traditional budget process is still the industry standard, there are other options that will be discussed later in this chapter.

Forecasting Customer Counts

One component of the budget process is forecasting how many customers or guests an operation will serve over a given budget cycle (*Exhibit 2.2*). Customer count or guest count can be forecast based on the historical guest count for the previous period—for example, a year,

Exhibit 2.2

24

a day, or a week. Managers should also remember to evaluate future business conditions. If the customer count for last year was 32,300 guests per year, does the operation expect the same level of business? If business conditions are deteriorating, a company may expect a decrease in total customer count. If managers expect an increase, then the percentage increase estimate will be positive.

Annual customer count forecast can be done using the following formula:

$$\begin{array}{c}\text{Historical} \\ \text{customer} \\ \text{count}\end{array} + \left(\begin{array}{ccc}\text{Historical} & & \text{\% of estimated} \\ \text{customer} & \times & \text{increase or} \\ \text{count} & & \text{decrease}\end{array}\right) = \begin{array}{c}\text{Customer} \\ \text{count} \\ \text{forecast}\end{array}$$

The following examples illustrate this concept:

Suzanne's Silver Seas restaurant had a total guest count of 32,300 for last year. If the manager expects a customer count increase of 2 percent for the upcoming year, what would the new customer forecast be?

$$\begin{array}{ccccccc}32{,}300 & + & (32{,}300 & \times & 2\%) & = & 32{,}946 \\ \text{Historical} & & \text{Historical} & & \text{\% of estimated} & & \text{Customer} \\ \text{customer} & & \text{customer} & & \text{increase or} & & \text{count} \\ \text{count} & & \text{count} & & \text{decrease} & & \text{forecast}\end{array}$$

However, if the manager expects a 4 percent decrease in sales for the upcoming year, then the estimate will be negative. The customer count with a decrease in sales would be as follows:

$$\begin{array}{ccccccc}32{,}300 & + & (32{,}300 & \times & -4\%) & = & 31{,}008 \\ \text{Historical} & & \text{Historical} & & \text{\% of estimated} & & \text{Customer} \\ \text{customer} & & \text{customer} & & \text{increase or} & & \text{count} \\ \text{count} & & \text{count} & & \text{decrease} & & \text{forecast}\end{array}$$

When forecasts show that customer count will decrease, managers have to work on increasing average sales per customer, also called average check per guest, to prevent total sales from dropping. Suzanne's Silver Seas had annual sales of $800,000 in 2011. Even with a 4 percent decrease in customer count, the establishment aims to generate the same amount of total sales. How much should average sales per customer be in order to achieve this goal? *Exhibit 2.3* details this calculation.

To calculate average sales per customer, divide the target sales by the number of expected customers:

$$\begin{array}{ccccc}\$800{,}000 & \div & 31{,}008 & = & \$25.80 \\ \text{Target} & & \text{Expected} & & \text{Average sales} \\ \text{sales} & & \text{customers} & & \text{per customer}\end{array}$$

Exhibit 2.3	
CALCULATING AVERAGE SALES PER CUSTOMER	
Target sales	$800,000
Customer count for last year (2011)	32,300
Expected decrease in customer count	4%
Anticipated customer count for this year	31,008
Average sales per customer	$25.80

The management at the Silver Seas restaurant now knows that to achieve the sales target, the operation must average $25.80 per customer. The next step for the manager would be to decide how to reach the established goal.

Forecasting Revenue

When forecasting revenue, managers must remember to take into account all sources of income for the operation. Food and beverage sales are the most obvious. Most customers go to restaurant and foodservice operations to dine. However, there are other sources of income depending on the concept. For example, merchandise is another method of boosting sales—think souvenir t-shirts or coffee mugs. Souvenirs, gifts, and other retail items unique to an establishment can increase sales and should be included in the revenue forecast.

Catering can also be a source of additional revenue. Off-site parties and events, as well as business functions (*Exhibit 2.4*), are a great way to increase sales and reach out to a new customer base. Box delivery or takeout lunch options work well for limited-service establishments. Establishments might be able to secure food sales opportunities at local high schools and sporting events. Such alternative income sources should be considered when forecasting revenue for a budget cycle. However, managers should be aware of additional expenses related to outside catering such as additional equipment, vehicles, and labor.

It is important to forecast some growth, because businesses that do not continue to grow normally are not in business for long. Most forecasters take sales history and add a percentage to account for growth, expansion, and possibly to adjust for inflation, which is considered negative growth. One of the best resources to make these projections would be to look at forecasts of major restaurant and foodservice industry consulting firms. For example, suppose that one firm reported in 2011 that the 2012 forecast for the limited-service segment of the U.S. restaurant and foodservice industry is 3 percent. It is important to understand that 3 percent is nominal growth that includes inflation. The inflation forecast for 2012 is 2.5 percent. Since customer demand is the key factor in sales, managers need to forecast the real growth of their operations.

In *Exhibit 2.5*, the manager will need to increase the price of some menu items to offset the effect of the 2.5 percent increase in goods prices due to inflation. The previous

Exhibit 2.4

Exhibit 2.5

GROWTH CALCULATION

Nominal growth	=	Real growth + Inflation
Nominal growth	=	3%
Inflation	=	2.5%
Real growth	=	Nominal growth − Inflation
Real growth	=	3% − 2.5%, or 0.5%

calculation shows that merely 0.5 percent of the growth in sales is due to customer demand. In some cases, a given operation may expect a much higher customer demand than the national average. Under those circumstances, managers can have some confidence that the establishment can achieve a much higher real growth than the national average (0.5 percent), which should be included in the revenue budget.

Most operations establish a target that is realistic and attainable; others believe a "stretch" budget drives better results. A stretch budget is a budget that is very optimistic and sometimes aggressive. It will be difficult, but not impossible, to achieve. However, it is important to keep projections reasonable. Expected revenues include not only the expected number of customers, but also what the average check will be. If a manager plans to increase prices, he or she also needs to determine the impact that change will have on customer counts. Change in consumer demand and lifestyles are often affected by economic conditions.

TYPES OF BUDGETS

There are a number of different types of budgets. Budgets that are defined by time period can be classified as long-term or short-term budgets. An organization may establish budgets for specific aspects of the operation as well. These might include sales and revenue budgets, operating budgets, capital expenditure budgets, and marketing budgets.

Long-Term versus Short-Term Budgets

There are no strict rules for determining the length of the budget cycle. It should generally be long enough to demonstrate the effect of management policies and procedures, yet short enough that forecasts can be made with reasonable accuracy.

Budgets are normally considered to be either long term or short term. **Long-term budgets** are plans from one year to five years in the future. Long-term budgets are often part of an organization's strategic plan.

An important part of long-term strategic planning is forecasting the need to purchase new equipment or make other large investments or renovations. **Capital expenditure budgets** allow an establishment to plan for the replacement of high-cost equipment that wears out, and to purchase new types of equipment that may come on the market. Items listed on a capital expenditure budget tend to be expensive and will last for several years. They include items such as walk-in coolers, gas ranges, chairs, and tables. Capital expenditure budgets help owners better plan and account for buying items of this type.

Manager's Memo

In busy establishments it can seem almost impossible for managers to find the time to handle all the required tasks each day. This is why smart managers know how to manage their time wisely. They need to look at the daily routines already built into their day and carve out time several times a week for budget work. They must also schedule time to meet with supervisors, executive management, and vendors, or just to do their own work.

For example, the purchase of a Combi oven steamer may be part of an owner's long-range plans for updating her kitchen. When purchased, the cost of this piece of equipment would not be listed as an operating expense in the month the owner bought it. The cost of the item instead would be listed on this owner's fiscal year capital expenditure budget and balance sheet. This is done because a Combi oven is an asset that has a useful economic life of several years, not just one month. As a result, this asset would be depreciated and expensed over a period of many months. If no new equipment is needed in the next two to three years, and the operation has been painted and refurbished recently, then a capital expenditure budget may not be needed for several years.

Another long-term budget is the five-year revenue budget. This offers managers a general business outlook and gives them a sense of direction while planning operations. In practice, as business conditions change, managers update its forecast but still use the long-term revenue budget as a strategic planning tool.

The most important type of long-term budget an establishment will prepare is the operating budget. The **operating budget** is a formal one-year operating plan to achieve the financial goals of an organization. It is prepared yearly and includes a forecast of sales activity and an estimate of costs that will be incurred in the process of generating those sales. The operating budget also includes the marketing plan for the operation.

Strategic plans typically influence the day-to-day operation of the business, which is covered by the **short-term budget**. Short-term budgets could be for a week, a month, or a quarter. Short-term operating budgets involve all levels of management, while long-term budgets typically involve only the top management.

Information for a short-term budget comes from the operating budget. For instance, weekly labor cost and sales projections come from the operating budget. However, since business conditions may have changed since the operating budget was prepared, managers may need to forecast weekly sales and labor expenses to update budgeted projections.

Fixed versus Flexible Budgets

Most businesses use a **fixed budget** that is based on a certain level of sales revenue. Expense estimates for food, labor, and other costs are then calculated based on that level of sales. With a fixed budget, managers do not consider any other scenarios or "what-ifs." A **flexible budget**, or variable budget, is prepared based on several possible levels of sales activity.

In stable economic times many management teams may speculate informally on how the business will evolve, but few actively debate scenarios or undertake the concrete short- and-long term financial analyses that would make such a debate meaningful. They rely instead on a fixed budget, usually one that reflects what has happened in the past. Unfortunately, this process is not very flexible and does not allow for quick responses to sudden, dramatic changes in the economy. Any revisions to the budget as the year unfolds are reactive and backward-focused rather than reflecting an informed view of alternative future scenarios.

Prepared managers are aware of the disadvantages of fixed budgets and instead develop flexible budgets based on different business scenarios. For example, managers can run different budget projections for three different revenue forecasts. One might show a decline in sales, another would show steady sales, and the third would reflect an increase in sales. The organization could then estimate a level of expenses for each. That is, while fixed expenses such as rent will stay the same, managers will calculate different labor, food, marketing, and utilities expenses for each scenario. With flexible budgets, managers would still have a single budget, but with a number of well-thought-out alternatives available. This approach lets businesses build flexibility into their cost structure.

INCOME STATEMENTS

The **income statement** reports an operation's sales, expenses, and profits or losses for a period of time, such as month, a quarter, or a year. The income statement gives managers a perspective on the health of a business, as reflected in its profitability. Managers use the profit formula to calculate an operation's profitability:

$$\textbf{Revenue} - \textbf{Expenses} = \textbf{Profit}$$

Remember that revenue is the amount of money generated from the sale of products and services and expenses are the costs incurred in the operation of the business.

For example, if an establishment takes in $150,000 in revenue over six months and incurs $138,000 in expenses over that same time period, the profit, or net income, would be $12,000, as shown:

$$\textbf{\$150,000} - \textbf{\$138,000} = \textbf{\$12,000}$$
$$\textbf{Revenue} \qquad \textbf{Expenses} \qquad \textbf{Profit}$$

Of course, if expenses exceed revenue, then the income statement will show a loss. The goal for managers is to find the most effective ways to maximize revenue and minimize expenses to maximize net income or profit. The income statement should provide managers with a picture of the bottom line, but it is also a tool to help determine the best ways to improve profitability.

Restaurant and Foodservice Income Statement

A restaurant and foodservice income statement is very different from the traditional business income statement. *Exhibit 2.6* shows a sample income statement.

Exhibit 2.6

SAMPLE INCOME STATEMENT

INCOME STATEMENT

	CURRENT PERIOD	
SALES	(in Dollars)	(% of Total Sales)
Food	$ 850,000	63.8%
Beverage	482,000	36.2
TOTAL SALES	$1,332,000	100.0%
COST OF SALES		–
Food	$ 288,750	21.7%
Beverage	135,700	10.2
TOTAL COST OF SALES	$ 424,450	31.9%
Gross Profit	$ 907,550	68.1%
PAYROLL		
Salaries & Wages	$ 346,785	26.0%
Employee Benefits	71,950	5.4
TOTAL PAYROLL	$ 418,735	31.4%
PRIME COST	$ 843,185	63.3%
OTHER OPERATING EXPENSES		
Direct Operating Expenses	$ 63,250	4.7%
Music & Entertainment	13,450	1.0
Marketing	29,500	2.2
Utilities	41,560	3.1
General & Administrative Expenses	42,645	3.2
Repairs & Maintenance	9,245	0.7
TOTAL OTHER CONTROLLABLE	$ 199,650	15.0%
CONTROLLABLE PROFIT	$ 289,165	21.7%
OCCUPANCY & DEPRECIATION		
Occupancy Costs	$ 168,920	12.7%
Depreciation	23,650	1.8
TOTAL OCCUPANCY & DEPRECIATION	$ 192,570	14.5%
Other (Income)	$0	0.0%
Interest Expense	42,500	3.2
INCOME BEFORE TAXES	$ 54,095	4.1%
Income Tax	18,000	1.4
NET INCOME	$ 36,095	2.7%

Prime Cost and Other Expenses

As mentioned in chapter 1, prime cost is extremely important since it is the largest expense managers need to control. All restaurant and foodservice managers should monitor their prime cost. As shown in *Exhibit 2.6*, the prime cost makes up 63 percent of total sales. The goal should be to keep prime cost at or below 65 percent for a full-service operation. Prime cost should be at 60 percent or below for a quick-service operation. Businesses that exceed these targets limit their chances of achieving growth or adequate profit.

Other expenses are grouped into categories such as direct operating expenses, marketing, and utilities. Most managers prefer to review a summary version of the income statement so they can quickly scan the key numbers and get a sense of how the business is performing. Management can then drill deeper into any category that does not make sense or appears to be a variance to budget. A **variance** is the difference between the budgeted amount and the actual result. A more detailed report would be available to show the data in each category that are included in the summary version. *Exhibit 2.7* is an example of the most common categories under direct operating expenses.

Exhibit 2.7	
COMMON DIRECT OPERATING EXPENSE CATEGORIES	
Direct Operating Expenses	**Monthly $**
1. Auto Expense	_____
2. Catering & Banquet Supplies	_____
3. Cleaning Supplies	_____
4. Contract Cleaning	_____
5. Pest Control	_____
6. Flowers & Decorations	_____
7. Kitchen Utensils	_____
8. Laundry & Linen	_____
9. Licenses & Permits	_____
10. Menus & Wine Lists	_____
11. Miscellaneous	_____
12. Paper Supplies	_____
13. Security System	_____
14. Tableware & Smallwares	_____
15. Uniforms	_____
Total Direct Operating Expenses	

As outlined in chapter 1, there are controllable and noncontrollable costs. Controllable costs are those that managers have the ability to influence to some degree. Noncontrollable costs include occupancy expenses such as rent, property taxes, and insurance, as well as other expenses like interest paid on loans and depreciation. Managers have little or no control over these expenses. In *Exhibit 2.6*, the line items under Occupancy & Depreciation are noncontrollable expenses.

Separating the controllable from noncontrollable costs allows managers to calculate one of the important margins on the income statement, the **controllable profit**. Controllable profit is a primary indicator of a manager's effectiveness in meeting operational and financial standards. Controllable profit reflects only those line items over which a manager has any influence or control.

Industry averages indicate that a full-service operation requires a controllable profit of 18 to 20 percent of total sales if it is to earn an acceptable net income before taxes. Quick-service restaurants have a little higher controllable profit number of 23 to 25 percent.

Reporting Periods

There are no rules about how often to report financial data or to create income statements. Instead, the frequency should be based on the operation's needs. Managers tend to want and need financial data on a regular basis, often once a month. However, some companies use different reporting periods. For example, a fast-food restaurant corporation uses a "4-4-5 week" quarterly reporting schedule for restaurant operations. That means the first two months of a given quarter consist of 4 weeks while the last month is composed of 5 weeks. In sum, the quarterly period consists of 13 weeks instead of 3 months.

Setting up reporting periods on a weekly cycle rather than every month has distinct advantages. First, it is difficult to compare the results of the current month with a previous month if there are a different number of days this month than last. Also, most restaurant and foodservice operations do as much as 50 percent of their weekly sales on the weekends. If one reporting month has four weekends and the next has five weekends, it becomes almost impossible to compare income statements.

As a result, more restaurant and foodservice operations find numbers based on a weekly reporting cycle more meaningful and useful. For example, using a monthly report that is based on four weeks, the sales and expenses of four Mondays, four Tuesdays, four Wednesdays, and so on. It is recommended that a manager end the four-week cycle on a Sunday. Sunday is normally the slowest day in an operation, which allows time for some pre-inventory organizational work. Plus, the inventory should be the lowest on a Sunday.

Reviewing the Income Statement

It should not come as a surprise that the majority of successful restaurant and foodservice managers know their prime cost every week, not just at the end of a reporting period. Technology today allows managers to keep track of revenues and expenses using point-of-sales (POS) systems. Prime costs can be tracked by inventory software for food and beverage costs and scheduling software for payroll costs. These will be discussed in greater detail later in this book. While weekly numbers are useful to a manager, the income statement that is produced every four weeks provides the clearest overview of operations and profitability. For example, *Exhibit 2.6* shows that an establishment made a net profit of $36,095. While this amount may seem reasonable, a further examination shows that the operation kept merely 2.7 cents as profit out of every sales dollar generated.

Therefore, the sooner managers review a new income statement, the more relevant the information and the more time they have to take corrective action if necessary. Income statements need to be completed on time and accurately. Sir Francis Bacon, an English philosopher and scientist, said it all: "Knowledge is power."

THE BUDGETING PROCESS

The **budgeting process** is the way managers go about developing a budget. It is a process of both planning and control. There are four stages in this process:

1. Resources are allocated.
2. Efforts are made to keep as close to the plan as possible.
3. The results are evaluated.
4. Corrective action is taken, if necessary.

It should be noted that budgeting is a continuous process. Any corrective action to the budget is very important for planning future operations and allocating resources to meet future budgeting goals. It is important to remember that a well-planned budget can contribute significantly to greater efficiency, effectiveness, and accountability in the overall management of an operation.

The budgeting process is also an opportunity to explore several courses of action, and to choose the one that will yield the best results. Ideally, budgeting causes managers to think ahead, have clear expectations that will help them measure performance, and coordinate the activities of the operation so that everyone is working to maximize outcomes.

In developing a budget, three key factors must be determined:

- What the revenue will be from sales
- What the expenses will be from food costs, labor costs, and other expenses
- What the desired profit must be

Once the budget has been established, managers can allocate resources according to the plan and manage with the budget figures in mind. They will also track actual sales, expenses, and profit against expectations.

Budgeting Revenue

Unless the manager is starting a new business or developing a new product, in which case there are no data to review, historical data will provide the best indication of what may happen in the next year. For budgeting, use historical data such as previous income statements as a starting point. Then develop reasonable assumptions. After a manager has reviewed the data collected and has considered any new trends or challenges, he or she will begin to formulate some assumptions about the future. Savvy managers use their own experiences and those of their colleagues to make educated guesses about the future of the business. Is the establishment anticipating an increase in customers? Is it possible to expand the operation's market, possibly by adding a new takeout service or catering? How effective will the operation's marketing program be? What will the establishment's competitors do?

The next step in the budget process is the sales forecast, which is the process of using historical information and knowledge of external factors to predict future sales (see *Exhibit 2.8*). It is extremely important for managers to develop an analysis of present and potential customers for the immediate area to become familiar with what other establishments are doing. Then they need to create three sets of revenue projections: conservative, moderate, and optimistic. The conservative projection is the worst-case scenario, the moderate forecast is the most likely case, and the optimistic projection is the best possible outcome. Customer counts and average check per guest by meal period should be objectively analyzed and forecasted. As previously mentioned, in most establishments the number of guests served can vary dramatically by day of the week and meal period. In many operations, as much as 50 percent of weekly revenue is generated on Friday and Saturday.

Exhibit 2.9 is an example of a weekly sales calculation. The first row shows customer count. The second row shows daily sales. The third row represents percentage of sales each business day contributes to total weekly sales. The last row indicates average sales per customer. An owner or manager can use these numbers to forecast sales for the coming week.

Exhibit 2.8

Exhibit 2.9

WEEKLY SALES CALCULATION

	Sunday	Monday	Tuesday	Wednesday	Thursday	Friday	Saturday	Totals/Avg.
Customer count	116	77	88	125	182	216	284	**1,088**
Daily sales ($)	$2,300.00	$1,563.00	$1,976.00	$2,844.00	$4,156.00	$5,600.00	$7,654.00	**$26,093.00**
Percentage of weekly sales	8.81%	5.99%	7.57%	10.90%	15.93%	21.46%	29.33%	
Average check per customer ($)	$19.83	$20.29	$22.45	$22.75	$22.83	$25.92	$26.95	**$23.98**

The weekly sales are calculated by adding together all of the daily sales. Managers can also calculate the total customer count using the same process. Finally, they can determine the average check per customer by dividing total weekly sales by total customer count. Managers may use one or all of these figures in forecasting revenue.

SALES FORECASTS FOR A NEW ESTABLISHMENT

A new operation's business plan revolves around forecasting realistic and achievable revenue figures. It is recommended that a new establishment create its budget using a conservative scenario. Under no circumstances should an establishment develop an opening budget based on a best-case scenario. If the operation is part of a chain it should use numbers from a comparable operation. If the operation is independent, it may use some information from its competitors or regional data that come from consulting companies.

Budgeting Expenses

As with budgeting revenue, budgeting expenses begins by reviewing prior period data. Managers must examine the income statement to see where improvements can be made. Reviewing market trends, including the forecasting of associations such as the National Restaurant Association and the State Restaurant Association, as well as those from various U.S. government departments, allows managers to anticipate surpluses or shortages of certain food items in the next year. For example, if a beef shortage has been forecast, a manager can anticipate that beef prices will increase. These increases must either be absorbed or passed on to customers.

There are two key calculations a manager must make to budget expenses. As noted earlier in this chapter, prime costs—food and labor costs—are a significant portion of an establishment's expenses. As a result, managers must budget in both of these areas.

FOOD AND BEVERAGE COSTS

There are two primary ways that managers can estimate food costs. These are the percentage of sales method, and the simple markup method. The **percentage of sales method** involves estimating expenses for a future period as a percentage of the sales forecast. This can help a manager determine whether food costs are in line with expectations. Food costs falls under the heading of **cost of sales**. This is the cost of the food and beverage products to a given operation.

Cost of food and beverage should be estimated as a percentage of the corresponding sales category. Then, based on expected costs and projected menu prices, managers should calculate the cost percentages for each category. For example, if food sales forecasts are for $100,000 per month, and projections show an average food cost of 34 percent, then the food cost portion of the budget would be $34,000:

$$\text{\$100,000} \quad \times \quad \text{34\%} \quad = \quad \text{\$34,000}$$

| Monthly food | Food cost | Monthly food |
| sales forecast | percentage | cost budget |

Remember, the percentage in each cost category for cost of sales should always be expressed in relation to the specific revenue category (i.e., food or beverage, not overall sales). Many restaurant and foodservice operations break down food cost by category—for example, meat, seafood, dry goods, and so forth. Beverages should be broken down into liquor, beer, and wine sales. See *Exhibit 2.10* for an example of how a manager might apply this approach.

Exhibit 2.10

BREAKDOWN OF COST BY FOOD CATEGORY

Operating Income Statements		
Last year		
Food sales	$800,000	
Food cost	280,000	35.0% (percentage of food sales)
Breakdown of Cost by Dollars and Percentage of Total Food Sales		
Meat	$ 88,400	11.1%
Seafood	78,400	9.9
Dairy	34,400	4.3
Produce	47,850	6.0
Groceries	26,450	3.3
Bakery	4,500	0.6
Total	**$280,000**	**35.0%**

The previous breakdown will come from a detailed income statement prepared at the end of each operating period. By using meat as an example, the formula to calculate the ratio of certain food items to total food sales is as follows:

$88,400	÷	$800,000	=	11.1% (rounded up)
Food cost		**Total food**		**Percentage of total**
(meat)		**sales**		**food sales (meat)**

The process of budgeting now becomes one of applying the same or new percentages to next year's forecast of food sales. For example, to estimate the cost of produce for next year, the manager needs to multiply expected total sales by 6 percent.

Calculating the cost of liquor, beer, and wine sales follows the same process, as shown in *Exhibit 2.11*.

Exhibit 2.11

BREAKDOWN OF COST BY BEVERAGE CATEGORY

Operating Income Statement		
Last year		
Beverage sales	$200,000	
Beverage cost	36,000	18.0%
		(percentage of beverage sales)
Breakdown of Cost by Dollars and Percentage of Total Beverage Sales		
Liquor	$ 10,400	5.2%
Beer	7,600	3.8
Wine	18,000	9.0
Total	**$ 36,000**	**18.0%**

The ratio of a beverage item cost to beverage sales is calculated the same way that the percentage of total food sales for meat was calculated. In the following example, the percentage of total beverage sales for beer is calculated by dividing the cost of beer by total beverage sales:

$7,600	÷	$200,000	=	3.8%
Beverage cost		**Total**		**Percentage of total**
(beer)		**beverage sales**		**beverage sales (beer)**

The second method used to calculate food and beverage cost is called the **simple markup method**. This method is based on expenses being increased by a predetermined amount, normally a percentage of last year's expense. For example, if this year's food cost is $280,000, and a 6 percent cost increase is projected, the adjusted food cost for the new budget period would be as follows:

$280,000	×	6%	=	$16,800
Current budget period food cost		**Percentage cost increase**		**Projected cost increase**

$280,000	+	$16,800	=	$296,800
Current budget period food cost		**Projected cost increase**		**Adjusted food cost**

Follow the same process for liquor, beer, wine, or any other expense category.

Of course, this method assumes that all costs in all categories are managed and controlled for maximum efficiencies. If they are out of line because of waste, theft, or poor management, the new budget does not take this into account. If a manager is aware of any unique increases, then the particular category or categories must be adjusted accordingly.

Until now, all food and beverage costs were calculated by assuming that all of the food and beverage items were used in operations. However, in reality most operations will not actually use 100 percent of the supplies purchased. For example, an operation may purchase a whole lamb that weighs 22.50 pounds at $4.30 per pound. This cost is called as purchased (AP) cost. However, not all parts of the meat will be used in food preparation. For example, some of the fat needs to be trimmed and some bones need to be removed before portioning meat for steaks or roast. In addition, some of the weight of the meat will decrease during cooking or trimming, which is called **shrinkage**. The actual amount of meat that is used to serve guests is called yield. Some foods may not be properly stored, which may result in spoilage (*Exhibit 2.12*). Last, food may be subject to theft, which will have an effect on food cost. Losses may result due to spoilage, theft, fire, and so on. To calculate the actual food cost of food, managers need to take into account all losses. **Utilization factor** is the percentage of an amount of a food item served to a guest. More details about determining actual food cost will be discussed in chapter 3.

For budgeting purposes, it is important for managers to review and consider historical trends pertaining to AP and actual costs. For example, if AP food cost is $30,000 and actual food cost was $24,000, then the utilization factor would be 80 percent:

$24,000	÷	$30,000	=	80%
Actual cost		**AP cost**		**Utilization factor**

As noted, the remaining 20 percent in food cost is lost due to shrinkage, theft, and other factors. Managers need to identify reasons for unfavorable utilization and, if possible, develop procedures to increase the utilization rate of foods. Restaurant and foodservice managers should determine the budgeted

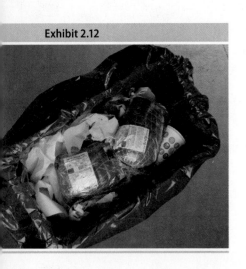

Exhibit 2.12

AP food and beverage percentage of sales first. This is done by dividing the AP food cost by the total sales:

$$\underset{\substack{\text{AP food cost}}}{\$400,000} \quad \div \quad \underset{\substack{\text{Total sales}}}{\$1,000,000} \quad = \quad \underset{\substack{\text{AP food cost} \\ \text{percentage}}}{40\%}$$

Then the next step would be to apply a historical utilization rate to obtain actual food cost. This is done by multiplying the AP food cost by the utilization factor:

$$\underset{\substack{\text{AP food cost}}}{\$400,0000} \quad \times \quad \underset{\substack{\text{Utilization} \\ \text{factor}}}{80\%} \quad = \quad \underset{\substack{\text{Actual food} \\ \text{cost}}}{\$320,000}$$

Finally, actual food cost percentage is obtained by dividing actual food cost by total sales:

$$\underset{\substack{\text{Actual food} \\ \text{cost}}}{\$320,000} \quad \div \quad \underset{\substack{\text{Total sales}}}{\$1,000,000} \quad = \quad \underset{\substack{\text{Actual food} \\ \text{cost percentage}}}{32\%}$$

Then the actual food cost percentage will be applied to budget the sales forecast. A large difference between as purchased cost and actual cost can increase food cost percentage of an operation and hurt its profitability. In practice, if an operation has been experiencing a high actual cost, management needs to carefully plan for better utilization, storage, and control of its foodservice items.

LABOR COSTS

The restaurant and foodservice industry is extremely labor-intensive, and hourly labor cost is one of the principal expenses of any operation. It is a variable expense that can fluctuate upward or downward based on changes in sales volume. Hourly labor wages consist of base pay and benefits such as social security taxes, unemployment, and vacation pay. Benefit levels vary by operation, but as an example, suppose each dollar of hourly labor wage has an additional benefit cost of $0.25. As a result, total labor cost of an employee paid $8.00 an hour with a 25 percent benefit cost would be $10.00:

$$\underset{\substack{\text{Hourly} \\ \text{wage cost}}}{\$8.00} \quad + \quad \left(\underset{\substack{\text{Hourly} \\ \text{wage cost}}}{\$8.00} \quad \times \quad \underset{\substack{\text{Benefit cost} \\ \text{percentage}}}{25\%} \right) \quad = \quad \underset{\substack{\text{Total} \\ \text{labor cost}}}{\$10.00}$$

Managers should take the time to project labor costs by position for each meal period in a typical week, based on the level of business expected. Remember to take into account operational standards, such as production times, service standards, food quality, and other quality standards established for the

Exhibit 2.13

operation. For example, a menu items served for lunch may take less time to prepare. Typically, a lunch period for customers is shorter since some of them need to get back to work or do other things. On the contrary, dinner is generally more relaxed and slower for most customers. In addition, labor for dinner may be higher because customers order appetizers or salads, and may order alcoholic and soft drinks several times. Therefore, managers need to consider not only the projected covers to be served, but also the complexity of the menu items and length of the mealtime when budgeting labor costs. In addition, style of service has an impact on labor cost. For example, in quick-service restaurants, a counter person is used, which results in lower labor cost. On the other hand, in fine-dining establishments, both a server and a bus person can be used to serve customers (*Exhibit 2.13*). This information is then used to estimate the hours and number of employees needed in each position to adequately staff the operation.

One of the simplest ways to determine labor budget is by using a target labor cost as percentage of sales that an establishment aims to meet. The calculation is similar to the budgeted food cost percentage. For example, if an establishment forecasts its weekly sales to be $50,000 and its labor target cost percentage is to be 23 percent, then its labor budget would be $11,500:

$$\underset{\substack{\textbf{Weekly sales}\\\textbf{forecast}}}{\textbf{\$50,000}} \times \underset{\substack{\textbf{Labor cost}\\\textbf{percentage}}}{\textbf{23\%}} = \underset{\substack{\textbf{Weekly labor}\\\textbf{cost budget}}}{\textbf{\$11,500}}$$

Some meal times may require more labor, which may mean that a target labor cost of 23 percent may not be achievable for all days and meal times. For example, the labor cost percentage for lunch on Tuesdays may be 28 percent due to lower level of sales and higher number of full-time employees on a payroll. On the other hand, labor cost percentage may be lower on Friday night because beverage sales can make up a significant contribution to total sales. As will be discussed in future chapters, the labor cost for preparing and serving beverages is much lower than that of the food cost.

As in food cost budgeting, managers can use a simple markup formula to budget labor cost. For instance, if an operation expects a 3 percent increase in number of labor hours, the manager can calculate labor cost for next year by using the markup formula.

Another formula to estimate labor cost is by using service standards of the operation. For instance, the manager can use total daily labor hours for each day the operation has been open. The formula used for that would be calculated as follows:

$$\underset{\substack{\textbf{Total annual}\\\textbf{labor hours}}}{\textbf{Total annual labor hours}} \div \underset{\substack{\textbf{Number of}\\\textbf{days open}}}{\textbf{Number of days open}} = \underset{\substack{\textbf{Total labor}\\\textbf{hours per day}}}{\textbf{Total labor hours per day}}$$

For example:

$$69{,}496 \div 365 = 190.4$$

Total annual labor hours	Number of days open	Total labor hours per day

To calculate average labor cost per day for full-time and part-time employees, managers first need to forecast labor hours per day for each type of employee. Last year's report shows that full-time labor hours account for 65.6 percent of total labor hours per day. Then, labor hours per day for full-time employees would be as follows:

$$190 \times 65.6\% = \$125$$

Total labor hours per day	Percentage of full-time labor hours	Labor hours per day for full-time employees

If full-time employees are paid on average $7.50 and receive 13 percent in benefits for a total labor cost of $8.50, then the daily wage cost for full-time employees would be as shown here:

$$125 \times \$8.50 = \$1{,}062.50$$

Labor hours per day for full-time employees	Average labor cost for full-time employees	Daily wage cost for full-time employees

We already know that full-time labor hours make up the 125 of the 190.4 total daily labor hours. Then, part-time employees account for 65.4 labor hours at an average labor cost of $4.20, which includes benefits. It should be noted that in this example the average pay rate for part-time employees is below minimum wage, since some part-time employees receive tips. Total daily labor cost for part-time employees would be as follows:

$$65.4 \times \$4.20 = \$274.68$$

Labor hours per day for part-time employees	Average labor cost for part-time employees	Daily wage cost for part-time employees

Thus, if the establishment assumes that labor hours will remain the same next year, average wage cost per day would be:

$$\$1{,}062.50 + \$274.68 = \$1{,}337.18$$

Daily wage cost for full-time employees	Daily wage cost for part-time employees	Total daily wage cost for all employees

It should be noted that daily labor hours and thus the labor cost can fluctuate between weekdays and weekends. For example, total labor hours may be

250 hours on weekends. In addition, part-time labor may comprise 100 of these 250 hours. As a result, it is recommended that management keeps track of historical labor hours and cost for weekdays and weekends separately.

As shown, labor costs may be a combination of different kinds of expenses, including wages and employee benefits such as insurance and vacation pay. Full-service operations can run hourly labor costs anywhere from 10 or 11 percent of sales on a busy night to as much as 25 percent of sales on a slow evening. However, the average weekly labor cost for hourly employees should be in the range of 18 percent of sales or less. Employee benefits include employer's portion of payroll taxes, workers' compensation, medical and other employee insurance premiums, plus all other employee-related expenses, such as meals. Employee benefits may run as much as 6 percent of gross sales and 25 percent of gross payroll. Industry standards recommend that management salaries should not exceed 10 percent of revenue. In many operations the general manager's salary may cost as much as 3 or 4 percent. Of course, an owner or manager may allocate a higher percentage to himself or herself.

OTHER EXPENSES

The sample income statement from this chapter included a line item for "Other Expenses." This category includes supplies, utilities, marketing, maintenance, rent, depreciation, insurance, and many other additional expenses. While insurance, depreciation, and rent are generally beyond restaurant and foodservice managers' control, they should carefully budget their controllable variable expenses such as marketing, supplies, maintenance, and utilities. As discussed before, most variable expenses can be estimated by using percentage of sales method. Marketing expenses is one category that is generally suitable for this method. For instance, in situations where the operation is both independent and new, managers may need to spend a considerable amount on marketing and advertising, such as 4 to 6 percent of total sales. However, an established operation may allocate only 1 percent of its total sales to its marketing budget.

Another method to estimate expenses in this category is historical average plus inflation. For a full-service establishment, if the annual cost of laundering linen is $2,000 and the expected increase due to inflation is 4 percent, the budget amount for next year will be $2,080.

A third method to estimate expenses is cost per customer method. If the supplies budget for last year was $1,800 and the operation served 40,000 customers, then a supplies cost per customer would be 4.5 cents ($1,800 ÷ 40,000). If the operation expects to serve 41,500 customers next year and assumes no increase in cost for next year, then the supplies budget would be $1,867.50 (41,500 × $0.045).

Budgeting Profit

The most basic goal of all business ventures is to make a profit. While some people may initially be uncomfortable about discussing profit, there is nothing threatening or negative about starting a plan by stating a profit goal. Guests, employees, vendors, and landlords all expect an establishment to make money. This is especially true of employees, since their welfare is directly tied to the operation's ability to make a profit. The majority of restaurant and foodservice operations define profits as the amount of funds left over after paying all expenses. Recall the profit formula from earlier in this chapter:

$$\textbf{Revenue} - \textbf{Expenses} = \textbf{Profit}$$

In an ideal world, running a business would be easy. An operation that offers a quality product backed by superior service in a wonderful atmosphere becomes popular, word spreads, and before the owner realizes it, sales and profits are growing rapidly. Unfortunately, in reality, few businesses are able to sit back and watch the profits roll in. Creating and consequently increasing profitability depends on doing all the little things better than the competition.

Some organizations use an approach where profit is treated as a "cost." This method determines the profit goal before calculating expenses. This may be a better choice if an operation is looking for a specific **return on investment (ROI),** or profit resulting from specific investments made in the operation. Entrepreneurs or corporations take risks for which they expect an adequate expected rate of return. The higher the risk and the longer the expected wait, the greater the expected return. Subtracting the required profit level from the forecasted revenue will determine ideal expenses:

$$\textbf{Revenue income} - \textbf{Required profit} = \textbf{Ideal expense}$$

Since managers know what the profit requirements are before beginning the budget process, they can plan accordingly by increasing revenue, decreasing expenses, or both. A manager also must consider the ROI needed to continue to grow the business.

HOW TO CALCULATE A BREAK-EVEN POINT

When calculating the required profit of an operation, it is also necessary to consider the operation's **break-even point**, which is the minimum amount of sales an establishment must generate in sales to cover all costs. Any revenue above this figure is considered profit.

To calculate the break-even point, first determine those expenses that are fixed and those that are variable (expenses that occur only if there are sales). Doing so allows managers to calculate the amount of sales it takes to keep from having a negative cash flow.

Exhibit 2.14

CALCULATING A BREAK-EVEN POINT

Fixed Costs	Per Week
Total management salaries	$2,200
Minimum hourly labor	6,000
Direct operating expenses	2,400
Marketing	750
Utilities	800
General and administrative	1,400
Repairs and maintenance	350
Occupancy costs	3,250
Loan and lease payments	1,600
Weekly fixed expenses	$18,750

Variable Costs	Percentage
Cost of sales	32.5%
Variable hourly labor	5.0
Credit card fees	2.0
Consumable supplies	1.0
Variable cost percentage	40.5%
Gross profit margin (100% − Cost %)	59.5%

Break-Even Calculation (divide fixed expenses by the gross profit margin %)	
Weekly fixed expenses	$18,750
Divided by gross profit margin	59.5%
Break-even point	**$31,512**

Fixed expenses are calculated in dollars, not a percentage of revenue. For example, occupancy costs may run $1,200 a month and the owner would need to pay those costs if he or she opened the doors or not. There are several other typical fixed expenses to consider:

- Management salaries
- Minimum staffing hourly labor
- Marketing expenses
- Administrative expenses
- Loan and lease payments

Variable expenses are calculated as percentages and can include several categories:

- Projected cost of linen
- Variable hourly labor (employees needed to accommodate additional sales volume)
- Energy costs

To calculate break-even, divide the fixed expenses by the gross profit margin percentage. The gross profit margin is the remaining percentage after subtracting the variable cost percentage from 100 percent. For example, a variable cost of 40 percent will result in a gross profit margin of 60 percent. *Exhibit 2.14* illustrates this formula.

As this example illustrates, the restaurant or foodservice operation would have to take in $31,512 in revenue to cover the fixed costs and the variable costs associated with sales. Any additional income during this period would be profit.

THE BUDGET AS A CONTROL TOOL

The budget sets the financial standards for an operation. It also helps the manager know when to review and revise plans, either because results are different from expectations or due to environmental, economic, market, or technological changes that no longer correspond to the original assumptions of the budget. Remember, effective control is based on having standards with which actual performance can be compared.

A budget provides a basis for comparing actual results with planned or desired results. As previously mentioned, the difference between the two is called a variance. A variance for each reporting period is calculated by subtracting budgeted data from actual results. Variances are easy to calculate. Managers use this formula:

Actual results − Budgeted data = Variance

These variances can be positive or negative. Consider an example where a manager had budgeted for $15,000 in sales, but achieved only $12,000 during the stated time period. In this case, the variance would be unfavorable:

$$\underset{\textbf{Actual results}}{\textbf{\$12,000}} \quad - \quad \underset{\textbf{Budgeted results}}{\textbf{\$15,000}} \quad = \quad \underset{\textbf{Variance}}{\textbf{$-$\$3,000}}$$

In this example, there is a negative revenue variance because the manager estimated that the establishment would generate more revenue than it actually did. Some managers use parentheses to express a negative variance. For example, they would write ($3,000) rather than $-$$3,000 when expressing a negative variance of $3,000.

Note how the formula works when calculating a favorable variance. Assume that the same manager had planned for $10,000 in revenue, but actually achieved $12,000 during that time period:

$$\underset{\textbf{Actual results}}{\textbf{\$12,000}} \quad - \quad \underset{\textbf{Budgeted results}}{\textbf{\$10,000}} \quad = \quad \underset{\textbf{Variance}}{\textbf{\$2,000}}$$

In this example, there is a positive revenue difference because the actual amount of revenue generated was greater than the amount planned.

Managers sometimes talk about variances in dollar figures. At other times, they may discuss variances in terms of a percentage difference. Variances can be calculated as a percentage difference using the following equation:

(Actual results $-$ Budgeted results) $\div$ Budgeted results = % Variance

What if a manager had planned for 10,000 customers in a given week, but actually serviced 11,000 customers in that time period? The percentage variance for this example is calculated as follows:

$$\underset{\substack{\textbf{Actual}\\\textbf{results}}}{\textbf{(11,000}} \quad - \quad \underset{\substack{\textbf{Budgeted}\\\textbf{results}}}{\textbf{10,000)}} \quad \div \quad \underset{\substack{\textbf{Budgeted}\\\textbf{results}}}{\textbf{10,000}} \quad = \quad \underset{\textbf{% Variance}}{\textbf{10%}}$$

In this example, the operation generated a 10 percent positive difference in weekly customer count because the actual weekly count was 10 percent greater than planned.

In most businesses, some variance between actual and budgeted numbers is normal and expected. Large variances, however, call for either adjusting the budgeted projections to represent the new reality, or controlling actual spending in future reporting periods so that the yearly variance comes closer to zero.

Assessing Results

Managers should review income statements regularly against budgeted figures. The information in *Exhibit 2.15* should be alarming to managers, especially the prime cost number, which is now dangerously close to the 65 percent cap. The issue appears to be the decline in beverage sales, which resulted in an increase to total cost of sales.

Exhibit 2.15

REVIEWING INCOME STATEMENTS AGAINST BUDGETS

	Budget	Actual	Variance	Budget %	Actual %
SALES					
Food	$ 850,000	$925,000	$75,000	63.8%	67.0%
Beverage	482,000	456,100	(25,900)	36.2%	33.0%
TOTAL SALES	$1,332,000	$1,381,100	$49,100	100%	100%
COST OF SALES					
Food	$288,750	$315,250	($26,500)	21.7%	22.8%
Beverage	135,700	142,200	(6,500)	10.2%	10.3%
TOTAL COST OF SALES	$424,450	$457,450	($33,000)	31.9%	33.1%
Gross Profit					
	$907,550	$923,650	$16,100	68.1%	66.9%
PAYROLL					
Salaries & Wages	$346,785	$358,900	($12,115)	26.0%	26.0%
Employee Benefits	71,950	74,600	(2,650)	5.4%	5.4%
TOTAL PAYROLL	$418,735	$433,500	($14,765)	31.4%	31.4%
PRIME COST	$843,185	$890,950	($47,765)	63.3%	**64.5%**

Exhibit 2.16

An examination of sales identified significant variance in beverage sales. While examining the numbers shown in *Exhibit 2.15*, the manager recalled that recently there had been above-normal turnover in service staff. After drilling down into the beverage sales numbers, he discovered that the slippage was in wine sales (*Exhibit 2.16*). That is, while wine sales remained below budget, cost of sales for wines exceeded the budgeted amount. The reason for misalignment between level of wine sales and wine costs was due to poor wine knowledge on the part of the service staff. Once the manager determined the problem, the next step was to determine what corrective action to take to fix the issue.

Taking Corrective Action

In the case of the slipping wine sales, the manager's corrective action was to conduct consistent training with an emphasis on wine. The objectives of this training were twofold: to increase wine sales and to control wine costs.

To conduct this training program the manager hired a sommelier, a wine professional with extensive training and knowledge who specializes in all aspects of wine service as well as wine and food pairing. To achieve the first objective, the program educated servers about wine varietals and pairings of food and wine. In addition, service staff was offered a bonus for selling "wine by the bottle" priced $40 or higher.

The second part of the program focused on wine costs. Due to high employee turnover, newly hired staff did not possess wine service competency, which resulted in poor wine recommendations, customer returns, and spilled wine. The sommelier conducted several demonstration and training sessions about wine service.

In the next budget year, the establishment was able to increase its wine sales, control wine costs, and increase employee retention due to the "wine sales" bonus system in place. This example clearly shows that variances can be a valuable catalyst for managerial action and thus help improve the profitability of operations.

SUMMARY

1. **Explain the purpose of budgets and forecasts.**

   Forecasting uses historical information and knowledge of external factors to predict future results. These forecasts are used to build a budget. Forecasting usually takes past numbers and builds in a certain additional percentage to account for growth. A budget is a plan that shows how managers expect to obtain and use resources to achieve the objectives of the business.

THINK ABOUT IT . . .

Expenses may be incurred during the year that are not part of the operating budget. For instance, how might a wine sales bonus be categorized, assuming it was not in the original operating budget?

Manager's Memo

Being able to compare an establishment's financial and operating data with industry averages allows owners and managers to get a feeling for how they are doing compared to other similar businesses. Preparing an income statement in a format consistent with the National Restaurant Association's Uniform System of Accounts for Restaurants (USAR) makes comparison with the Restaurant Industry Operations Report simple and meaningful, with several critical advantages:

- Allows for a "common language" based on industry specific standards

- Allows for the easy comparison of operating numbers in the same format

- Provides detailed instructions for accurately classifying (cost-coding) the different expenses associated with operating a restaurant

- Gives restaurant and foodservice managers credibility when presenting to investors

2. **List and describe the forecasting methods used by restaurant and foodservice managers.**

    There are two major forecasting methods that are used by restaurant and foodservice managers. The percentage of sales method forecasts cost of sales and labor cost relative to expected revenue. The simple markup method forecasts sales and expenses by adding the expected growth rate to last year's figures.

3. **Describe types of budgets.**

    Budgets may be long or short term, and cover a whole operation or only one business segment. The main budget for most restaurant and foodservice operations is the operating budget. This budget presents a plan for revenues and expenses for a period of time. Most operations will find a four-week cycle to be the most useful. However, budgets must be examined cyclically for accuracy and to find areas in which to improve. Budgeting for shorter cycles, such as a week or a month, should be fairly accurate, while yearly budgets and five-year plans will need to be adjusted to accommodate changing or unexpected conditions.

4. **Identify the purpose of the income statement.**

    Actual spending and revenue data are used to create an income statement to compare with the budgeted target numbers. The difference between the two figures is called a variance.

    Variances may be caused by factors that are outside managers' control, such as economic conditions or stronger than expected demand. However, managers should make every effort to attempt to meet their target, or adjust the budget to better reflect current conditions.

5. **Describe how to prepare food and labor cost budgets.**

    Food and labor costs should include historical trends when establishing budgets. Managers should analyze trends for differences between as purchased and actual cost. If there is a decrease in utilization factor for food items, managers need to identify the reasons for a loss (i.e., shrinkage, theft, spoilage, etc.).

    When budgeting labor, managers should first assign wage rates for both part-time and full-time employees. Next, total labor cost for full-time and part-time employees should be calculated. Since benefit costs of full-time employees are higher, managers should carefully adjust schedules of employees based on meal times, menu complexity, and service level.

6. **Explain the importance of variance and its use in operations.**

    When actual results differ from budget projections, that difference is called a variance. A variance may be positive or negative. A significant variance is a sign that a manager may need to take corrective action to address the problem.

APPLICATION EXERCISE

Golda's Skillet Diner has the following information: customer count, daily sales, food cost percentage, and labor cost percentage information. The establishment does not estimate beverage cost separately. Given the following information, prepare a sales forecast, a food cost budget, and a labor cost budget.

	Sunday	Monday	Tuesday	Wednesday	Thursday	Friday	Saturday	Totals/Avg.
Customer count	104	62	76		146	200	222	
Daily sales ($)	$2,300.00	$1,563.00	$1,876.00	$2,694.00	$4,151.00	$5,183.00		
Average check per customer ($)								
Food cost (%)	27%	28%	29%	28%	30%	31%		
Food cost budget ($)								
Labor cost (%)	25%	28%	30%	29%	29%		32%	
Labor cost budget ($)								
Prime cost (%)								

A. It is assumed that the customer count for Saturday is twice as high as Wednesday. What is the total weekly customer count?

B. It is also assumed that daily sales for Saturday are triple than sales on Tuesday. How much are total weekly sales?

C. How much is the average check for each day, and for the whole week?

D. Food cost percentage is 10% higher on Saturday than on Thursday. How much is the daily food cost percentage for the week?

E. How much is the food cost budget for the week?

F. Labor cost percentage is 20% higher on Friday than on Monday. What is the labor cost percentage for the week?

G. What is the total labor cost budget for the week?

H. What is the average prime cost percentage on a weekly basis?

REVIEW YOUR LEARNING

Select the best answer for each question.

1. Which of the following is a labor cost forecasting method?

   A. Sales forecast

   B. Labor hours per day

   C. Percentage of sales

   D. Break-even point

2. Which of the following is a long-term budget?

   A. Monthly labor budget

   B. Weekly food cost budget

   C. Operating budget

   D. Monthly marketing budget

3. Generally, what is the highest expense in restaurant and foodservice operations?

   A. Prime cost

   B. Beverage cost

   C. Linen cost

   D. Wage cost

4. Calculate the average check per customer if an operation has weekly sales of $9,300 and a weekly customer count of 258.

   A. $25.80

   B. $35.75

   C. $27.74

   D. $36.05

5. At a local bistro, total fixed costs for June were $176,432. In that month, 8,652 covers were served. What was fixed cost per cover for June?

   A. $17.64

   B. $20.39

   C. $23.90

   D. $26.38

Questions 6, 7, 8, 9 and 10 are based on the following sample income statement for the PanPan Noodle House:

Description	Dollars	Percentages
Revenues	$800,000	100%
Food and beverage costs	$300,000	37.5%
Labor costs	350,000	43.7
Other costs	50,000	6.25
Total expense	**$700,000**	**87.5%**
Profit	$100,000	12.5%

6. How much is the prime cost for PanPan Noodle House?

    A. $300,000

    B. $400,000

    C. $650,000

    D. $750,000

7. If the Other costs category increases by 40%, how much would profits for PanPan Noodle House be, assuming that all other items do not change?

    A. $60,000

    B. $70,000

    C. $80,000

    D. $140,000

8. If the desired profit is 15%, what is the ideal total expense?

    A. $100,000

    B. $120,000

    C. $680,000

    D. $700,000

9. If revenues are expected to increase by 3% and total expenses by 2.5%, what is the budgeted profit for next year?

    A. $75,500

    B. $97,500

    C. $103,000

    D. $106,500

10. If the budget for food and beverage costs drops to $280,000 and the budget for total revenue remains at $800,000, what is the new food and beverage cost as percentage of sales?

    A. 32%

    B. 35%

    C. 37%

    D. 39%

3 Calculating Food Cost

INSIDE THIS CHAPTER

- **What Is Food Cost?**
- **Calculating Basic Food Cost**
- **Calculating Food Cost Percentage**
- **Standardized Recipes**
- **Standardized Recipe Files**
- **Costing Standardized Recipes**
- **Calculating Plate Costs**
- **Calculating Buffet and Salad Bar Costs**

CHAPTER LEARNING OBJECTIVES

After completing this chapter, you should be able to:

- Define food costs and explain how managers track and analyze food costs.

- Explain how to calculate the cost of sales and how to calculate the actual cost of sales.

- Describe how to calculate the food cost percentage.

- Explain the importance of standardized recipes to cost control and product consistency.

- Contrast the three types of standardized recipe files.

- Describe why and how managers create recipe cost cards.

- Outline the process for calculating plate cost.

- Explain how managers calculate food costs for buffets.

KEY TERMS

CASE STUDY

Chef Paul was recently hired by a local steakhouse. During his first week of work, Chef Paul asked the restaurant's general manager about the state of the business. She told him that the restaurant was struggling. In fact, the establishment had not turned a profit for the past three years.

Chef Paul was puzzled. His first impression was that the restaurant had a pleasant ambiance, experienced staff, and appropriate equipment. He wondered why the restaurant was struggling.

The general manager explained that the restaurant uses family recipes that are ideal for a party of four. In addition, the food costing is based on the sale price of a dish. Customers like the restaurant's generous portions, but the operation continues to lose money.

Thanks to his training and experience, Chef Paul recognized several places where procedures could be improved to make the restaurant profitable again. He suggested that he and the general manager sit down and discuss the issues in more depth, and then draw up an action plan.

1. What are some of the things that the general manager overlooked in her explanation? Explain.

2. What corrective actions can the general manager take together with Chef Paul?

WHAT IS FOOD COST?

What exactly is food cost? Many people, including some restaurant and foodservice managers, think that when food is purchased, it becomes food cost. It is true that purchases are an important part of food cost; however, food cost refers to food that is actually used. Food cost is the actual dollar value of the food used by an operation during a certain period. Food cost is sometimes referred to as cost of sales, or cost of goods sold. It includes fruit, vegetables, dairy, protein (meat, fish, poultry), and other categories of food expenses. However, it should be noted that cost of sales includes two types of costs: food cost and beverage cost. Therefore, food cost and cost of sales cannot be used interchangeably if an operation has beverage sales. This chapter will focus on food cost.

CALCULATING BASIC FOOD COST

To calculate the basic food cost, a manager needs to know three key pieces of information:

- **Opening inventory:** the value of how much food product exists at the start of a given period
- **Purchases:** the value of how much the operation spent on food product in a given period
- **Closing inventory:** the value of how much food product exists at the end of a given period

Inventory

Inventory represents the dollar value of a food product in storage. It can be expressed in terms of units, values, or both. Most operations will have hundreds of food items in inventory at any given time. Opening inventory, also called beginning inventory, is the physical inventory at the beginning of a given period, such as the month of April. The closing inventory is the inventory at the end of a given period. It is important to remember that when one period ends, a new period begins. Therefore, the opening inventory is always equal to the closing inventory of the previous period.

A period can consist of a day, week, month, quarter, or year. Most operations conduct inventory and figure food cost monthly or every 28 days, but some quick-service operations may do it weekly. A more detailed discussion on storeroom operation, storeroom reconciliation, and inventory control will appear in later chapters.

Purchases

In addition to taking inventory on a regular basis, managers must also keep a record of food purchases. Remember to post any credits for returns or invoice adjustments. Credit is issued by the supplier to the purchaser for returns of food items, while invoice adjustments are done when the amount of food items received is different from the amount of food items ordered. For example, if an establishment ordered 50 pounds of T-bone steaks but received 40 pounds, an invoice adjustment reflecting the 10 pounds' difference should be made. Also, managers need to log the amount paid for each. At the end of the period, the manager will have a record of total purchases of food. The same holds true for beverages such as liquor, beer, and wine. See *Exhibit 3.1* as an example.

Exhibit 3.1

PURCHASES FOR PAUL'S GRILL

			Paul's Grill Purchase Log				
Week of May 20–26							
Date	**Invoice Number**	**Vendor**	**Invoice Amount**	**Food**	**Liquor**	**Beer**	**Wine**
5/20	5164	Bobbie's Produce	$402.60	$402.60			
5/20	415661	Cliff Liquor	500.00		$500.00		
5/24	5923	Mary Meats	734.25	734.25			
5/24	5204	Bobbie's Produce	325.60	325.60			
5/25	12000	C-Control Distributors	628.75			$425.35	$203.40
5/26	11913	Heimly Foods	1,462.00	1,462.00			
5/26	477415	El General Supply	240.40	240.40			
		Total Purchases	$4,293.60	$3,164.85	$500.00	$425.35	$203.40

Cost of Sales Formula

Once a manager knows the opening and closing inventories, as well as the purchases made in a given period, he or she can quickly calculate the cost of sales. The formula for cost of sales is simple:

(Opening inventory + Purchases) − Closing inventory = Cost of sales

Assume that the House of Noodles started the month of July with an inventory worth $2,500 and made $6,500 worth of purchases in that month. At the end of the month, the establishment held $1,800 in inventory. Calculating the cost of sales for the House of Noodles would look like this:

$$
\begin{array}{ccccccc}
(\$2,500 & + & \$6,500) & - & \$1,800 & = & \$7,200 \\
\text{Opening} & & \text{Purchases} & & \text{Closing} & & \text{Cost of} \\
\text{inventory} & & & & \text{inventory} & & \text{sales}
\end{array}
$$

The overall cost of sales for the House of Noodles in July was $7,200. By using the same formula, managers can separately calculate food costs and beverage costs for any operation.

Calculating Actual Cost of Sales

Recall that cost of sales is the actual dollar value of the food and beverage used by an operation during a certain period. In addition to costs associated with purchases, a manager needs to know the expense incurred when food and beverages are consumed for any reason. These expenses include purchases plus food given away, wasted, or even stolen (*Exhibit 3.2*). Expenses can be further broken down into purchases and transfers.

Exhibit 3.2

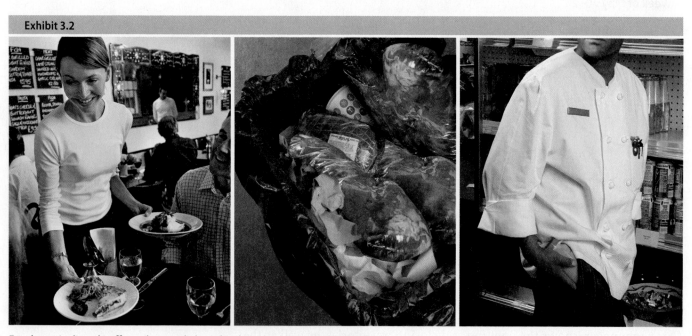

Food cost is directly affected not only by sales, but also by waste and theft.

Purchases and Credits

Recall that purchases are the amount spent on all food purchased during the reporting period. As demonstrated, total purchases are calculated by adding all invoices for that specific reporting period. An operation will also have credits to cost of sales. These are food and beverage expenses or revenues that are not directly related to restaurant or foodservice operations. These can be subtracted from purchases to give managers a more accurate picture.

CREDITS TO COST OF SALES

Credits to cost of sales will vary from operation to operation. Following are some typical categories of credits:

- **Employee meals (at cost):** If an operation feeds its employees, this number is part of its cost of sales. In the case of a hotel, this could be a substantial amount, considering the large numbers of housekeeping, front desk, maintenance, and food and beverage staff.

- **Comp (at cost):** An abbreviation of the word *complimentary*, this term is used to describe managers giving a free meal to a guest. It could be because the guest was disgruntled, or merely because the person is prominent in the community and it is good for business to have this caliber of person in the establishment. Some operations comp public safety officers or persons on active military duty. Often comps are recorded as promotional expenses. There should be a budget standard for the amount of comps allowed during any reporting period.

- **Grease sales:** Old oil from the deep fryers, as well as fat or bones (if an operation does its own meat cutting) can be sold to rendering companies. Since these items were a food cost originally, when they are sold the amount of the sale is taken as a credit to cost of sales.

Transfers

Transfer refers to the process of moving food, and its associated cost, from one part of the operation to another. Transfers might be used in larger operations in which there is more than one outlet for food. If kitchen A were to transfer goods to kitchen B, the loss would be subtracted from kitchen A's food cost. Kitchen B would then add the transfer to its food cost.

FOOD-TO-BAR TRANSFERS

This type of transfer is used primarily where food items are moved to the bar for use in drink preparation. Some examples are limes and strawberries, or food items such as cream, whipped cream, or olives. This should not be confused with a customer ordering and paying for food eaten in the bar.

COST TRANSFERS FROM OTHER UNITS

Sometimes, food or beverage costs will be transferred to the kitchen from another unit or area. One example of this might be alcoholic beverages being transferred from bar to kitchen. The use of alcoholic beverages in the kitchen is generally referred to as *cooking liquor.* Beer might be used for onion ring batter. Wine is often used for risotto or deglazing pans to prepare meat sauce. For menu items that use a large amount of cooking liquor, managers should communicate with the bar to make sure that there is enough in stock. In addition, managers should make sure that the cost of cooking liquor is included in the recipe cost.

THINK ABOUT IT ...

What are some other factors or circumstances that would add to or subtract from an operation's food cost? How might these factors be accounted for?

Why Managers Care about Cost of Sales

Calculating the cost of sales on a regular basis allows an operation to identify problems. This gives managers the opportunity to compare actual results with targets and take corrective action if necessary. Managers who take inventories and calculate their cost of sales on a regular basis, usually weekly, are far more profitable than those who do not. Establishments that conduct inventory and calculate cost of sales can increase profits from 2 to 10 percent. There are two primary reasons for this. As noted, managers can take action sooner when they have accurate information. The second reason is that excess inventory takes money out of the bank and keeps it on the shelves. Extra inventory is also susceptible to spoilage, waste, and theft. Establishments that have an accurate record of actual cost of sales can better plan their future operations by paying more attention to products that are both expensive and perishable, such as truffle mushrooms.

Food and beverage sales are the two main profit centers of just about any restaurant or foodservice operation. However, for many operations, food sales must cover not just the actual cost of the food product, but also expenses such as payroll, rent, insurance, repairs, marketing, utilities, and so on and still produce a profit. It is essential that a manager control costs of sales as effectively as possible.

CALCULATING FOOD COST PERCENTAGE

Once the actual food cost has been determined, the next step is to calculate the food cost percentage. Food cost percentage is the relationship between sales and the cost spent on food to achieve those sales. Food cost percentage is often the standard against which food cost is judged. Food cost percentage may be analyzed by comparing it to company standards, historical costs, or even industry standards. In most cases, the standard food cost percentage is a target determined by managers.

By expressing the cost of food sold in percentages, it can be compared on a month-to-month or week-to-week basis regardless of any fluctuation in sales. Controlling the food cost percentage becomes paramount if the operation is to be profitable. Remember that food cost is a key component of prime cost. To calculate food cost percentage, divide the food cost by food sales:

Food cost ÷ Food sales = Food cost percentage

Thus, if food cost is $8,500, and food sales are $27,490, the food cost percentage is 30.9 percent:

$$\underset{\textbf{Food cost}}{\textbf{\$8,500}} \quad \div \quad \underset{\textbf{Food sales}}{\textbf{\$27,490}} \quad = \quad \underset{\substack{\textbf{Food cost} \\ \textbf{percentage}}}{\textbf{30.9\%}}$$

Note: *To convert a decimal into a percentage, simply move the decimal two places to the right or multiply the answer by 100.*

Another way to state this is to say that out of every dollar of sales, food cost accounted for about $0.31. This example indicates an average food cost percentage for a given period. The calculation can be broken down into further levels of detail, such as by menu item, menu category, or meal period. For instance, the average breakfast food cost percentage might be lower than the average dinner food cost percentage. Note that automated systems exist to help managers track, calculate, and differentiate food cost percentages (*Exhibit 3.3*).

How Costs and Sales Affect Food Cost Percentage

Food cost is identified as a variable expense in the previous chapter. This means that it increases or decreases as sales increase or decrease, and does so in direct proportion. That is, it *should* do so in direct proportion if all of the standards and controls are followed. If the cost controls are not followed, food costs will not change in direct proportion to sales.

Therefore, if an operation meets its standard food cost percentage month after month, its standards are set properly and the control system is working. If it does not meet its standard, then either the standards are set wrong or the controls are not working, or both.

For example, if a three-ounce hamburger has a food cost of $0.50 and sells for $1.50, the food cost percentage is 33.3 percent:

$0.50 ÷ **$1.50** = **33.3%**
Food cost   **Sale price**   **Food cost percentage**

Assuming that this percentage is the standard set by managers, if the prep cook portions the hamburger at four ounces, thereby increasing the food cost to $0.60, the food cost percentage increases to 40 percent:

$0.60 ÷ **$1.50** = **40%**
Food cost   **Sale price**   **Food cost percentage**

The food cost percentage does not increase or decrease in direct proportion to the selling price because the standard was not met. Instead, the food cost increased while the selling price stayed the same. In this case, the standard was set correctly. However, the control was not met, and the food cost percentage increased.

Exhibit 3.3

THINK ABOUT IT ...

What should an operation's food cost percentage be? How might you set different standards, depending on the operation and its type of service, location, and specific business goals?

The following problems involve figuring food cost percentages.

1. Food cost: $5,722

   Sales: $18,900

What is the food cost percentage of the establishment?

2. Menu item cost: $1.35

   Selling price of an item: $4.00

What is the food cost percentage for the menu item?

(Answers: 1. 30.3%; 2. 33.7%)

To look at it another way, assume that the server charged $2.00 for the hamburger, and it was made according to standard. The food cost percentage would be 25 percent:

$$\$0.50 \div \$2.00 = 25\%$$

Food cost   **Sale price**   **Food cost percentage**

At first glance, managers might say that this is good because the food cost percentage is below the standard of 33.3 percent and more profit will be made. In the long run, however, this is not good, since the restaurant and foodservice industry is very competitive. The customer will not pay $2.00 for an item that is only worth $1.50, especially if they could get it elsewhere for that amount. It is critical to remember that lost sales result in lost profit.

Managers may consider cost control as the elimination of any expense that will not diminish a guest's overall experience. So an operation needs to be careful to not reduce quality or portion size to the point that they impact the expectations of the guest and become unacceptable.

Food cost is important, specifically when considering prime cost, but do not forget to look at the big picture. Managers who chase only food cost percentage often lose profit. For example, if a chicken item is listed on the menu for $12 and it costs $3, the food cost percentage would be 25 percent:

$$\$3 \div \$12 = 25\%$$

Food cost   **Sale price**   **Food cost percentage**

If a rack of lamb on the menu sells for $32 and costs $12, the lamb item has a food cost percentage of 37.5 percent:

$$\$12 \div \$32 = 37.5\%$$

Food cost   **Sale price**   **Food cost percentage**

Looking only at food cost percentage, the chicken item would seem to be the preferred item to sell, given a 25 percent food cost compared to 37.5 percent. However, *Exhibit 3.4* shows the contribution margin for each item.

With the chicken, the operation takes in $9, but with the lamb the gross profit, or contribution margin, is $20. Higher-cost menu items may have a higher food cost percentage because the markup must be smaller, but often they are more profitable. This is also the case on most wine lists.

Exhibit 3.4			
Item	**Sales Price**	**Food Cost**	**Contribution Margin**
Chicken	$12	$ 3	$ 9
Lamb	32	12	20

Exhibit 3.5 demonstrates a final example. Rose either has not set her controls correctly or is not following them correctly. These examples show how important it is that standards are met exactly. There are a number of standards that must be monitored and controlled constantly. This task is one of the more difficult ones for managers.

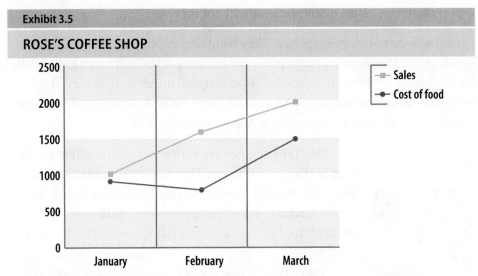

Exhibit 3.5

ROSE'S COFFEE SHOP

This graph show the sales and food costs for the first three months of this year for Rose's Coffee Shop. Notice that food cost is not in direct proportion to sales.

Food cost is normally considered to be in good shape if the current food cost percentage is consistent or in line with past periods. Unfortunately, the people who have accountability for food cost do not always have control over all factors that could have caused food cost to be higher or lower. These factors include changes in menu offerings, **sales mix** of menu items, which is the percentage of sales volume each menu item contributes to total sales, and raw product costs.

During the budgeting process, every operation should establish a food cost percentage standard or benchmark that reflects the current menu, prices, recipes, raw product costs, and sales mix that can be compared with the operation's actual food cost. This type of food cost percentage standard is often referred to as "ideal" or "theoretical" food cost. Managers can compare actuals against the ideal costs to assess the operation. *Exhibit 3.6* shows an example of such analysis.

Costing out an operation's menu is the only way to calculate **ideal food cost**, or the target cost an operation is aiming for. Recipes consist of many different items, and most establishments have hundreds of raw products. Costing out these recipes must be done to see the intricacies of what makes up food cost.

Exhibit 3.6

Percentage	
Ideal food cost	31.5%
Actual food cost	33.4
Variance (Unfavorable)	(1.9%)
Dollar	
Ideal food cost	$12,450
Actual food cost	13,215
Variance	($ 765)

STANDARDIZED RECIPES

Why do people return to any establishment? Normally, they return because they enjoyed something about the experience they had the last time they visited. National Restaurant Association surveys have found that the average fine-dining establishment gets around 60 percent of sales from repeat customers. Among casual operations, that figure increases to around 80 percent. Without repeat customers, most establishments will not survive.

Customers do not want surprises. They want and expect consistency. Many quick-service restaurants are popular not because of the culinary skill of their cooks, but rather because people know exactly what they will be served when they visit. When people return to an establishment and the dining or service experience is different, they rarely give it another chance.

Standardized recipes are a formalized, consistent guide to preparing menu items. They list the ingredients and quantities needed for a menu item, as well as the methods used to produce it and its appropriate portion size. Standardized recipes are essential for any establishment to be consistent and prepare food that looks and tastes the same every time, day after day, week after week, and year after year. While the number one reason for using standardized recipes is because it increases customer satisfaction, there are a number of other important reasons.

Developing Standardized Recipes

The purpose of the recipe development process for restaurant and foodservice operations is to commit current production procedures to a written or computerized form to take advantage of costing, scheduling, training, and other benefits. The steps of developing a standardized recipe are shown in *Exhibit 3.7*.

Step 1: Observe Menu Item Preparation Process.

Food-production employees can be observed as they prepare the menu item (*Exhibit 3.8*). What ingredients are used and in what quantities? How and when are the ingredients weighed and measured? What small and large equipment is needed and when? How is the item portioned after preparation? When different cooks produce the same item, production techniques used by each employee should be observed.

Exhibit 3.7

STANDARDIZED RECIPE DEVELOPMENT: CURRENT MENU ITEMS

Step 1: Observe Menu Item Preparation Process

Step 2: Consider Preparation Details

Step 3: Write Recipe Draft

Step 4: Review and Revise Recipe Draft

Step 5: Use Recipe for Preparation

Step 6: Evaluate Recipe

Step 7: Consider Further Revisions (If Necessary)

Step 8: Implement and Consistently Use the Recipe

Step 2: Consider Preparation Details.

Can some preparation tasks be combined? If utensils needed for several recipe steps are all stored in the same general area, include a procedure suggesting, "Obtain all necessary utensils [state what they are]." This can increase productivity by saving the time needed for repeat trips to the utensil storage area. **Productivity** refers to the quality and quantity of output compared to the amount of input such as labor hours needed to generate it.

Step 3: Write Recipe Draft.

A first draft of the recipe that incorporates observations from step 1 and details from step 2 now becomes important. This is the first attempt that lists all ingredients, utensils, and so on, and lists production procedures. This is the step at which the recipe should be costed.

Step 4: Review and Revise Recipe Draft.

The recipe draft should be reviewed by the production personnel who prepare the item. At this step, any revisions to production procedures should be made.

Step 5: Use Recipe for Preparation.

The recipe draft should be carefully followed to prepare the menu item. This stage can be referred to as a recipe testing stage where all directions are put into action.

Step 6: Evaluate Recipe.

The food item produced in step 5 should be carefully evaluated to determine if quality standards have been attained. At this step, production personnel evaluate any deviations from established quality standards, such as meat being dry or vegetables being overcooked.

Step 7: Consider Further Revisions, If Necessary.

If the recipe does not yield a product meeting quality standards, further revisions to the recipe are necessary. For example, if cooking time for steamed vegetables is too long, chefs will need to shorten cooking time and record the change in the standardized recipe.

Step 8: Implement and Consistently Use the Recipe.

After the recipe is developed with agreement about desired quality, it should be used each time the product is prepared.

Exhibit 3.8

Advantages of Using Standardized Recipes

The **standardized recipe form** includes a set of directions for preparing a food or beverage item, along with a list of ingredients. The recipe should account for the type of operation, available kitchen equipment, and skill levels of the kitchen or beverage staff. There are some tangible advantages of using standardized recipes:

Exhibit 3.9

- **Simplifies costing of menu items:** The only way to establish effective menu selling prices is to know the cost of each item. The information on standardized recipes allows for precise calculation of portion costs. These are also important data when developing budgetary guidelines.

- **Encourages consistent plate presentation:** Standardized recipes include portion sizes and serving details, which helps ensure that menu items look the same each time a guest orders the item (*Exhibit 3.9*).

- **Promotes consistent food-production quality:** Standardized recipes should be thoroughly tested, which reduces the possibility of the finished dish being affected by the personal preferences or skill level of the cook. The more information employees have, the more likely they are to repeatedly produce the item correctly. No one in the operation should include personal preferences in standardized recipes, nor should anyone be allowed to substitute amounts, ingredients, or cooking techniques.

- **Promotes consistent yields:** As part of the development of a recipe, the total yield is tested and determined.

- **Increases productivity of the kitchen staff:** Standardized recipes include procedures that are clear and simplified to eliminate confusion among kitchen staff. Cooks using standardized recipes work smarter, cleaner, and faster, which helps reduce the overall labor needed in the kitchen.

- **Improves job satisfaction:** Cooks and kitchen staff using standardized recipes know what to do, how to do it, and what the end product should be. Clear expectations and a measurable way to meet them increase employees' overall job satisfaction.

- **Simplifies the training of kitchen staff:** Correctly written standardized recipes with detailed, accurate procedures reduce the time and energy required when training new personnel. Recipe cards reduce the amount of information that must be committed to memory, which allows the cook to concentrate on producing a great product, not remembering what the ingredients and procedures are.

- **Saves money by controlling inventory levels:** Standardized recipes help determine the amount of food to order. Appropriate inventory levels keep money in the bank, not on stockroom shelves.

- **Saves money by controlling overproduction:** Standardized recipes enable operations to achieve a consistent yield, even when preparing meals in large amounts. This is particularly the case for occasions such as celebration parties, business dinners, or weddings.

Product Specifications

Product specifications describe the quality requirements of the products that are purchased. They help ensure that staff, managers, and vendors have the same understanding about quality needs. Before developing purchase specifications, managers need to use recipe cards to identify which items are needed. Depending on the complexity of the menu, sometimes managers need to prepare product specifications for several items in one recipe. Once product needs are identified, the next step would be to identify what products are available in the market. Managers may search the database of their vendors to determine availability of given products.

It is important to search for availability item by item. Identified products sold by vendors are then matched against desired specifications of a given item. For example, an establishment may be looking for lamb rack from Australia, Frenched with 10 ribs per rack in packs of 6. The grade should be Prime. However, a vendor may sell lamb rack Frenched with 8 ribs from New Zealand in packs of 10. The USDA grade is Choice, which is below Prime. Another vendor offers Prime Grade lamb rack Frenched with 10 ribs in packs of 8 from California. In such situations, managers need to sort available items based how available items match recipe needs.

Finally, managers need to develop several criteria that are important about items of interest, such as the lamb rack. For example, how important is number of items in a pack? How about the origin of an item? Is it acceptable to have a lower-grade item? All these considerations are the foundation of developing purchase specifications.

Effective purchase specifications must meet several requirements:

- They must be simple and short while providing accurate product descriptions.
- They must be capable of being met by several vendors to encourage competitive bidding.
- They must be capable of being verified to ensure that proper quality is received.
- They must be written to permit reasonable compliance with quality requirements.

Product specifications inform vendors about the operation's required quality standards. They allow vendors to quote applicable prices for products when quantity and other order requirements are known. Specifications can be described in several ways:

Exhibit 3.10

- **Brand or trade name:** Managers who specify a specific brand of ketchup are indicating a quality preference.

- **Certification with industry specification:** Consider the North American Meat Processors Association (NAMP) and its Meat Buyer's Guide (MBG) numbers. When a manager specifies, for example, NAMP #1185, then a bottom sirloin butt steak meeting specific quality standards is identified. Federal grading standards such as Prime, Choice, and Select are additional examples of widely circulated and recognized specifications and are available for many products.

- **Careful description of the required product:** There are many products such as fresh seafood, meat, and dairy products that cannot be identified by a brand name or a trade-recognized product number. Written purchase specification statements are needed for these items.

- **Use of samples:** Samples of products currently used by a restaurant or foodservice organization may serve as specifications. For example, a manager may want to buy ready-made specialty bread products, and samples may be given to possible vendors as an example of the quality standards required by the operation (*Exhibit 3.10*).

STANDARDIZED RECIPE FILES

Recipes must be easy to read or they will not be used. There are a number of different formats that can be used for recipe standardization. They should be readable at a distance of 18 to 20 inches by a person in a standing position. Staff should not have to pick up the recipe for a closer look. This generally eliminates smaller cards. To keep recipes clean, they should be placed in a plastic cover or laminated for use in the kitchen.

The standardized form, as seen in *Exhibit 3.11*, includes a list of all ingredients at the top with numbered procedural steps listed below. However, the drawback of the standardized recipe form is that it requires the eyes to constantly shift between two places—the procedural steps and the ingredients list.

Exhibit 3.11

STANDARDIZED RECIPE FORM

Black Sea Bass with an Herb Crust and Salsify

Original total yield:	28 oz
Portion size:	7 oz
Number of portions:	4
Equipment required:	Scale, baking sheet, food processor, 12-inch sauté pan, broiler
Preparation time:	20 minutes
Cooking time:	10 minutes

10 Portions	25 Portions	Original Amount	Unit	Ingredient	Preparation Method
2.50	6.25	1	oz	Chives	
1.25	3.13	0.5	oz	Chervil	Herbs picked clean
2.50	6.25	1	oz	Parsley	Leaves only
1.25	3.13	0.5	oz	Tarragon	
1.25	3.13	0.5	oz	Rosemary	
2.50	6.25	1	oz	Basil	
2.50	6.25	1	oz	White bread, sliced	Trimmed of crust
12.50	31.25	5	oz	Sweet butter	Softened
				Salt and pepper	To taste
2.50	6.25	1	lb	Salsify	Peeled, sliced ¼ inch
4.38	10.94	1.75	lb	Black sea bass, 1 ¼ lb whole fish	Cut to 7-oz fillets
1.25	3.13	0.5	oz	Vegetable oil	

Procedure:
1. Place the herbs in the food processor and chop finely. Reserve 1 Tbsp of the chopped herb mixture for the salsify and 4 sprigs of chervil for garnish.
2. Add the bread to the herbs in the food processor and finely chop. Add 80% of the butter and salt and pepper to the mixture and process until smooth. Reserve.
3. Boil the salsify slices in salted water until tender. Drain and toss with remaining butter and herbs, and salt and pepper to taste. Reserve.
4. Salt and pepper the sea bass fillets. Sear them in the vegetable oil on both sides, and then transfer them to a broiling pan.
5. Spread the bread and herb mixture evenly over the skin of each fillet. When ready to serve, broil the fillets until the herb crust has melted and starts to brown.

Portioning, plating, and garnishing instructions:
Arrange 4 oz of the salsify and herb mixture on a warmed serving plate. Place the sea bass fillet over the salsify, and drizzle 1 oz of the melted butter from the broiling pan all around. Garnish with sprigs of fresh chervil and fried salsify.

Breakdown, cleanup, and storage instructions:
Prepare only what will be consumed immediately, as this dish is fragile and cannot be reheated. Any extra peeled raw salsify should be held under refrigeration in a mixture of half water and half milk. The herb paste may be tightly covered and refrigerated for up to three days. Raw fish fillets must be tightly wrapped in plastic and iced in a perforated hotel pan.

Another commonly used recipe format is called the narrative form. Procedures and ingredients are presented as needed in the recipe. Procedural statements will include ingredient amounts and are written in a paragraph format. An example of the narrative form is shown in *Exhibit 3.12*.

Exhibit 3.12

NARRATIVE RECIPE FORM

Blueberry Yogurt Smoothies

Line a rimmed baking sheet with parchment paper. Arrange 1 peeled medium banana and 3 ½ cups blueberries (about 16 oz) in a single layer on the baking sheet. Freeze the fruit until very cold, but not frozen, about 10 minutes. Blend the cold fruit, ½ cup yogurt, ½ cup pineapple juice, a pinch of salt, 1 tablespoon sugar, 1 teaspoon lemon juice, and 3 cups ice until uniformly smooth, 10 to 15 seconds.

Taste for sugar and lemon; if desired, add more sugar or lemon and blend until combined, about 2 seconds longer.

Serve immediately. Makes 4 cups (servings).

The descriptive or block form, shown in *Exhibit 3.13*, is the preferred format in high-quantity operations. Ingredients are listed on the left side of the recipe and the procedures associated with each ingredient are written directly across from them on the right side. Ingredients to be combined can be grouped, divided by horizontal lines that form visual "blocks." Many chefs believe that the block form is easier to read.

Regardless of form, a standardized recipe should contain the following information:

- Name of the food item or recipe.
- Ingredient details, including grades and brands of products needed, precise descriptions, etc.
- Total quantity and the number of portions of a specific size.
- Ingredients by weight and/or measure, volume, or count. This will depend partly on portion size, or the size of an item's individual serving, such as "six ounces of fish fillet."
- Equipment and tools needed, including everything from pots to utensils.
- Procedures and approximate prep time, including information on thawing, the types of cuts to be made, etc.
- Cooking method, such as blanching, sautéing, deep-frying, etc.
- Cooking or baking temperatures and times.
- Portioning, plating, and garnishing instructions.
- Cleanup directions.

Exhibit 3.13

BLOCK RECIPE FORM

Black Sea Bass with an Herb Crust and Salsify

Total yield:	24 oz
Portion size:	6 oz
Number of portions:	4

Equipment required:	Scale, baking sheet, food processor, 12-inch sauté pan, and broiling pan
Preparation time:	20 minutes
Cooking time:	10 minutes

Ingredients	Amount (U.S.)	Amount (Metric)	Procedure
Fresh chives, parsley, and basil leaves only	1 oz each	28 g each	Place the herbs in the food processor and chop finely. Reserve 1 Tbsp chopped herb mixture for the salsify and 4 sprigs chervil for garnish.
Fresh chervil, tarragon, and rosemary leaves only	½ oz each	14 g each	
White bread, sliced and trimmed of crust	1 oz	28 g	Add the bread to the herbs in the food processor and finely chop.
Butter, unsalted, softened	5 oz	140 g	Add 5 oz (140 g) to the herb mixture, process until smooth, and season with salt and pepper.
Salt and pepper	To taste		
Salsify, peeled, sliced ¼ inch	16 oz	448 g	Boil in salted water until tender. Drain and toss with remaining butter and reserved chopped herbs and season to taste with salt and pepper. Reserve.
Black sea bass, boneless, skin on fillets	24 oz (4 6-oz fillets)	672 g (4 168-g fillets)	Heat sauté pan over medium high heat and add vegetable oil. Season fillets with salt and pepper. Sear fish fillets 45 seconds on each side and transfer to a broiling pan. Spread bread–herb mixture evenly over the skin side of each fillet. When ready to serve, broil fish until herb crust has browned.
Vegetable oil	4 oz	120 ml	
Portioning, plating, and garnishing instructions:			Arrange 4 oz of the salsify and herb mixture on a warmed serving plate. Place the sea bass fillet over the salsify, and drizzle 1 oz of the melted butter from the broiling pan all around. Garnish with sprigs of fresh chervil.
Breakdown, cleanup, and storage instructions:			Prepare only what will be consumed immediately, as this dish is fragile and cannot be reheated. Any extra peeled raw salsify should be held under refrigeration in a mixture of half water and half milk. The herb paste may be tightly covered and refrigerated for up to three days. Raw fish fillets must be tightly wrapped in plastic and iced in a perforated hotel pan.

COSTING STANDARDIZED RECIPES

A key control in the relationship between the cost of a menu item and its selling price is the use of a **recipe cost card**. A recipe cost card is a tool used to calculate **standard portion cost** for a menu item, or the exact amount that one serving or portion of a food item should cost when prepared according to the item's standardized recipe. A recipe cost card is a table of ingredient costs for each item in the standardized recipe. If recipe cost cards are not used, the selling price is nothing more than a guess. Several methods for determining menu prices will be discussed in greater detail later in this book.

As with the standardized recipe, there should be a recipe cost card for every multiple-ingredient item listed on the menu. To properly fill out a recipe cost card and figure an item's standard portion cost, follow these steps:

1 Copy the ingredients from the standardized recipe onto the recipe cost card. All ingredients should be recorded. The ingredients listed on the recipe cost card should match exactly the ingredients listed on the standardized recipe card.

2 List in the appropriate columns the amount and unit used for each ingredient needed to prepare the recipe.

3 From the invoice(s), list the cost of each ingredient as well as the unit listed on the invoice. It is important to note that the unit called for in the recipe is quite often different from the unit listed on the invoice.

4 Convert the invoice unit to the unit used for the recipe in the recipe column, and figure the cost per recipe unit. For example, if the invoice unit is gallons and the recipe unit is pints, convert the gallon cost into cost per pint and record this number on the recipe cost card.

5 In the last column, figure the extended cost by multiplying the number of units needed for the recipe by the cost per recipe unit.

6 Add the cost of all ingredients together in the extended column. This gives managers the total cost for preparing the entire recipe.

7 Divide the total cost by the number of portions the recipe will produce to get the standard portion cost.

Refer to *Exhibits 3.14* and *3.15* as you read the following steps to set up a recipe cost card for pasta sauce based on its standardized recipe.

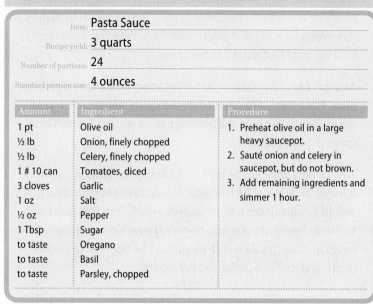

Exhibit 3.14

STANDARDIZED RECIPE FOR PASTA SAUCE

Item: Pasta Sauce

Recipe yield: 3 quarts

Number of portions: 24

Standard portion size: 4 ounces

Amount	Ingredient	Procedure
1 pt	Olive oil	1. Preheat olive oil in a large heavy saucepot.
½ lb	Onion, finely chopped	
½ lb	Celery, finely chopped	2. Sauté onion and celery in saucepot, but do not brown.
1 # 10 can	Tomatoes, diced	
3 cloves	Garlic	3. Add remaining ingredients and simmer 1 hour.
1 oz	Salt	
½ oz	Pepper	
1 Tbsp	Sugar	
to taste	Oregano	
to taste	Basil	
to taste	Parsley, chopped	

Exhibit 3.15

RECIPE COST CARD FOR PASTA SAUCE STANDARDIZED RECIPE

Item Pasta Sauce

Recipe Amount	Recipe Unit	Ingredients	Invoice Cost	Invoice Unit	Recipe Cost	Recipe Unit	Extended Cost
2	2	1	3	3	4	4	5
1	pt	Olive oil	$ 112.00	4 gal	$ 3.50	pt	$ 3.50
0.5	lb	Onion, finely chopped	16.50	50 lb	.33	lb	0.17
0.5	lb	Celery, finely chopped	27.85	30 lb	.93	lb	0.46
1 can	#10	Tomatoes, diced	18.00	6/ #10	3.00	#10	3.00
3	cloves	Garlic	0.05	clove	.05	clove	0.15
1	oz	Salt			.10		0.10
0.5	oz	Pepper			.10		0.10
1	Tbsp	Sugar			.10		0.10
to taste		Oregano			.10		0.10
to taste		Basil			.10		0.10
to taste		Parsley, chopped			.10		0.10
					Total	6	$ 7.88
					# portions		24
					Cost/portion	7	$ 0.33

1. Copy the ingredients from the standardized recipe to the third column of the recipe cost card.

2. List the amount and unit used for each ingredient in the appropriate column. For example, the first ingredient is olive oil, which is listed in the third column. In the first and second columns of the first row, put the amount and unit of the olive oil, 1 pint. The next ingredient is chopped onion, and the amount and unit is 0.5 (1/2) pound, which goes into the first and second columns respectively. Repeat this for the entire recipe as shown.

3. Next, look up the price for each ingredient on the invoice. Put the price and unit from the invoice in the fourth and fifth columns, respectively.

4. The recipe cost column is calculated next. In the case of the first ingredient, olive oil, the recipe unit is pints but the invoice unit is 4 gallons. This is typical of oils since they are commonly packed 4 gallons to the case. There are several ways this number can be converted. The easiest is to divide the cost of the case, $112.00, by 32 (the number of pints in 4 gallons) to arrive at $3.50. A slower way, but just as accurate, is to take the cost of the case, $112.00, and divide by 4 (4 gallons in a case) to get the cost of a gallon, $28.00. Then divide by 4 (4 quarts to a gallon) to get the cost per quart, $7.00. Finally, divide by 2 (2 pints in a quart) to get the cost per pint, $3.50.

5. Since the recipe calls for only 1 pint of oil, the $3.50 is placed in the extended cost column. The second ingredient, onion, comes in 50-pound sacks. A half-pound is needed. A 50-pound sack costs $16.50. Divide $16.50 by 100 (the number of half-pounds in 50 pounds) to get 0.165, which is rounded to 0.17 in the extended cost column. Celery comes 30 pounds to the case. A half-pound is needed. The case costs $27.85, which divided by 30 equals $0.93 per pound, and divided by 2 equals $0.46.

    Diced tomatoes are packed 6 #10 cans per case. One can is needed. A case costs $18.00, which divided by 6 (cans per case) equals $3.00 per can.

    The salt, pepper, and sugar are small amounts. In this case, a cost of $0.10 each is assigned. The last three items are also assigned a cost of $0.10 each as the amount used is tiny and not worth the time to calculate.

6. Next, add the numbers in the last column to get the total cost of the recipe, which is $7.88.

7. Finally, take the total cost ($7.88) and divide by the number of portions that the recipe will make (24) to get the standard portion cost for pasta sauce, which is $0.33.

Portion Size

One of the most important standards that any restaurant or foodservice operation must establish is the **portion size**, which is the quantity of any item that is to be served each time that item is ordered. The portion size for any item is the fixed quantity of a menu item given to each customer in return for the fixed selling price identified in the menu. It is possible and desirable for managers to establish these fixed quantities in very clear terms. Every item on a menu can be quantified in one of three ways: weight, volume, or count.

WEIGHT

Weight, normally expressed in ounces, or in grams if the metric system is used, is frequently used to measure portion sizes for a number of menu items. Meat and fish are two of the most common. Steak, for example, is served in portion sizes of varying weights, typically ranging from 8 to 16 ounces, with the particular size being set by managers. The same is true of roasts, often served in 4- or 5-ounce portions. Vegetables, particularly those purchased frozen, are commonly portioned by weight as well.

VOLUME

Volume is used to measure portion size for many menu items. Liquids such as soups, juices, coffee, and milk are commonly portioned by volume expressed as liquid ounces, or in milliliters in the metric system. A cup of soup may contain 5 ounces, and a bowl of soup may contain 8 ounces. A portion of orange juice may be 3 or 4 ounces. Coffee may be served in a 5-ounce portion (*Exhibit 3.16*). A glass of milk may contain 8 or 10 ounces. Volume for nonliquid items such as sausage and mushrooms on a pizza may be measured by a cup. A portion scoop may be used to scale muffins or cupcakes.

Exhibit 3.16

COUNT

Count is also used by restaurant and foodservice managers to identify portion size. Such items as bacon, link sausage, eggs, chops, shrimp, and asparagus are portioned by count. Some foods are purchased by count, and this plays a major role in establishing portion size. Operations purchase shrimp, for example, by number per pound. A common purchase size is 16 to 20 per pound. The shrimp is then portioned by number per shrimp cocktail, often four or five in one order.

Potatoes and grapefruit are purchased by count per purchase unit, which clearly serves as a determinant of portion size. Potatoes for baking, for example, can be purchased in 50-pound boxes with a particular number per box specified. The higher the count per box (e.g., 120 rather than 90), the smaller the size of the portion served to the customer. Count is important even with some dessert items, such as pie, with the portion size expressed in terms of the number of slices of equal size to be cut from one pie.

Determining Standard Portion Cost

One of the most important reasons for using standardized recipes is to determine how much each serving costs to produce. The selling price for each menu item is directly related to its food cost. Without a standardized recipe, a manager cannot arrive at an accurate standard portion cost for each item. As previously mentioned, the standard portion cost is the exact amount that one serving, or portion, of a food item should cost when prepared according to the item's standardized recipe.

There are two methods used to determine the cost of ingredients in a standardized recipe. These two methods are the AP method, which means "as purchased," and the EP method, which stands for "edible portion." There is a significant difference between these two methods that affects both the quality of the recipe and the costs of the ingredients.

AS PURCHASED (AP) COST

The **as purchased (AP) method** is used to cost an ingredient at the purchase price prior to any trim or waste being taken into account. In the AP method, all ingredient quantities are listed on the standardized recipe in the form in which they are purchased. "Ten pounds of onion, diced" is an example of AP, as the recipe is calling for 10 pounds of onion, as purchased. In this case, the chef would start with 10 pounds of whole onion, peel and dice it, and add the onion to the recipe. The manager would calculate the cost of 10 pounds of onion using the AP method.

EDIBLE PORTION (EP) COST

The second type of costing method is called **edible portion (EP) cost**. The edible portion (EP) method is used to cost an ingredient after it has been trimmed and waste has been removed so that only the usable portion of the item is reflected.

Many fruit, vegetable, meat, poultry, and seafood items lose volume and weight when cooked. This may be referred to as shrinkage, which is simply the amount of loss incurred when a product is trimmed and cooked. When breaking down a whole snapper, for instance, weigh the whole fish and calculate the price paid for it whole (the AP cost). Then, after cleaning, weigh the two fillets. The EP cost of the two fillets is the price paid for the whole fish, divided by the final weight of the cleaned and trimmed fillets. Managers can then use the EP cost when calculating menu pricing and food cost per serving.

Using the EP method, the quantity is listed on the standardized recipe using only the edible portion of that particular ingredient. For example, "10 pounds of diced onion" involves taking some quantity of onion, and then peeling, dicing, and weighing the results until there are 10 pounds of peeled, diced onion. This ingredient would be costed using the EP method because the recipe is based on the edible portion of the onion only. To obtain a cost in this case, the original weight of the product would have to be used. So if starting with 11 pounds of onion in order to obtain 10 pounds EP of diced onion, the cost for 11 pounds would be used to determine the cost of the onion used in the recipe.

It is imperative for a manager to know whether to use the AP method or the EP method to determine the costs of the ingredients in a standardized recipe. If the AP method is used to determine costs, but the recipe is actually written following the EP method, the selling price will be incorrect and the operation will lose money. The same will be true if the recipe is written using the AP method and the manager uses the EP method to determine the ingredient costs.

Unfortunately, most recipes do not come with the headings AP or EP. It is up to managers to decide how to cost them. Normally there are clues in the directions of the recipes themselves. To further confuse the issue, quite often AP and EP directions may both be used within a single recipe; one ingredient is listed as AP and the next ingredient is listed as EP, as seen in *Exhibit 3.17.*

THINK ABOUT IT ...

The EP method, in spite of being more time-consuming for figuring costs, is more precise than the AP method. Under what circumstances might the AP method be preferable?

Exhibit 3.17

| 10 lb onion, diced | 10 lb diced onion =
11 lb onion with skin on |

CONVERTING AP QUANTITIES INTO EP QUANTITIES

To determine the AP quantity that is needed to result in a given EP quantity, a manager must know the cooking or cutting loss for the item. Many quantity cookbooks, purchasing textbooks, and yield books include charts of average cooking loss for common food items. A conversion chart is a list of food items showing the expected, or average, shrinkage from AP amount to EP amount. These charts are tools that a manager can use, and they work well in most cases. However, it is wise for an operation to conduct its own tests periodically to get the exact AP amount for that specific operation. A **butcher's yield test** is used to measure the amount of shrinkage that occurs during the trimming of a meat product. This trimming includes deboning and removing fat and gristle (*Exhibit 3.18*). A **cooking loss test** is a way to measure the amount of product shrinkage during the cooking or roasting process. A **yield test** is used to measure the amount of shrinkage that occurs during trimming and cutting products that are not cooked, such as produce. The amount of shrinkage due to trimming and cutting is usually expressed in terms of a percentage. For example, a yield test of 65 percent for lettuce denotes that 35 percent of the purchase weight of lettuce was lost during trimming and cutting.

Exhibit 3.18

These tests are particularly important if the product is a high-cost item and if it is a product sold in high volume at the operation. If these two variables are true, the item has a profound effect on the operation's food cost percentage and should not be left to chance. For example, if beef brisket is a house specialty, a conversion chart might not be accurate because there are many variables that determine the amount of shrinkage, such as the length of time the product is cooked and at what temperature. *Exhibit 3.19* is an example of the results from conducting both a cooking loss and a yield test for beef brisket.

Exhibit 3.19

COOKING LOSS AND YIELD TEST FOR A BEEF BRISKET

Piece	Weight (lb)				Yield %
	Raw	Cooked	Trim	Usable	
1	9.4 lb	6.3 lb	1.2 lb	5.1 lb	54.2%
2	11.6	7.3	1.6	5.7	49.1
3	9.8	6.4	1.4	5.0	51.0
4	10.7	6.7	1.8	4.9	45.7
5	8.8	5.4	1.1	4.3	48.8
Average	10.0 lb	6.4 lb	1.4 lb	5.0 lb	50.0%

Using five pieces of brisket, each piece was weighed before and after cooking. The weight of the trim and the amount of brisket available to sell is also determined. When conducting a similar analysis, most managers use several pieces from different packages to arrive at an average. This exercise is important because it shows that the cost per pound or ounce of a product may increase significantly due to preparation and cooking steps. With brisket, a customer's 8-ounce serving actually costs as much as a full pound of brisket delivered to the operation.

Consider the yield for tomato slices on a sandwich or hamburger. A case of tomatoes at 5 × 6 tomatoes (5 layers of 6 tomatoes per layer) has 30 tomatoes:

$$
\underset{\text{Layers per case}}{5} \quad \times \quad \underset{\text{Tomatoes per layer}}{6} \quad = \quad \underset{\text{Tomatoes per case}}{30}
$$

If yield tests show an average of 6 per tomato, then the yield would be 180 slices per case if every tomato was usable or a 100 percent yield:

$$
\underset{\text{Tomatoes per case}}{30} \quad \times \quad \underset{\text{Average slices per tomato}}{6} \quad = \quad \underset{\text{Slices per case}}{180}
$$

There are normally a few rotten tomatoes in each case, so count on a 96 percent yield or 173 usable slices per case:

$$
\underset{\text{Slices per case}}{180} \quad \times \quad \underset{\text{Usable percentage}}{96\%} \quad = \quad \underset{\text{Usable slices per case}}{173}
$$

If the cost per case was $24.90, then the cost per slice would be $0.14 per slice:

$$\underset{\text{Price per case}}{\$24.90} \quad \underset{}{\div} \quad \underset{\text{Usable slices per case}}{173} \quad \underset{}{=} \quad \underset{\text{Price per slice}}{\$0.14}$$

This may seem like a lot of work, but to calculate food cost, it is best to drill deep into the details to have better information and more reliable results when these data are applied and used. Many opportunities to control food cost will occur during purchasing, which will be covered in chapter 5.

Updating Recipe Cost Cards

Because of cost changes, it is imperative that recipe cost cards be updated periodically. If a cost goes up and the selling price is not adjusted accordingly, the standard food cost percentage will not be met and the profit of the operation will be reduced. While this seems like a lot of work, once the initial setup of the recipe cost cards is complete, they are quite easy to maintain. Once managers update the purchase price of a given item such as rib-eye steak, all recipes using this food item are updated. Recipe cost card software is explained in more detail later in this chapter.

Ingredient costs vary from area to area and, in many cases, change from day to day. This is usually true of meat, seafood, and produce, especially for high-cost items. The impact of these price changes can be particularly large when they affect popular menu items. Recipe cost cards for these items should be reviewed weekly to make sure that menu cost is updated if there is a significant price change for main ingredients of a menu item. Other recipe cost cards that are made up primarily of low-cost and consistently priced goods should be reviewed monthly.

HANDLING CUSTOMER SUBSTITUTIONS AND ADDITIONS

In addition to creating recipe cost cards for each menu item, managers will need to determine how to account for food costs when customers ask for substitutions or additions to standard menu items. Suppose, for example, that an establishment offers fettuccine Alfredo as a standard menu item. How should the operation account for the cost when a customer requests that chicken breast be added to the dish? Or, how will it account for food cost if a customer requests that the mashed potato accompaniment be replaced with a more expensive vegetable? In the case of fettuccine Alfredo, managers might create a standardized recipe and cost card for the standard menu item and another standardized recipe and cost card for the fettuccine Alfredo with chicken. Another possibility is to create a cost card for the substituted ingredient only. Regardless of how it is done, the important point is to account for the cost so that the operation maintains its standard food cost and desired profit.

Manager's Memo

All aspects of food costing operate as a system in which they are interrelated. Standardized recipes determine product specifications for each ingredient of a menu. On the other hand, target food cost percentage influences quality of ingredients to be used in standardized recipes. Another food cost factor that should be considered in restaurant and foodservice operations is the difference between as purchased (AP) and (EP) edible cost, called shrinkage. That is, managers should strive to balance their menu with items that presumably have low shrinkage (i.e., high yield percentage) and high contribution margin. It should also be noted that customer demand should be taken into account when making cost-related decisions. This is because discontinuing a popular menu item that has low yield percentage and low contribution margin may have a negative impact on customer loyalty.

Recipe Cost Card Software

More and more establishments, especially larger operations and chains, are moving toward automating many of these processes. There are a wide variety of software programs available that will produce recipe cost cards. Some of the more sophisticated programs will also make automatic adjustments. Alternately, a recipe cost card can be set up on any spreadsheet program. These programs can save time and labor compared to manual methods.

In operations that use recipe card software, when an ingredient is purchased, received, and the invoice is put into the system, the price of that ingredient will be adjusted on the recipe cost card. When the standard portion cost of the recipe reaches a predetermined level, the software will notify the manager that the cost of an item and the selling price are no longer in balance, and that the standard food cost percentage is in jeopardy. Managers can then take action to correct the problem.

CALCULATING PLATE COSTS

A **plate cost** is the total sum of product costs included in a single meal, or plate, served to a guest. For example, if the beef brisket dinner includes a dressed baked potato, biscuits, butter for the biscuits, and side salad, all parts of the dinner must be included to accurately establish a menu selling price.

To arrive at the plate cost for a given menu item, managers create a menu item cost worksheet. This worksheet allows a manager to calculate each menu item's ideal food cost based on ingredients, portions, and current cost. *Exhibit 3.20* shows three menu items: hamburger basket, dinner salad, and beef brisket. Suppose a manager wants to calculate the plate cost of the hamburger basket. When preparing the worksheet, the manager first lists all ingredients for a particular menu item. All ingredients used in preparing the hamburger basket are listed under the name of the menu item. Then the units or measures and quantity are added. The second column includes unit measures such as count (each), weight (oz, lb), or cooking measures (e.g., tablespoon). The third column shows actual quantity used. For example, the hamburger basket uses three slices of pickle. The next column shows unit cost and the last column includes the recipe cost. Unit cost for pickle slices is $0.05. Menu cost is calculated by multiplying quantity (3.0) by unit cost ($0.05). Thus, menu cost for pickles is $0.15. As a last step, the manager totals the costs to arrive at the overall plate cost. Adding up all ingredients for the hamburger basket results in a total menu item cost, or plate cost, of $3.26. When using menu costing software or a spreadsheet program, it is advisable to link the menu items to an ingredient's recipe unit cost from a master inventory list.

Exhibit 3.20

MENU ITEM COST WORKSHEET

Menu Items/Ingredients	Units	Quantity	Unit Cost	Recipe Cost
Hamburger Basket				
Beef patty	oz	5	$0.13	$0.65
Hamburger bun	each	1	0.17	0.17
Tomatoes slices	each	2	0.14	0.28
Pickles	each	3	0.05	0.15
Lettuce	oz	0.5	0.30	0.15
French fries	oz	6	0.24	1.44
Cooking oil	oz	0.5	0.20	0.10
Ketchup	Tbsp	4	0.08	0.32

Menu Item Cost: $3.26

Dinner Salad				
Lettuce	oz	4.00	$0.30	$1.20
Cherry tomatoes	oz	2.00	0.19	0.38
Red onion	oz	0.25	0.15	0.04
House salad dressing	oz	2.00	0.35	0.70
Croutons	oz	2.00	0.08	0.16

Menu Item Cost: $2.48

Beef Brisket Dinner				
Beef brisket	oz	6.00	$0.49	$2.94
BBQ sauce	oz	2.00	0.21	0.42
Baked potato	each	1.00	0.34	0.34
Sour cream	oz	2.00	0.18	0.36
Butter	oz	1.00	0.21	0.21
Cheddar cheese, grated	oz	1.00	0.15	0.15
Biscuits	each	2.00	$0.08	$0.16
Dinner salad (half size)	each	0.50	2.47	1.24

Menu Item Cost: $5.82

Exhibit 3.21

Managers can use the individual plate costs to determine the overall food cost forecast for an establishment. Once each plate cost is known, the manager can multiply that cost by the estimated number of that menu item likely to be sold in a given time period. For instance, if the plate cost for a chicken dinner (*Exhibit 3.21*) is $4.50 per plate and the manager forecasts selling 100 chicken dinners in a given time period, that manager can assume that his or her food cost for the chicken dinner will be $450.00 for that time period:

$4.50	×	100	=	$450.00
Plate cost		**Forecasted quantity**		**Forecasted food cost**

The manager can make this calculation for each menu item to arrive at a forecasted food cost. When the time period is over, the manager can compare the forecasted food costs with actual costs to determine whether additional considerations or controls need to be put into place.

CALCULATING BUFFET AND SALAD BAR COSTS

Buffet service can be found in many different types of operations: "budget" steakhouse chains, country club and hotel Sunday brunches, and salad-focused chains are a few examples. It can be challenging for managers to calculate food costs for these types of establishments because customers may eat as much or as little as they desire. Food costs for "all-you-can-eat" buffets typically have food costs 4 to 6 percent higher than standard cook-to-order operations because leftovers and waste from buffet-style service is typically higher. Managers must consider that a quality buffet must be just as fully stocked five minutes before closing as it is when the buffet line opens. Plus, items served on the buffet often are not the same as those served on the à la carte service menu. Despite the challenges, there is a method for determining food cost for this style of service: price-per-person.

Price-per-Person Model

The **price-per-person model** is the most widespread method used to determine pricing for all-you-can-eat food bars. Operations typically charge one price for all that a single person can eat. To determine food cost based on a price-per-person model, start by calculating the food cost for all the items included on the buffet and the backup inventory used to replenish the buffet during the service period. For example, assume that the cost to stock the buffet for service and have the necessary backup inventory is $800. That becomes the opening inventory. At the end of service, the closing inventory, or food that can be reused, is worth $200. So, the overall food cost is the difference between the opening inventory and the closing inventory, which in this case is $600.

If the number of customers served on the buffet during that service period was 225, the average cost per customer served can be determined by dividing the number of customers into the overall food cost:

$600	÷	225	=	$2.67
Overall food cost		**Number of customers**		**Average food cost per customer**

In this example, $2.66 is the average food cost per customer. Managers would need to repeat this process for each meal service for at least three weeks. The average food cost per customer will vary slightly from day to day due to the mix of customers, the meal period, and day of the week, but the average over time will give managers a good approximation of the food costs on any given day.

SUMMARY

1. **Define food costs and explain how managers track and analyze food costs.**

   Food cost is the actual dollar value of the food used by an operation during a certain period. It includes the expenses incurred when food is consumed for any reason. Food cost includes the cost of food sold, given away, wasted, or even stolen. Controlling food cost requires analyzing an operation's income statement to highlight any spending issues and compare current results with previous periods and the budget. Food cost is normally considered to be in good shape if the current percentage-to-sales ratio is consistent or in line with past periods.

2. **Explain how to calculate the cost of sales and how to calculate the actual cost of sales.**

   The formula for calculating cost of sales starts with adding the opening inventory plus purchases, which is all of the food and beverages purchased during that period. The total of these two numbers equals the total food available, or the dollar amount of all food available for sale. The closing inventory is then subtracted from the total food available. This results in the cost of sales. Most operations inventory and figure food cost monthly, but some quick-service operations conduct inventory on a weekly basis.

   In addition to purchases, there are several other factors that should be considered in calculating the actual cost of goods sold. These factors include credits such as employee meals, comps, and grease sales. Transfers to and from other units also impact the cost of sales.

3. **Describe how to calculate the food cost percentage.**

    Food cost percentage is the relationship between sales and the cost of sales. To calculate the food cost percentage, managers divide the food cost by the sales revenue. Food cost percentage is often the standard against which food cost is judged. Food cost percentage is generally analyzed by comparing it to company standards, historical cost percentage, or even industry standards.

4. **Explain the importance of standardized recipes to cost control and product consistency.**

    The standardized recipe is one of the key tools used in the control process. A standardized recipe is a written format used for consistently preparing and serving a given menu item. It includes a complete list of ingredients, their quantities, and the procedures to be followed each time that recipe is produced. Since a standardized recipe is so important, it must be clearly written and very detailed so that different cooks using the recipe will produce an identical product time after time.

5. **Contrast the three types of standardized recipe files.**

    The standardized form includes all ingredients at the top, with numbered procedural steps listed below. This form requires the user to shift attention between two spots on the recipe. The narrative form presents procedures and ingredients as needed in the recipe. Finally, the block form lists ingredients on the left side of the recipe, and the procedures associated with each ingredient are written directly across from them on the right side. The block form is often the preferred form because many chefs find it easier to read.

6. **Describe why and how managers create recipe cost cards.**

    Managers create recipe cost cards to understand the costs for each menu item. They create a recipe cost card by listing each ingredient and its associated cost for a given recipe, then dividing by the total number of portions to determine the per portion cost. Managers must understand as purchased (AP) and edible portion (EP) units, sometimes translating between the two, when arriving at recipe costs.

7. **Outline the process for calculating plate cost.**

    Plate cost is the total cost included in a single meal (or "plate") served to a guest. A menu item worksheet calculates each menu item's ideal food cost based on ingredients, portions, and current cost. Managers can use individual plate costs to come up with forecasts of overall cost of sales.

8. **Explain how managers calculate food costs for buffets.**

    Buffet and salad bar service creates a challenge for managers because the customers can eat as much of any food on the buffet as they want. The most common method for determining food cost for this style of service is the price-per-person method, with operations charging one price for all that a single person can eat. To calculate the price-per-person, the total cost of food served during a period is divided by the number of customers served during that period. The result is the average food cost per customer.

APPLICATION EXERCISES

Exercise 1

Splendid Burgers restaurant had monthly purchases of $20,000 in March. The operation had an opening inventory of $5,200 and closing inventory of $9,400. It also offered employee meals valued at $1,200 and generated $2,800 from grease sales.

1. What is the actual cost of sales for Splendid Burgers?

2. If the restaurant had $40,000 in sales, what is the sales cost percentage for Splendid Burgers?

Exercise 2

Complete the butcher's yield test for veal scallopini.

BUTCHER'S YIELD TEST: VEAL LEG TO SCALLOPINI

	Item	Weight (lb & oz)		Weight (lb)		Value per Pound	Total Value (Weight × Value per lb)
Original item before trimming	Veal leg (as purchased)	34 lb	0 oz	34	lb	$2.79	$94.86
Trim, salvage and waste	Fat	2 lb	12 oz	2.75	lb	$0.02	
	Bone	3 lb	12 oz	3.75	lb	0.25	
	Ground veal	2 lb	8 oz	2.5	lb	2.89	
	Stew meat	3 lb	0 oz	3	lb	3.29	
	Unusable trim	lb	15 oz	0.938	lb	0.00	
	Cutting loss					0.00	
Total:							
Item after trimming	Scallopini	Total yield of item (Original weight) − (Total weight of trim, salvage, and waste):				Net cost per pound (Net cost of item / Total yield of item)	Net cost of item (Original total value) − (Total value of trim, salvage, and waste)
		20 lb	12 oz	20.75	lb		

REVIEW YOUR LEARNING

Select the best answer for each question.

1. **Inventory represents the dollar value of**
    A. items ordered in a given time period.
    B. items purchased in a given time period.
    C. food products used in a given time period.
    D. food products in storage for a given time period.

2. **Which is used in determining cost of sales?**
    A. Food and beverage purchases
    B. Per-pound pricing
    C. Customer counts
    D. Edible portions

3. **Which is a credit to cost of sales?**
    A. Grease sales
    B. Edible portion
    C. Food-to-bar transfer
    D. Food cost percentage

4. **Given the following data, determine the food cost percentage:**

    Opening inventory = $3,890
    Purchases = $74,381
    Closing inventory = $2,996
    Sales = $233,479
    A. 31.1%
    B. 32.2%
    C. 33.7%
    D. 35.6%

5. **What is the major advantage of developing standardized recipes?**
    A. Improve guest satisfaction
    B. Improve employee satisfaction
    C. Help maintain consistency of food production
    D. Help prepare more food with fewer ingredients

6. **Who is in charge of developing product specifications?**
    A. Suppliers
    B. Customers
    C. Managers
    D. Produce growers

7. **Which recipe form lists all ingredients at the top with numbered procedural steps listed below?**
    A. Block form
    B. Narrative form
    C. Standardized form
    D. Descriptive form

8. **What is the major benefit of the EP costing method?**
    A. It is less time-consuming than the AP costing method.
    B. It is more accurate than the AP costing method.
    C. It is used only in smaller operations.
    D. It helps reduce labor costs.

9. **Which test measures the amount of shrinkage that occurs during the trimming of a meat product?**
    A. Butcher's yield test
    B. Meat cutting test
    C. Cooking loss test
    D. Food yield test

10. **Which statement describes plate cost?**
    A. Total sum of product costs included in a single meal
    B. How much food product exists at the start of a given period
    C. Actual dollar value of the food used by an operation during a certain period
    D. Relationship between sales and the cost spent on food to achieve those sales

FIELD PROJECT

Work through the following steps:

1. Visit a restaurant or foodservice operation (or research online) to find a standardized recipe.

2. Call actual food suppliers or use online resources to cost each of the ingredients in the recipe.

3. Calculate plate cost for a menu item that includes the items from the standardized recipe.

4. What percentage of plate cost is composed of recipe cost? (Note: *This is the proportion of recipe cost to plate cost.*)

4 Determining Menu Prices

INSIDE THIS CHAPTER

- Why Menu Prices Matter
- Factors Affecting Menu Prices
- Establishing Food and Beverage Prices
- Analyzing the Menu Mix
- Implementing Revised Prices

CHAPTER LEARNING OBJECTIVES

After completing this chapter, you should be able to:

- Describe external and internal factors that influence menu pricing.

- List and explain different menu pricing formulas.

- Describe the menu product mix and menu engineering.

- Explain the process used to identify food cost percentage problems.

- Describe the process for determining menu modifications and price adjustments.

KEY TERMS

composite (potential)
food cost percentage,
p. 99

contribution margin (CM),
p. 94

contribution margin
method (pricing), p. 94

demand-driven pricing,
p. 89

factor method (pricing),
p. 93

food cost percentage
method (pricing), p. 93

market-driven pricing,
p. 89

market price, p. 92

markup, p. 93

markup differentiation,
p. 91

menu engineering, p. 103

menu matrix, p. 103

menu product mix,
p. 99

price–value relationship,
p. 90

prime cost method
(pricing), p. 96

Q factor, p. 98

ratio pricing method,
p. 95

value perception, p. 90

CASE STUDY

The manager at Polo Bistro restaurant was reviewing last month's menu engineering spreadsheet with Chef Bob. Both were interested in the liver and onions sales numbers. The report indicated that only 62 items were sold last month.

"You know we bring liver in only for that one dish and we caramelize onions only for the liver. Do we really need to keep that item on the menu?" asked Chef Bob. The manager mentioned that Mr. Tomas, the owner's father, really likes that dish. After reviewing last month's invoices, both agreed it did not cost much to maintain the item, but that it was a "dog" because of its poor sales.

1. If you were the chef, would you leave the item on the menu based on sales numbers only?

2. If you were the manager, would you consider other factors when considering a menu change?

3. Should either Chef Bob or the manager consider the fact that Mr. Tomas likes liver and onions?

WHY MENU PRICES MATTER

The menu and its prices have a direct influence on an operation's profit. In business, companies make money by selling the product that generates the greatest amount of profit. Knowing the cost of everything on the menu is the only way to accurately identify high- or low-profit items. This information allows managers to maximize the menu as a marketing tool.

In the restaurant and foodservice industry, the selling price of an item is based on its cost: not only food cost, but also labor and overhead needed to run the operation. The selling price must be enough to cover all of the costs and result in some profit.

However, managers must not forget that it is the buyer, not the seller, who ultimately determines the price. Customers do not care what it costs to deliver a great meal. They do not care what margin is needed to stay in business. Managers must keep costs as low as practical when pricing the menu. This is done in order to maximize customers' perceived value.

Exhibit 4.1

FACTORS AFFECTING MENU PRICES

Market factors, what potential customers are willing to pay for specific menu items, and what the competition is charging will all influence pricing decisions (see *Exhibits 4.1* and *4.2*). These factors will result in many menu items selling at lower prices than managers might desire, and those items having a higher food cost percentage. Since some menu items will sell at higher prices with lower-than-average cost, the goal is for the total menu to average out to an acceptable food cost percentage. Menus should be designed around high-profit items and managers should train their staff to effectively sell those items.

Menu pricing should be primarily market-driven; however, knowing what the food cost is to produce all menu items is an important part of the process. Knowing what it costs to produce individual items provides managers with the necessary data to make informed decisions based on facts. With true cost numbers, managers can decide to either charge a higher price for a specific item, regardless of competition, or drop an item from the menu altogether.

Exhibit 4.2

MARKET FORCES AFFECTING SELLING PRICE

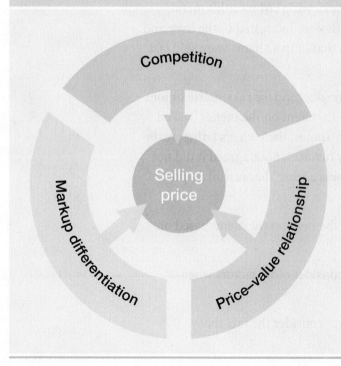

External Factors

Competition is one external factor that can play a role in menu pricing. Many customers purchase goods based solely on price, and a competitor can force an operation to charge a lower price. For example, quick-service establishments will often have price wars to compete for customers. To get customers to choose their operation, managers will match or beat a competitor's price.

This does not mean that an establishment should automatically charge at or below a competitor's prices. Managers must first figure out what the price needs to be in order to meet the standard food cost percentage. This is done by completing a recipe cost card and calculating a markup. These calculations are covered in chapter 3. Only when these numbers have been determined can managers make a rational decision about whether to meet or beat the competition's price on an item, or to possibly not carry that item at all.

Competitive pricing is especially prevalent in the quick-service segment of the industry. This is because customers in this segment may be more concerned with lower prices than with quality. It is used to a lesser degree in the casual dining segment, and rarely in the fine-dining segment, since people purchasing on the high end are more concerned with quality and less concerned with price.

In addition to direct competition, there are two other external factors that affect menu prices: market and demand. **Market-driven pricing** is pricing that is determined by the market, which is usually regional. For items that are offered in many competing establishments, a price point will exist in the market and in the mind of the customer. For example, when offering a grilled chicken sandwich, an establishment might change the bun, spice mixture, sauce, or sides. Consumers, however, will still perceive it as similar to other grilled chicken sandwiches, and will have a definite idea about what they are willing to pay. Prices that are market-driven tend to be on the moderate to low end of the pricing range.

Demand-driven pricing is the theory that an operation can set pricing based on demand for the product or service. For example, food and beverage prices in airports and sports stadiums are more expensive than those in an establishment located in a strip mall. Higher prices are partly due to high overhead, but also because the clientele is a captive crowd. Demand is high because consumers cannot leave to buy a food or a beverage item once they have entered the airport security area or stadium gates. Establishments that offer unique items or unusual concepts can create demand-driven pricing; however, most are never able to maintain it over the long run. Competition will eventually adopt unique menu items or match the concept.

Not all competitive situations will force a lower price. After costing out an item, managers may find that they can sell it at a higher price than the standard markup because the competition is also selling it at a higher price. Another reason could be that no one else in the market is selling the item. But under normal conditions, managers must price menu items at what the market will bear.

PRICE–VALUE RELATIONSHIP

Value perception is customer's opinion of a product's value to him or her. Typically, high prices are associated with high quality and low prices with lower quality. However, the total restaurant or foodservice package helps establish value perception. Guests consider factors including service, ambiance, conveniences, and reputation when determining what they feel is a fair value for their dining experience.

For an operation to be profitable, it must also sell its goods at the right price from the customers' perspective. If the selling price on the menu is set too high, sales will be lost, and lost sales mean lost profit. The connection between the selling price of an item and its worth to the customer is known as

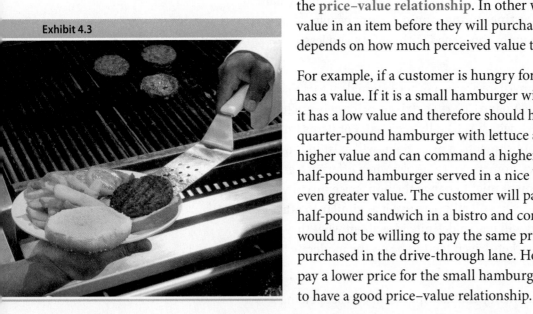

Exhibit 4.3

the **price–value relationship**. In other words, customers must see value in an item before they will purchase it. How much they will pay depends on how much perceived value they see in an item.

For example, if a customer is hungry for a hamburger, the hamburger has a value. If it is a small hamburger with onion, pickle, and mustard, it has a low value and therefore should have a low selling price. If it is a quarter-pound hamburger with lettuce and tomato added, it has a higher value and can command a higher price (*Exhibit 4.3*). If it is a half-pound hamburger served in a nice bistro atmosphere, it has an even greater value. The customer will pay a certain price for the half-pound sandwich in a bistro and consider it a good value, but would not be willing to pay the same price for the smaller hamburger purchased in the drive-through lane. However, the customer would pay a lower price for the small hamburger, and consider that purchase to have a good price–value relationship.

Actually, there is a narrow price range for what people will pay for any given item. This is true in quick-service restaurants, fast casual, casual, and even fine-dining establishments. Moving outside the acceptable price range usually results in the consumer deciding to purchase a substitute (ordering the farm-raised salmon rather than the line-caught halibut), patronize the competition, or eat at home.

What makes this situation difficult is that the price–value relationship is not a static formula. A good value for one person may not necessarily be considered a good value by the next person. When pricing the menu, managers need to focus on the norm and ask, "Will the average customer perceive this as a good price value?" Much of the price–value relationship comes from competition, which affects the mindset of the customers as to what they are willing to pay for an item. To charge more for an item, an establishment must add value by giving it a new name, offering interesting sides, or changing the sauce or garnish, for example.

MARKUP DIFFERENTIATION

Because there is a range of expectations in the market, different categories of food can get different markups. This is known as **markup differentiation**. Two extreme examples are beverages and steaks. A cup of coffee can be produced for less than $0.10 per cup and sold for $1.00, which is approximately a 10 percent food cost and a 90 percent markup. If the same markup were used on a rib-eye steak that costs $7.00, it would have to be sold at $70.00. Obviously, an operation would not sell very many steaks at that price.

In general, lower-cost items have a higher markup. This can be explained by the fact that a cup of tea that costs $0.12 can be sold for $1.50 without facing any price resistance from customers. While these are lopsided examples, the point is that different categories on the menu bring different markup expectations and levels of tolerance from customers. *Exhibit 4.4* shows the widely accepted markup percentages for different menu categories.

Exhibit 4.4	
COMMON MARKUP PERCENTAGES	
Menu Item Category	**Markup**
Soups/Appetizers	20–50%
Salads	30–45%
Entrées/Sandwiches	25–50%
Desserts	20–50%
Beverages	30–90%

Internal Factors

Costs are probably the most important internal factor when it comes to establishing menu prices. A business should know the cost of the products it sells. Therefore, it is necessary to calculate the actual food and beverage cost of every item on the menu in order to maximize profit. Costing every item can be time-consuming and laborious; however, if done correctly it will return managers' investment many times over. Effective managers make the commitment to ongoing, accurate menu costing that provides valuable information and allows them to make better, more informed decisions.

COSTS

One of the most important ways managers control costs is to determine if the menu items are priced appropriately. To calculate the menu price, a manager first needs to know the cost of one standard portion. Remember that standard portion cost is the dollar amount that a standard portion should cost, based on the standardized recipe. Recall from chapter 3 that a standardized recipe yields a predetermined number of standard portions. First, managers calculate as purchased costs of the ingredients used in each item. Once the cost of each ingredient has been established, the total cost of preparing the recipe is determined by adding the costs of the individual ingredients. The

Manager's Memo

Low-price perception is an important pricing strategy. Odd-cents pricing is a technique used for everything from clothing to cars and real estate. Have you ever noticed that most prices end in an odd number, usually nine or five?

Psychologically, it is perceived as a lower cost than if the price ended in a zero. For example, $8.95 is preferred to $9.00. Prices under $5.00 have four ideal price ending points: $0.29, $0.49, $0.79, and $0.99. Prices above $5.00 have only two: $0.49 and $0.99.

Establishments run the risk of losing customers when they increase prices. If a menu item is priced ending in five, consider moving to an ending price of nine. Menu prices increased in this manner are less likely to be noticed by the customer and it is an easy way to add to the profit line.

total, divided by the number of portions or yield, gives the cost of one standard portion:

Total recipe cost ÷ Number of portions = Standard portion cost

Remember that costs change: A drought in California or heavy rains in Arizona can cause the cost of lettuce to jump 200 percent in just one week. Therefore, it is very important that recipe cost cards are updated periodically. If the cost goes up and the selling price is not adjusted accordingly, the standard food cost percentage will not be met and the profit of the operation will be reduced. Recipes with high-cost items or items that are seasonal should have their recipe cost cards reviewed weekly. Items that are made up mainly of low-cost and consistently priced products should have their recipe cost cards reviewed monthly.

Other major costs that should be considered in menu pricing would be labor cost and operating expenses. Particularly, menu items that are more complicated to prepare will have higher costs and should be priced accordingly. In addition, operating expenses such as utilities should be considered, especially for menu items that have long cooking times.

To gain some control over food prices that move up and down, an operation may use **market price**. Market price is a menu pricing strategy where the price of a menu item changes based on the current market. Typically, market price is applied to fresh seafood or highly seasonal items; the words "market price" are listed on the menu where the price would be. Market price allows an establishment to charge what is necessary to make a reasonable profit without dropping a menu item. However, this type of menu pricing is normally reserved for more expensive items, and should be applied to a very small percentage of the menu.

Exhibit 4.5

PORTION SIZE

Portion size must be controlled or it will impact food cost and profit. For example, if the standard portion size for a roast beef sandwich is four ounces and the cooks consistently prepare it with five or six ounces instead, the food cost for the roast beef is 25 to 50 percent higher than it should be, even if they are doing everything else perfectly. Consistent overportioning leads to higher food costs and a lack of consistency, both of which are bad for business.

Portion size may also help control food cost if prices go up. If the price of an ingredient goes up, the portion size could be adjusted downward to accommodate the cost increase (see *Exhibit 4.5*). However, managers should be careful to maintain an acceptable price–value relationship. When it is necessary to increase menu prices, consider increasing the portion size or adding an accompaniment when increasing the price. This creates a new improved version of the item and adds value to justify the increased price.

ESTABLISHING FOOD AND BEVERAGE PRICES

Setting menu prices is more of an "art" than a mathematical equation. New managers may think it is only about food costs, labor costs, operating expenses, and using menu pricing formulas based on what is necessary for a reasonable return on the investment. However, there are quantifiable and nonquantifiable approaches to setting menu prices. Establishments use a variety of methods to calculate markup and determine selling prices:

- The factor method, also called the food cost percentage pricing method or the simple markup method
- The contribution margin (CM) pricing method
- The ratio pricing method
- The prime cost pricing method

The **markup** is the difference between the actual cost of producing an item and the price listed on the menu. To understand the relationship better, look at the following example of an income statement (*Exhibit 4.6*) that is pro forma, or prepared before the fact. It is an estimate of what managers expect to happen. Pro forma income statements are used when opening new operations and are also used in preparing budgets.

The statement shown in *Exhibit 4.6* indicates what the Slippery Noodle expects to happen in the upcoming year. If the establishment hits its sales budget of $1,450,000 and controls food cost percentage at 34 percent, labor expenses at 29 percent, controllable expenses at 6 percent, and noncontrollable expenses at 23 percent, then the operation will show a profit of 8 percent, or $113,500. In other words, these are the standard costs: the targets that managers will try to achieve.

Exhibit 4.6

SAMPLE PRO FORMA INCOME STATEMENT

Pro Forma Income Statement Slippery Noodle Restaurant		
Sales	$1,450,000	100%
Cost of food sold	− 493,000	34%
Gross profit	**$ 957,000**	**66%**
Labor expenses	$ 420,500	29%
Other controllable expenses	93,000	6%
Noncontrollable expenses	+ 330,000	23%
Total expenses	**$ 843,500**	**58%**
Profit	**$ 113,500**	**8%**

Factor Method

The **factor method** is a popular formula used to determine menu prices based on the standard food cost percentage. This method is also called simple markup or **food cost percentage method**. The factor method is best suited to operations with historical data showing that the difference between sales and food costs is sufficient to cover all other expenses and to generate net profit.

To calculate the factor method, managers follow a two-step process:

Step 1: Divide 100 percent by the desired food cost percentage.

The result of this step is the factor. Again, 1.00 is 100 percent, which represents sales or the menu item's selling price:

1.00 ÷ Standard food cost percentage = Factor

Step 2: Multiply the factor by the menu item cost (from the recipe cost card).

This step gives a menu selling price for the item:

Factor × Menu item cost = Selling price

Using the cost of food sold (or food cost percentage) from the Slippery Noodle's pro forma income statement (see *Exhibit 4.6*), and using $3.22 as a meal or item cost, the two steps would look like this:

1.00	÷	34%	=	2.94
		Standard food cost percentage		**Factor**

2.94	×	$3.22	=	$9.47
Factor		**Menu item cost**		**Selling price**

In this case, the selling price would probably be rounded up to $9.49. Assuming that the standard food cost percentage for the operation across the board is 34 percent, the only step that needs to be taken to determine all menu prices is to multiply each item's standard portion cost by the factor of 2.94. (*Exhibit 4.7* shows the relationship between various food cost percentages and their factors.)

If all food cost controls are effective and the food costs remain constant, the desired food cost percentage will be correct. If costs change, the new food cost needs to be multiplied by the factor to determine a new selling price.

Contribution Margin (CM) Method

Contribution margin (CM) is what is left over after the food cost of a menu item is subtracted from the menu selling price. That amount is what each item contributes to paying for labor, other operating expenses, and profit.

CM is often referred to as gross profit because that is the amount each item can contribute to paying for labor and all other operating expenses and to providing a profit. Using the **contribution margin method**, the CM figure, once known, is then added to the cost of each item to determine that item's price.

Exhibit 4.7

FACTOR METHOD

Food Cost %	Factor
20%	5.00
25	4.00
28	3.57
30	3.33
32	3.12
34	2.94
36	2.77
40	2.50
42	2.38

The CM pricing method is easy to use if managers know or can estimate several variables:

- The number of customers they will serve in a budget or time period
- Their nonfood operating costs
- Their desired profit

To illustrate, assume that a manager has created a budget that indicates the operation will serve 10,000 customers in the coming year and that all nonfood costs including labor and all other operating expenses will be $28,000. The operation's target profit goal is $5,500. To use CM pricing, managers would follow these two steps:

Step 1: Calculate the average CM per customer.

$$\left(\begin{array}{c}\text{Nonfood}\\\text{costs}\end{array} + \text{Profit}\right) \div \begin{array}{c}\text{Number of}\\\text{customers}\end{array} = \begin{array}{c}\text{Average CM}\\\text{per customer}\end{array}$$

In this example:

$$\underset{\text{Nonfood costs}}{(\$28,000} + \underset{\text{Profit}}{\$5,500)} \div \underset{\text{Customers}}{10,000} = \underset{\text{CM per customer}}{\$3.35 \text{ Average}}$$

Step 2: Determine the selling price for the menu item by adding the food cost to the CM.

For example, the base selling price for a menu item with a $3.22 food cost would be:

$$\underset{\text{Food cost}}{\$3.22} + \underset{\substack{\text{Contribution}\\\text{margin}}}{\$3.35} = \underset{\text{Selling price}}{\$6.57}$$

CM menu pricing is easy to use because the necessary information is generally in the establishment's operating budget or forecast. CM is practical when the nonfood costs required to serve each customer are basically the same and the only difference in menu items is the food cost itself. Managers who use the CM pricing method consider the contribution margin per menu item to be as important as, if not more important than, food cost in the individual menu item pricing decision. This pricing method reduces the range of selling prices because the only difference in the selling price is the cost of the individual food item.

Ratio Pricing Method

The **ratio pricing method** centers on combined expenses, both food and nonfood, and on profit. Managers need three key components to arrive at selling price using this method: food costs, nonfood costs (labor, etc.), and target profit. First, take the sum of all nonfood costs, including labor cost, other controllable costs, and noncontrollable costs, and add it to the target profit. Next, divide the resulting number by the cost of food sold in dollars. This results in a ratio.

For example, a local establishment has food costs of $32,000, nonfood costs of $64,000, and target profit of $5,100.

Step 1: Calculate the ratio of food cost to nonfood costs and profit.

(Nonfood costs + Target profit) ÷ Food costs = Ratio

In this example:

($64,000   + $5,100)   ÷ $32,000   =   2.16
Nonfood costs   Target profit   Food costs   Ratio

Now the manager knows that for each $1.00 of revenue generated to cover food costs, he or she must generate an extra $2.16 in revenues to cover nonfood costs and realize target profit requirements.

Step 2: Calculate the nonfood and profit requirement amount for the menu item.

In this next step, the manager multiplies the menu item's food cost by the ratio determined in step 1:

Food costs × Ratio = Nonfood costs and target profit

In this example, assume that the food cost is $3.20. The formula applied would look like this:

$3.20   ×   2.16   = $6.91
Food costs   Ratio   Nonfood costs
and target profit

Step 3: Determine the menu item's selling price by adding the nonfood and profit requirement to the menu item's food cost:

Food costs + Nonfood costs + Target profit = Selling price

In this example:

$3.20   + $6.91   = $9.91 ($9.99 menu price)
Food costs   Nonfood costs and target profit   Menu price

Prime Cost Method

The **prime cost method** focuses on the labor costs involved in food preparation. This method requires managers to determine the amount of direct labor spent in preparing an item. Once that number is known, it is added to the food cost to arrive at the prime cost:

Direct labor + Food cost = Prime cost

For example, if food cost is $3.00 and direct labor cost is $0.50, then prime cost is $3.50.

To determine direct labor cost, managers and employees need to track the actual time spent preparing an item by conducting a time-and-motion study. This may be more than most operations are willing to commit to in the modern restaurant and foodservice environment. However, if the operation does not commit to that research, then the cost of meat cutting or salad preparation will be charged to the menu items that did not benefit from the labor. Prime cost menu pricing assigns the cost of direct labor only to the items that required the labor.

To determine the selling price, managers must establish a desired combined food and direct labor cost percentage. If the operation desires a 35 percent food cost and 10 percent direct labor cost, the prime cost percentage would be 45 percent. The prime cost is then divided by that percentage to arrive at the selling price:

Prime cost ÷ Prime cost percentage = Selling price

So, the earlier example of an item with a $3.50 prime cost would be divided by 45 percent to arrive at a $7.77 or $7.75 menu selling price:

$3.50	**÷**	**45%**	**=**	**$7.77 ($7.75 Menu price)**
Prime cost		**Prime cost percentage**		**Selling price**

An example closer to real-world conditions might look like this: A recipe requires two hours of labor at $9.50 per hour to produce 30 portions and has a food cost of $118.50. The direct labor cost would be $19.00:

$9.50	**×**	**2**	**=**	**$19.00**
Hourly labor cost		**Total hours**		**Direct labor costs**

The direct labor cost is then combined with the food cost of $118.50, which gives a prime cost of $137.50:

$19.00	**+**	**$118.50**	**=**	**$137.50**
Direct labor costs		**Food cost**		**Prime cost**

The prime cost per portion would be divided by the number of portions the recipe made:

$137.50	**÷**	**30**	**=**	**$4.58**
Prime cost		**Portions**		**Portion cost**

Finally, the selling price would be the portion cost divided by the prime cost percentage:

$4.58	**÷**	**45%**	**=**	**$10.17 ($10.25 Menu price)**
Portion cost		**Prime cost percentage**		**Selling price**

Exhibit 4.8

Q Factor

When a customer orders an entrée, he or she gets more than just the main attraction. For example, starch and vegetable, tossed salad, and bread and butter may be served (*Exhibit 4.8*). "**Q" factor** refers to the quotient or cost of all other food items served with an entrée. The cost of these food items must be included in the final plate cost for an operation to be profitable. But it is not just side and garnishes; all costs should be included. The Q factor also includes all complimentary items such as ketchup, mustard, soy sauce, steak sauce, hot sauce, coffee creamer, sweetener, and even salt and pepper. Plus, managers need to factor in the cost of the most popular dressing choice, extra bread and butter, or the difference in the cost of sides (baked potato rather than rice) if a choice is offered.

The Q factor is a way to recapture the cost of everything in an establishment that the customer sees as free, because it is not on the final bill. Thus, when calculating Q factor it is convenient to create a master recipe that may be used with every entrée (see *Exhibit 4.9*).

Exhibit 4.9

MENU ITEM COST WORKSHEET WITH Q FACTOR

Menu Items/Ingredients	Units	Quantity	Unit Cost	Recipe Cost
Q Factor				
Bread	each	3.00	$0.15	$0.45
Starch	each	1.00	0.65	0.65
Vegetable	each	1.00	0.55	0.55
Dinner salad	each	1.00	0.75	0.75
Salad dressing	oz	2.00	0.15	0.30
Butter	oz	2.00	0.24	0.48
Condiments	each	1.00	0.25	0.25
			Q Factor Cost:	**$3.43**

Most operations include the Q factor only in the entrée plate cost. However, even those operations that do not offer sides, bread or butter, and so on still need to capture the cost of condiments (see *Exhibit 4.10*). While these operations may include a small Q factor on the majority of menu items, the number should be small enough so as not to skew menu prices too high.

Exhibit 4.10				
MENU ITEM COST WORKSHEET WITH Q FACTOR				
Menu Items/Ingredients	**Units**	**Quantity**	**Unit Cost**	**Recipe Cost**
Beef Brisket Dinner				
Beef brisket	oz	6.00	$0.485	$2.91
BBQ sauce	oz	2.00	0.205	0.41
Q Factor *(Includes bread,* *vegetable, starch, etc.)*	each	1.00	$3.43	$3.43
			Menu Item Cost:	**$6.75**

ANALYZING THE MENU MIX

Recall that in order for a restaurant or foodservice operation to be profitable, the menu as a whole must produce a certain standard food cost percentage. So how do managers measure the overall average food cost percentage when the menu includes some items that sell at lower or higher food cost percentages? They measure by looking carefully at the menu product mix. The **menu product mix** is a detailed analysis that shows the quantities sold of each menu item, along with their selling prices and standard portion costs. A sample menu mix percentage (MM%) might look like this:

$$405 \div 4{,}845 = 8.4\%$$

No. of pork chop entrées sold   Total entrées sold   MM%

The menu product mix is used to determine the **composite (potential) food cost percentage**. The composite (potential) food cost percentage is the weighted average food cost percentage for all items sold. It is this average, not each individual item, that must meet the operation's standard food cost percentage. It is important to remember that an operation should not simply total the food cost percentage column and divide by the number of menu items. The result would not be accurate because these percentages are not weighted by the quantity of each item sold. The menu product mix allows managers to see how each individual item contributes to the overall sales and cost-effectiveness of the menu. The markup of each item on the menu tells managers where that item stands in relationship to the overall product mix and the standard food cost percentage.

In the factor method–food cost percentage examples in the previous section of this chapter, the menu item's standard portion cost is $3.22. It was determined that the item would have to sell for $9.47 to get a 34 percent food cost, which is the operation's standard, with a menu price that would most likely be

RESTAURANT TECHNOLOGY

The POS (point-of-sale) system is a very effective control tool. If managers know the menu cost for each item that is sold, the POS allows managers to calculate an estimated cost of goods sold from the item sales reports. Managers who use a POS system, track purchases, and conduct a physical inventory each week can calculate profit and loss on a weekly basis. This would allow them to respond to cost increases before they become a real problem.

rounded to $9.50. If the menu item is a rib-eye steak sandwich, and the operation's manager looked at the competition, considered the price–value relationship, and decided that the local market would bear only $9.00 for this item, the menu selling price would be set no higher than $9.00. The manager now knows that for every rib-eye steak sandwich sold, the operation needs to make up $0.47 somewhere else to offset the fact that the item is priced below the standard food cost percentage. The manager must now look at other menu items to make up this difference.

Determining Item Popularity

A manager can assume that a menu item is popular if it produces sales that are at least 70 percent of its percentage share within the menu mix:

$$\text{Item popularity} = 0.70 \times \text{Share \% of total sales}$$

For example, if a given menu item has an expected share of 20 percent of total weekly sales for next week, it has to make up at least 14 percent of total weekly sales (0.20×0.70) to be considered popular. The result is the menu mix popularity percentage: the percentage of total menu items that must be sold for a menu item to be considered popular when sales mix analysis is performed.

For example, the Caddie Diner features eight entrées (see *Exhibit 4.11*). Therefore, the expected sales percentage is 12.5 percent:

100%	÷	8	=	12.5%
Total sales		No. of different entrées		Expected sales mix %

Then, to calculate the menu mix popularity of a single entrée, take 70 percent of the expected sales mix percentage:

12.5%	×	70%	=	8.75%
Expected sales mix %		Allowable sales %		Menu mix popularity %

After the menu mix popularity percentage is calculated, the MM percentage of each menu item is compared to this benchmark to determine whether the item is popular or unpopular (see *Exhibit 4.12*):

- Items with an MM percentage at or above the menu mix popularity percentage are considered popular sellers.

- Items with an MM percentage below the menu mix popularity percentage are considered unpopular.

Exhibit 4.11

MENU MIX AT THE CADDIE DINER

Caddie Diner: Menu Mix Worksheet (Partial)

Menu Items: Entrées	Number Sold	Menu Mix Popularity %
Chicken Breast Dinner	867	17.9%
Seafood Platter	253	5.2
Steak Dinner	721	14.9
Turkey Sandwich	346	7.1
Pork Chop	405	8.4
Hamburger	659	13.6
Cheeseburger	1,376	28.4
Meatloaf	218	4.5
Weekly Total	**4,845**	**100.0%**

If an item is considered popular, *High* is recorded in the Rating category. If an item is considered unpopular, *Low* is recorded.

In this example, the MM percentage of the Pork Chop entrée is 8.4 percent. This is just below the MM popularity percentage of 8.75 percent, so the popularity of the Pork Chop entrée is low. On the other hand, the Chicken Breast Dinner has an MM percentage of 17.9, meaning its popularity is high.

Determining Item Contribution Margin

To identify how menu items contribute to the composite (potential) food cost percentage, managers use a simple chart or spreadsheet. On this spreadsheet, the number sold of each item is multiplied by the item's standard portion cost to get the total cost:

Exhibit 4.12		
MENU MIX POPULARITY RATING		
Caddie Diner: Menu Mix Popularity Rating		
Menu Items: Entrées	**Menu Mix Popularity %**	**Rating**
Chicken Breast Dinner	17.9%	High
Seafood Platter	5.2	Low
Steak Dinner	14.9	High
Turkey Sandwich	7.1	Low
Pork Chop	8.4	Low
Hamburger	13.6	High
Cheeseburger	28.4	High
Meatloaf	4.5	Low

$$
\left(\begin{array}{c} \text{Number} \\ \text{of item} \\ \text{A's sold} \end{array} \times \begin{array}{c} \text{Item A's} \\ \text{standard} \\ \text{portion} \\ \text{cost} \end{array}\right) + \left(\begin{array}{c} \text{Number} \\ \text{of item} \\ \text{B's sold} \end{array} \times \begin{array}{c} \text{Item B's} \\ \text{standard} \\ \text{portion} \\ \text{cost} \end{array}\right) = \begin{array}{c} \text{Total} \\ \text{(weighted)} \\ \text{food cost} \end{array}
$$

Likewise, the number sold is multiplied by the selling price to get total sales:

$$
\left(\begin{array}{c} \text{Number} \\ \text{of item} \\ \text{A's sold} \end{array} \times \begin{array}{c} \text{Selling} \\ \text{price} \\ \text{for A} \end{array}\right) + \left(\begin{array}{c} \text{Number} \\ \text{of Item} \\ \text{B's sold} \end{array} \times \begin{array}{c} \text{Selling} \\ \text{price} \\ \text{for B} \end{array}\right) = \begin{array}{c} \text{Total} \\ \text{food} \\ \text{sales} \end{array}
$$

Total cost is then divided by total sales to get the product mix for this entire menu:

$$
\begin{array}{c} \text{Total (weighted)} \\ \text{food cost} \end{array} \div \begin{array}{c} \text{Total} \\ \text{food sales} \end{array} = \begin{array}{c} \text{Product mix} \\ \text{for entire menu} \end{array}
$$

Note that the product mix for the entire menu is also a weighted food cost percentage for the menu. The menu product mix spreadsheet shown in *Exhibit 4.13* on the next page illustrates that each of the items sold has a different food cost percentage. In this case, the composite (potential) food cost percentage for the entire menu at Mel's Quick-Bite Grill is 36 percent.

Exhibit 4.13

MENU PRODUCT MIX SPREADSHEET FOR MEL'S QUICK-BITE GRILL

Item	Number Sold	Cost	Selling Price	Food Cost Percentage	Total Cost	Total Sales
Hamburger	250	$ .60	$1.50	40%	$ 150.00	$ 375.00
Hot dog	190	.37	1.00	37%	70.30	190.00
French fries	225	.42	.85	49%	94.50	191.25
Onion rings	157	.61	1.25	49%	95.77	196.25
Carbonated beverages	428	.15	.85	18%	64.20	363.80
Ice cream cone	118	.26	.75	35%	30.68	88.50
Total				**36%**	**$505.45**	**$1,404.80**

To further understand how this tool can be used, change the standard food cost for the establishment to 35 percent. There are many ways to lower the food cost percentage, but assume that the manager wants to do it by increasing the selling prices of French fries and onion rings. By increasing the price of each serving of French fries or onion rings by $0.10, the results will change as shown in *Exhibit 4.14*. The operation now has a composite (potential) food cost percentage of 35 percent and is therefore meeting its standard.

Exhibit 4.14

CHANGING THE SELLING PRICE AFFECTS FOOD COST PERCENTAGE

Item	Number Sold	Cost	Selling Price	Food Cost Percentage	Total Cost	Total Sales
Hamburger	250	$ .60	$1.50	40%	$ 150.00	$ 375.00
Hot dog	190	.37	1.00	37%	70.30	190.00
French fries	225	.42	**.95**	44%	94.50	213.75
Onion rings	157	.61	**1.35**	45%	95.77	211.95
Carbonated beverages	428	.15	.85	18%	64.20	363.80
Ice cream cone	118	.26	.75	35%	30.68	88.50
Total				**35%**	**$505.45**	**$1,443.00**

Assessing Individual Item Performance

There are numerous software programs that analyze menu product mix as well as several different versions of menu engineering programs. **Menu engineering** is similar to analyzing the menu product mix, but additionally it takes into account an item's contribution margin and its popularity.

Menu engineering is a concept developed to help restaurant and foodservice professionals track variables that influence a menu's profitability. In 1982, Michigan State University School of Hospitality professor Michael Kasavana and Donald Smith published *Menu Engineering: A Practical Guide to Menu Pricing.* The authors wanted to know if it was possible to influence the customers' decisions toward menu items that have a greater contribution margin and therefore generate more profit. Menu engineering is a tool that provides managers with the necessary data to make decisions about menu items to improve the overall profitability of the menu.

On the menu, items actually compete against one another: Some items are more profitable, others are high sales items, some items offer both, and a few are neither. Kasavana and Smith developed four categories of menu items:

Exhibit 4.15

- Stars: Menu items with high popularity and high CM

- Plow horses: Menu items with high popularity and low CM

- Puzzles: Menu items with low popularity and high CM

- Dogs: Menu items with low popularity and low CM

Since the menu is the primary marketing tool an operation has, menu engineering helps determine layout and product mix. Where items are placed on a menu will affect how many are sold, so it would make business sense to place the high-selling, high-grossing items, or "stars" according to Kasavana and Smith, in the best position to maximize sales (*Exhibit 4.15*).

The first step in menu engineering is to develop a **menu matrix**, where menu items are placed in different categories based on their popularity and profitability. The menu matrix will help determine what to keep on the menu, where there may be opportunities to make price increases, and where to eliminate items. As mentioned, menu items are placed in one of four performance classifications based on popularity and contribution margin. The more managers can influence the sales toward stars, the more profitable the operation will be. The Steak Dinner from the Caddie Diner, shown in *Exhibit 4.16*, is one such "star." Again, service staff should be trained to emphasize these items and managers should be mindful about making significant changes, whether in ingredients, presentation, or price.

Items that sell well but have a lower-than-average gross profit contribution are called "plow horses" or loss leaders, and every operation must have them. These items often are the top-selling menu items. Plow horses are very price-sensitive, which means that even small price increases could reduce sales volume. However, if the food cost on a loss leader could be reduced without affecting perceived value, this type of item could easily move into the "star" classification.

A third classification, "puzzles," includes menu items that have greater-than-average gross profit, but lower-than-average popularity. Typically, these are the more expensive items on the menu. Too many puzzles could cause problems and managers may need to think about whether these menu items should be repackaged, have the price adjusted, or be eliminated.

The final classification is "dogs," or menu items that have lower-than-average popularity and produce a lower-than-average contribution to gross profit. These items do not sell well, do not contribute much toward the bottom line, and should be repackaged or replaced. However, there may be reasons for maintaining a dog on the menu. For example, these items may be important to a particular market segment such as kids' meals or senior favorites, and it may be necessary for an operation to keep these items in order to remain competitive.

An operation should consider eliminating an item from the menu if it accounts for less than 3 percent in its category. For example, if steamed artichokes account for 3 percent or less in the appetizer category, managers should consider removing it from the menu. Items that are seldom ordered risk increased spoilage, often have poor quality because they may not be fresh, and cost additional labor because they are often not prepped when needed.

Menu engineering may point to problems on the menu, but decisions on how to manage those challenges should not be based only on quantitative data. There are a number of nonquantifiable factors that must be considered during menu planning and the pricing phase. Customer preferences, regional practices, competition, the establishment's history or tradition, and marketing policies are all factors that should influence purely quantitative factors and may keep certain items on the menu regardless of costs or contribution margins.

Exhibit 4.16 shows an example of a menu engineering worksheet.

Exhibit 4.16

MENU ENGINEERING WORKSHEET

Restaurant: Caddie Diner

	A	B	C	D	E	F	G	H	I	P	R	S
	Menu Item	Number Sold Menu Mix	Menu Mix % (Popularity)	Food Cost	Menu Price	Item CM (Profit)	Menu Costs	Total Menu Revenue	Menu CM Total Profit	CM Category	MM% (Popularity) Category	Menu Item Categories
		# Sold Total Covers		(from Cost Cards)	(from Menu)	Menu Price – Food Cost	Food Cost × Number Sold	Menu Price × Number Sold	Item CM × Number Sold	Item CM or Average CM	Compare to MM% Popularity Rate	Compare Stars, Dogs, Puzzles, or Plow Horses
Chicken Breast Dinner	867	17.9%	$2.81	$ 7.95	$ 5.14	$ 2,436.27	$6,892.65	$ 4,456.38	Low	High	Plow Horse
Seafood Platter	253	5.2	4.31	10.95	6.64	1,090.43	2,770.35	1,679.92	High	Low	Puzzle
Steak Dinner	721	14.9	6.24	24.95	18.71	4,499.04	17,988.95	13,489.91	High	High	Star
Turkey Sandwich	346	7.1	1.56	6.95	5.39	539.76	2,404.70	1,864.94	Low	Low	Dog
Pork Chop	405	8.4	3.06	7.95	4.89	1,239.30	3,219.75	1,980.45	Low	Low	Dog
Hamburger	659	13.6	1.88	4.50	2.62	1,238.92	2,965.50	1,726.58	Low	High	Plow Horse
Cheeseburger	1376	28.4	2.19	5.50	3.31	3,013.44	7,568.00	4,554.56	Low	High	Plow Horse
Meatloaf	218	4.5	1.56	6.50	4.94	340.08	1,417.00	1,076.92	Low	Low	Dog
	Total Number of Covers						Total Menu Food Cost	Total Menu Revenue	Menu Power Index			
Totals	**4,845**						$14,397.24	$45,226.90	$30,829.66			

FINDING THE RIGHT PRICE

While doing consulting work overseas, I found myself working with a restaurant owner who really had no restaurant or business experience. The quantity of items on the menu was extensive; the pricing was all over the place. Quite frankly, the menu was so extensive it was unmanageable. The pricing was very confusing. For example, some appetizers were considerably more expensive than most of the entrées. Conversely, there were entrées that were priced into the appetizer range.

Actually, the pricing was done with just straight food cost calculations. We took the time to reengineer some of the items, remove others, and tighten up the pricing. We also added a formula for rotating in and out different specials and theme nights.

What was the end result? Production in the kitchen was smoother; the quality of the food produced increased; guest satisfaction improved; the comfort level of the service staff was more relaxed; and ultimately, sales and profits increased.

Menu Modifications and Price Adjustments

Now that you understand how pricing affects the composite (potential) food cost percentage for the menu, the next step is to examine how managers can identify possible concerns. There are three factors that should be examined and compared:

- Standard food cost percentage for the operation
- Composite (potential) food cost percentage based on the menu product mix
- Actual food cost percentage calculated from the income statement

If all three match, then there are no apparent problems for the operation regarding food cost. If they do not match, however, this indicates problems that need to be investigated. The variance among these factors will give managers insight into where the problem lies, and whether it is related to the menu or to the actual activities within the operation.

IS THE MENU THE PROBLEM?

To see if the problem is with the menu itself, such as the items listed or the prices at which the items are being sold, the composite (potential) food cost percentage should be compared with the operation's standard food cost percentage. The formula looks like this:

$$\text{Standard food cost percentage} - \text{Composite (potential) food cost percentage} = \text{Variance}$$

Compare that variance to any variance between the standard food cost on the budget and the actual food cost, found on the income statement:

$$\text{Standard food cost (on budget)} - \text{Actual food cost (on income statement)} = \text{Variance}$$

Then compare the two variances against one another. If they are equal, it will be necessary to adjust the menu pricing structure. There are several possible solutions:

- Increase prices.
- Eliminate high-cost/low-selling items and replace with low-cost items that have higher sales potential.
- Evaluate portion sizes.

Using the previous formulas in this chapter for standard food cost and product mix, assume that an operation's standard food cost percentage is 28 percent. The operation's income statement calculation results in an actual percentage of 32 percent for the month. If the manager analyzed the menu product mix and found a composite (potential) food cost percentage of 32 percent, then his or her only solution in this case is to adjust the items or prices on the menu to eliminate any future variance and bring the actual food cost percentage back down to 28 percent.

This is an extremely important concept to master. Many managers, particularly in chain operations where they have little control over menu pricing, have struggled to attain the company's standard food cost when there is no realistic way to do so. The product mix and the standard food cost must match if there is any expectation of achieving the standard on the income statement.

IS THE PROBLEM OPERATIONAL?

Now consider a different scenario. In this case, the operation's composite (potential) food cost percentage as calculated through the menu product mix is equal to its standard food cost percentage, but, by comparing the budget to the income statement, the manager has identified a variance between the standard food cost and the actual food cost. Under these circumstances the variance is usually caused by an operational problem within the establishment.

For example, if the composite (potential) food cost percentage calculated through the menu product mix analysis is 35 percent, and it matches the establishment's standard of 35 percent, but the actual food cost percentage calculated from data on the income statement is 40 percent, then the issue is not related to the menu. In theory, the operation should be able to achieve the standard food cost percentage based on its current menu offerings. The variance between these figures rests with one or more of the operational controls that will be discussed in detail later in this book.

IMPLEMENTING REVISED PRICES

Assuming that managers do have control of the menu, there are several solutions that can be explored to bring the menu into agreement with the desired percentages. The first inclination would be to increase prices. Although this could certainly be a solution to the problem, it may not be the wisest choice. When increasing prices, an operation must be careful not to exceed the price–value relationship as it is perceived by the customers.

Another alternative would be to eliminate high-cost/low-selling items (the "dogs" of menu engineering) and replace them with low-cost items that have higher sales potential. Lower-cost items can also be marketed in such a way as to encourage the customer to choose them over higher-cost items. Another consideration would be to evaluate the portion sizes. However, as with increasing prices, managers must be careful not to affect the price–value relationship by cutting portions to the extent of causing customer discontent.

Revenue Forecast Adjustments

Factors that affect either sales or costs may invalidate the original forecast targets. A menu matrix will help managers either confirm that an operation is meeting its targets or show that they need to adjust revenue forecasts. If, for whatever reason, the sales mix of menu items is not what was originally forecasted, revenue will be affected. Menu engineering can provide managers

RESTAURANT TECHNOLOGY

POS systems are an important tool for costing and tracking sales of menu items. The success of a POS is determined by the quality of programming that goes into it. Managers must communicate with the POS vendor what they want and expect. The POS can be programmed to track all sales, provide report breakdown by menu category, or retrieve any other data required. In addition, good reporting practices are essential to assess past data.

Exhibit 4.17

with the necessary data to make decisions about menu items to improve the overall profitability of the menu.

Menu Revisions

If the menu needs to be revised, the first task for the manager is to gather information (see *Exhibit 4.17*). Sales information gives the manager the tools to make price adjustments with some measure of confidence. It is necessary to keep good records to determine a menu's stars and dogs. A POS system can help with the data tracking and storage.

When making menu item price revisions, there are a number of actions that managers can take to reduce negative customer reactions:

- Changing menu prices and menu design at the same time will highlight the price increases. This can affect perceived value in the mind of the customer.

- Use odd-cents increments in prices such as $0.25, $0.50, $0.75, and $0.95. If that is already the pricing structure, consider $0.29, $0.59, $0.79, and $0.99. Menu item increases within this range are less likely to be noticed.

- Reposition menu items that are increased by a dollar or more. Move the item to a spot less visible on the menu and move a low-price item into the vacated spot.

Besides tracking data, managers should always keep open lines of communication with the service staff. They know what the guests are saying about the establishment and the menu items. Managers can also benefit from spending time with guests and listening to their comments.

SUMMARY

1. **Describe external and internal factors that influence menu pricing.**

   The selling price on the menu is not always the same price that is derived from one of the formulas. Other factors must also be taken into account when pricing a menu, including the market, location, economic climate, competition, and the perceived value by the customer. One of the most important ways managers use a menu as a cost control device is to determine if the menu items are priced appropriately. Food costs change, so it is very important that recipe cost cards are updated regularly. If the cost goes up and the selling price is not adjusted accordingly, the standard food cost percentage will not be met and the profit of the operation will be reduced. Portion size must also be controlled or it will impact food cost and profit.

2. **List and explain different menu pricing formulas.**

   Establishments use a variety of methods to calculate markup and determine selling prices. The factor method, also known as the food cost percentage method, is a popular formula used to determine menu prices based simply on the standard food cost percentage. The contribution margin (CM) method calculates what is left over after the product cost of a menu item is subtracted from the menu selling price. That amount is what each item "contributes" to paying for labor and other expenses and providing a profit. The ratio pricing method considers the relationship between all expenses and profit, whereas the prime cost method calculates labor costs involved in food preparation, as well as food cost.

3. **Describe the menu product mix and menu engineering.**

   The menu product mix is a detailed analysis that shows the quantities sold of each menu item, their selling prices, and their standard portion costs. It is used to determine the composite (potential) food cost percentage for all items sold. It is this average, not each individual item, that must meet the operation's standard food cost percentage.

   Menu engineering identifies the buying habits of customers, and how their choices affect profitability. Menu engineering places each of the menu items into one of four categories based on their sales volume and contribution to profits: stars, plow horses, puzzles, and dogs. This process helps determine which items to feature more prominently on the menu, which items need repackaging, and which items may need to be removed from the menu.

4. **Explain the process used to identify food cost percentage problems.**

   Managers can identify concerns directly related to food cost percentages. There are three factors that should be examined and compared: standard food cost percentage for the operation, composite (potential) food cost percentage based on the menu product mix, and actual food cost percentage calculated from the income statement. If they do not match, this indicates problems that need to be investigated. The manner in which these factors do not match will give managers insight into where the problem lies, and whether it is related to the menu or to the actual activities within the operation.

5. **Describe the process for determining menu modifications and price adjustments.**

   Managers should be cautious and methodical in making price adjustments. They need to listen to the customers and service staff, track sales mix and profitability, as well as employ common sense. By adjusting specific variables, such as cost, pricing, menu placement, and presentation, an operation can maximize the profitability of each menu item.

APPLICATION EXERCISE

You are the general manager of Burrito Biggies, a popular quick-service restaurant, and have been given this assignment.

1. Calculate the missing information and complete the menu product mix spreadsheet that follows.

2. What is the composite (potential) food cost percentage for Burrito Biggie's menu?

part – food cost
whole – selling price

MENU PRODUCT MIX SPREADSHEET

Item	Number Sold	Cost *part*	Selling *whole* Price	Food Cost Percentage	Total Cost	Total Sales
Taco	890	*132*	$0.89	36%	*284.80*	$ 792.10
Burrito	775	$0.42	*1.62*	26	$325.50	1,255.50
Tamale	800	0.29	0.79	*36*	232.00	*632*
Chili con queso/chips	520	*40*	1.49	27	208.00	774.80
Salsa/chips	780	0.26	0.89	29	*202.80*	694.20
Beverages	1,650		0.89	18	264.00	
Total	*5915*	*276*				

3. You have just found out that the cost of cheddar and Monterey Jack cheese will be going up substantially due to a major strike by your dairy distributor's delivery personnel. You have refigured the recipe cost cards for the items using these ingredients and have come up with new costs: tacos at $0.35, burritos at $0.46, and chili con queso at $0.46. Butch Biggs, the owner of Burrito Biggies, will not stand for any increase in the standard food cost percentage, nor will he let you change the recipes or portion sizes. You are therefore limited to price increases.

Refigure the menu product mix information using the revised costs and determine what you will do to offset these increases.

Note: *You are not limited to changing the selling price of those items that have an ingredient cost increase. You can change the selling price of anything on the menu.*

Fill in the following worksheet to reflect changes in the product mix:

WORKSHEET TO REFLECT CHANGES IN THE PRODUCT MIX: MENU PRODUCT MIX SPREADSHEET

Item	Number Sold	Cost	Selling Price	Food Cost Percentage	Total Cost	Total Sales
Taco	890	$0.35				
Burrito	775	0.46				
Tamale	800	0.29			$232.00	
Chili con queso/chips	520	0.46				
Salsa/chips	780	0.26			202.80	
Beverages	1,650	0.16			264.00	
Total						

4. Create a short presentation, including a new menu product mix analysis that you will give to Mr. Biggs regarding the cost increase on cheese. Your presentation should describe how you plan to offset the cost increase, while maintaining the operation's standard food cost percentage. You also want to reassure Mr. Biggs that customers will not be able to tell any difference in product quality or consistency.

5. Use the following menu product mix spreadsheet for your presentation. Be able to fully explain and justify your proposal.

Use this menu product mix spreadsheet for your presentation to Mr. Biggs:

WORKSHEET PRODUCT MIX SPREADSHEET FOR PRESENTATION TO MR. BIGGS: MENU PRODUCT MIX SPREADSHEET

Item	Number Sold	Cost	Selling Price	Food Cost Percentage	Total Cost	Total Sales
Taco	890	$0.35				
Burrito	775	0.46				
Tamale	800	0.29			$232.00	
Chili con queso/chips	520	0.46				
Salsa/chips	780	0.26			202.80	
Beverages	1,650	0.16			264.00	
Total						

REVIEW YOUR LEARNING

Select the best answer for each question.

1. **Which is an internal factor that might affect the final selling price of an item?**
   A. Competition
   B. Price–value relationship
   C. Regional economic climate
   D. Standard food cost percentage

2. **Demand-driven pricing refers to a theoretical statement that states that**
   A. the market will determine the prices an operation can charge.
   B. customers will pay only a certain amount based on a perceived value.
   C. competition can demand that an operation lower its prices.
   D. an operation can set pricing based on demand for the product or service.

3. **A hotdog has a food cost percentage of 24.5%. What is the factor for this item, if the manager uses the factor method?**
   A. 1
   B. 2.5
   C. 4
   D. 6.1

4. **What information is used to determine the menu product mix?**
   A. The list of food items in inventory
   B. All of the ingredients that go into a standardized recipe
   C. An average of the number of items in each category on a menu
   D. Food costs of all items on the menu and their quantities sold

Use the following pro forma income statement data to answer questions 5 and 6.

Sales	$450,690
Food cost	110,575
Labor cost	125,989
All other expenses	150,500

5. A menu item's cost is $4.50. Using the ratio method, what should the item price be?

   A. $11.23

   B. $18.31

   C. $21.49

   D. $45.00

6. A menu item's prime cost is $6.50. Using the prime cost method, what should the item price be?

   A. $9.99

   B. $11.99

   C. $12.99

   D. $16.99

7. If the food cost on the income statement and the composite (potential) food cost are each 4% higher than the standard, then there is a potential problem with the

   A. recipe.

   B. menu.

   C. standard.

   D. inventory.

8. In menu engineering, a low-CM/high-popularity item is referred to as a

   A. dog.

   B. star.

   C. puzzle.

   D. plow horse.

9. What term refers to the amount left after a menu item's food cost is subtracted from its selling price?

   A. Plate cost

   B. Prime cost

   C. Contribution margin

   D. Accompaniment cost

10. Based on the following chart, what is the composite (potential) food cost percentage for Burrito Biggie's menu?

   A. 36%

   B. 30%

   C. 27%

   D. 18%

BURRITO BIGGIES MENU PRODUCT MIX SPREADSHEET

Item	Number Sold	Cost	Selling Price	Food Cost Percentage	Total Cost	Total Sales
Taco	890	$0.32	$0.89	36%	$ 284.80	$ 792
Burrito	775	0.42	1.62	26	325.50	1,255.50
Tamale	800	0.29	0.79	36	232.00	
Chili con queso/chips	520	0.40	1.49	27	208.00	774.80
Salsa/Chips	780	0.26	0.89	29%	202.80	694.20
Beverages	1,650	0.16	0.89	18	264.00	1,468.50
Total					**$1,517.10**	**$4,985.00**

FIELD PROJECT

Visit three different nonfranchised establishments in your area. Choose a similar item that appears on each menu. Ask the manager or owner of each operation how he or she came up with the costs for the item on the menu.

Some sample questions are:

1. How did you determine the selling price?

2. What internal factors helped you determine the price?

3. What external factors helped you determine the price?

4. How do you track your sales to determine if you are charging enough or too much?

Write a paper comparing the different ways each establishment chose its pricing. End the paper with your recommendation on which operation used the best pricing method.

5 Controlling Food Costs in Purchasing

INSIDE THIS CHAPTER

- Developing Purchase Procedures
- Implementing the Ordering System
- Improving the Ordering System

CHAPTER LEARNING OBJECTIVES

After completing this chapter, you should be able to:

- Explain the purchase process and determine who should make purchasing decisions.

- Describe the importance of par levels and how to establish them.

- Explain different types of purchasing methods and their uses.

- Describe the parts of a purchase specification and of a purchase order.

- Explain the importance of maintaining an ordering system.

KEY TERMS

CASE STUDY

Chef Bob Schmidt and Chef Linda Wiley were discussing Bob's new position at the Polo Bistro restaurant during a recent Chef Association meeting. Chef Smith had just moved to the area, and was hoping Chef Wiley could help with contacts for vendors and suppliers.

"Foodservice Meats and Betty Poultry are two very good sources," Linda said. "I use B&B Broadline Suppliers for most of my goods."

"What about local produce or specialty houses?" asked Bob.

"My sales guy with B&B takes good care of me, and I really look forward to baseball tickets he gives me each year," Linda replied. "So, I don't really shop around much. Besides," she said in a low voice, "the chef before you used only B&B."

1. Chef Smith has an employment contract that includes a bonus if he meets specific food cost targets. Should he be concerned that B&B has had a long-term vendor relationship with the Polo Bistro? Why or why not?

2. Do you think that the salesperson with B&B Broadline Suppliers believes his accounts are partnerships? Explain why or why not?

Exhibit 5.1

Buyers select the food needed to produce menu items that satisfy customers' expectations.

DEVELOPING PURCHASE PROCEDURES

Purchasing is one of the key areas in the cost control process of the restaurant and foodservice industry. When a customer orders an item from the menu, he or she has certain expectations. If size, shape, color, grade, or portions are mentioned, then those food characteristics are what the customer should receive. The person responsible for purchasing items for the operation must be aware of these customer expectations and procure exactly what is stated on the menu (see *Exhibit 5.1*).

In addition to the correct item, the buyer must also purchase the correct amount. If too many goods are purchased, not only is the operation's capital tied up in inventory, but if the goods are perishable, they might spoil. This is one way for operations to lose money. However, if too few goods are purchased, there is the danger of running out and disappointing guests. Purchasing, like every other section in the operation, is an area where costs can get out of line. Controls and procedures must be instituted to prevent this from happening. The purchasing procedure consists of the following steps:

1. Designating a purchasing person
2. Determining which products to buy by establishing product specifications
3. Estimating how often and how much to order
4. Choosing purchasing methods based on organizational needs
5. Selecting vendors

Who Should Buy

The first step in the purchasing process is designating who will do it. It could be one or several people, depending on the size of the operation. In very large restaurant or foodservice operations such as major hotels, hospitals, and college foodservices, a purchasing agent will do the buying. In smaller operations, it could be the general manager, production manager, or chef. Regardless of who does it, this person is referred to as the buyer and is the sole person responsible for purchasing particular goods.

While the buyer's responsibility may be shared, clearly designating who will be the buyer for which items eliminates confusion and minimizes the risk of running out of a product or having too much of it on hand. For example, in a larger operation, the chef might purchase meat, seafood, and produce, while the sous chef orders dairy, baked goods, dry goods, and supplies. Although two people are purchasing, only one person is the buyer in each category.

Buyers need to possess a variety of skills:

Exhibit 5.2

- **Balanced communication skills:** They must be able to listen to the needs of stakeholders in their operation (*Exhibit 5.2*), including the preparation staff, accounting staff, receiving and storing staff, ownership, and management. They must also be able to articulate those needs to vendors.

- **Excellent math skills:** Math is basic to all of the primary functions of the buyer and storeroom staff: buying, receiving, storing, and issuing.

- **Computer skills:** Computers are widespread in purchasing. Tracking inventory is the heart of control and purchasing, and is mainly done with computer software.

- **Product knowledge:** Buyers can develop their food knowledge by spending time at trade shows, farmer's markets, and food distributor's warehouses. Attending food shows is an efficient way to keep up on the latest food and equipment developments.

While it is common for managers to delegate purchasing, it is extremely important that the person selected to purchase products is trained and knowledgeable about the subject. Only by following correct purchasing procedures and having controls in place can the establishment get the right item at the right price. For this reason, if the manager is going to delegate this responsibility, it must be passed on to someone who has been trained in the operation's purchasing procedure.

What to Buy

To know what to purchase, a buyer must work with a number of variables. The buyer needs to know the growing seasons for produce and that beef prices are lower in the spring than in the fall. The buyer must be familiar with varieties, grades, and forms in which the products can be purchased. And the buyer needs to be able to judge if a distributor **quotes**, or offers, a fair price. An experienced buyer can "read the market" for signs of supply, demand, and price fluctuations and does not rely on supply-and-demand information received from **suppliers**. Suppliers, also called vendors, are the companies that provide products purchased for use in restaurant and foodservice operations. Some examples for products provided by suppliers are meat, dairy, vegetables, fruit, utensils, and paper products.

The buyer also needs to organize product specifications by vendor. That is, products that will be ordered from the same vendor should be grouped together. The buyer must also have a working knowledge of grading terminology, labeling terms, and standards used to judge quality. A buyer's responsibilities go beyond getting the best price and ensuring that sufficient quantities are available; standards of quality must be upheld as well.

Product Specifications

The second step in the purchasing process is determining which products to purchase by establishing product specifications. Because there is such a wide variety of food available, the specification (or spec) is an important control device. Through this device managers set policy as to which brands, grades, and variety of food products will be ordered for the operation. A specification ties together what is written on the menu and what is called for in the standardized recipe. It also controls the purchasing and receiving procedures.

Everyone uses specifications in their everyday lives. If someone wanted to buy some clothes, for example, he would have a specific size, preferred style, and color in mind. In contrast, the specifications used in the restaurant and foodservice industry are much more formal.

A **specification** explains or describes the desired product name, its intended use, grade and size, and other product characteristics. It also includes general instructions regarding delivery, payment procedures, and other pertinent data. Basically, it tells the supplier exactly what the buyer wants. A specification should be documented so that both the buyer and the supplier are clear on the buyer's purchase requirements.

Managers, with input from the chef or production manager, must write the specifications for all the food needed to produce the standardized recipes of the menu items. It is important to match product specifications to the desired use. One example of a mismatch might be ordering Grade A tomatoes for spaghetti sauce, when Grade B tomatoes would suffice and save the operation money. Large operations typically write formal specifications; smaller operations might use verbal specifications. A detailed formal specification includes the following information:

- **Product name**
- **Intended use:** the component of the standardized recipe the item will be used to make
- **Grade:** U.S. Department of Agriculture (USDA), brand name, trade association endorsement
- **Product size:** could include portion size; weight ranges for food items such as roasts, ribs, whole chickens, or whole fish; size of produce
- **Packaging:** size of pack, type of packaging material
- **Product characteristics:** color, amount of trim, type of preservation, degree of ripeness, point of origin

- **Acceptable substitutions ("or equal"):** substitutions previously agreed upon by both buyer and vendor
- **General instructions to bidders:** Restaurant and foodservice establishments receive bids from several vendors on the same product in order to purchase at the best possible price. These vendors are competing with each other for the operation's business.

To understand the importance of clear specifications, imagine if a buyer were to order simply "a case of fresh apples" from a produce company. The company could possibly ship any type of apple. Purchasing the correct fresh apples requires buyers to know the following:

- What is the intended use? Are the apples for baking, puree, or eating raw? Red Delicious apples are among the most popular apples, but they are the wrong variety for cobbler, pie, or applesauce.
- What are the grade standards? Do they need to be U.S. Fancy or U.S. No. 1?
- What varieties are available? Produce companies may carry as many as 18 to 20 different varieties of apples.
- How are they packed, by count or by weight? Generally, vendors refer to apples by count. The higher the number of apples per case, the smaller the apple.
- When are they in season? Most apples are available year-round, but some varieties, such as Gravenstein, are seasonal.
- Are there any additional considerations? Should the apples be organic? Should they be fresh cut in order to reduce labor costs and waste? Should they be unwaxed?
- Should they be sourced locally, and if so, what is the distance they may be shipped?

A specification for apples might look like *Exhibit 5.3*.

Developing quality standards is time-consuming and tedious. It is also one of the most important ways to consistently get the quality desired by any operation. Tools exist to help buyers and managers develop specifications, such as *The Meat Buyers Guide*, published by the North American Meat Processors Association (see *Exhibit 5.4* on the following page). Specifications identify exactly what the buyer should purchase.

WHAT'S THE FOOTPRINT?

In recent years, many operations have turned to using locally sourced products on their menus. Using locally sourced products can have several advantages:

1. Restaurant and foodservice operations are supporting the local economy, which improves stakeholder relationships.
2. Using terms such as "farm fresh" or "locally grown" on menus is a great marketing tool, which helps increase sales.
3. Local products travel shorter distances, and may reduce the environmental impact associated with long-distance shipping.

Exhibit 5.3

PRODUCT SPECIFICATION

Type: Apple	Water content: 85%
Variety: Fuji	Cultivation type: Organic
Maturity: 100%	Grade: Fancy
Weight (lb): 10–13 oz	Color: Red
Style: Fresh	Packaging: Cases (15-lb)

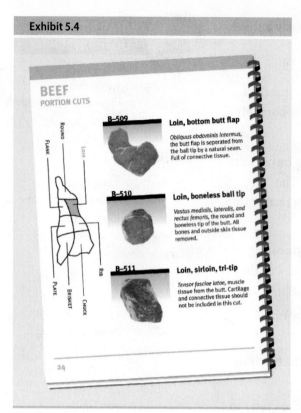

Exhibit 5.4

BEEF
PORTION CUTS

ROUND
FLANK
Loin
Rib
PLATE
BRISKET
CHUCK

B–509   **Loin, bottom butt flap**

*Obliquus abdominis internus,
the butt flap is seperated from
the ball tip by a natural seam.
Full of connective tissue.*

B–510   **Loin, boneless ball tip**

*Vastus medialis, lateralis, and
rectus femoris, the round and
boneless tip of the butt. All
bones and outside skin tissue
removed.*

B–511   **Loin, sirloin, tri-tip**

*Tensor fasciae latae, muscle
tissue from the butt. Cartilage
and connective tissue should
not be included in this cut.*

24

PRODUCT SUBSTITUTIONS

Acceptable substitutions ("or equal") are an important part of purchasing specifications. An operation's vendor may experience shortages or "outs," which is a product that has not been delivered. Establishing acceptable substitutions, "or equal," allows the vendor to fulfill an order with previously agreed-upon substitutions. Vendors can do a thorough review of the products an operation uses and provide the buyer with other options. Substitutions also help the buyer. For example, fresh seafood fluctuates in price. Allowing the buyer to purchase an acceptable substitute can result in a lower price.

Once the specifications are written, they are circulated to suppliers to determine which suppliers will provide each product. Acceptable substitute products should be written into the specifications. In addition to the supplier, specifications are used by the buyer, the receiving clerk, the kitchen, and accounting. Remember, specifications are an internal communication tool, as well as one for outside vendors.

How Much and How Often to Buy

The third step in the purchasing process is estimating how often and how much to order. This is also one of the controls in purchasing. Consider that the act of purchasing costs money, not only in product, but in organizational costs as well. It takes time and labor to receive bids, complete purchase orders, phone in or electronically transmit orders, receive the goods, store the goods, and pay the invoices.

To obtain the best prices for products and to decrease the time spent on researching prices, restaurant and foodservice operations often use a bidding process. The first step in bidding is a request for proposal (RFP) that is prepared by an establishment. An RFP is a document that shows the amount, variety, and specification of products that an operation needs. The RFP is distributed to solicit bids from suppliers, who then can submit their bids or proposals to an operation. Then the manager selects the bid that offers the best prices for the desired specifications. The bidding process is important, but can be time-consuming to both the operation and the supplier.

Every time a supplier's truck stops, the costs to the supplier, and consequently the restaurant or foodservice operation, go up as well. It would stand to reason, then, that less-frequent orders would be best for the organization. However, this is not always true for two reasons. First, if fewer orders are being placed, the inventory level must be higher. High levels of inventory tie up cash, not only in the cost of the food but also in the cost of the storage space. Storage space, while necessary, does not generate sales, costs money to build and maintain, and may take space away from other functional areas such as dining space. In addition, some storage, such as cold storage, requires cooling and ventilation equipment that runs on electricity, thereby increasing utility costs. All of these costs associated with storage space must be covered by the sales brought in by the operation. Finally, some goods cannot be stored for an extended length of time and may need to be ordered frequently. Consequently, the buyer needs to create an order guide that identifies vendors that best satisfy the needs for specific products.

To optimize the timing of purchases, goods are broken down into two categories. **Perishable goods** are products that have a relatively short shelf life—usually one to three days, as shown in *Exhibit 5.5*. Some perishable goods might last a few days longer, but their quality and yield may be considerably diminished. Perishable goods should be purchased as often as possible. In larger restaurant or foodservice operations, perishable goods could be purchased daily. In smaller operations, purchasing perishable goods every two to three days is considered reasonable. However, even smaller operations should not put off purchasing perishable goods such as cream and milk longer than three days.

Nonperishable goods are products that have a relatively longer shelf life. Nonperishable goods can last for a few months to a year if stored and handled properly. Nonperishable goods should be purchased as seldom as possible for reasons previously given. The size of the storage area, the operation's cash flow, and location such as urban versus rural are all factors that the buyer must consider when determining how often to order nonperishable goods. Some operations purchase nonperishable food weekly, some bimonthly, and others monthly.

Exhibit 5.5

Examples of perishable goods

Examples of nonperishable goods

DETERMINING PRODUCT USAGE

Every server dreads having to tell a guest, "We just ran out of the filet mignon about 10 minutes ago. Would you like to try the red snapper?" With guest expectations increasing every day, managers cannot afford to disappoint them on any level. Purchasing the correct amount of product at the correct time for the correct price is the goal of every restaurant or foodservice manager.

These are the steps used in accurately estimating the amount to purchase:

1. Determine the amount of product needed until the next delivery.

2. Check inventory to determine what is on hand.

3. Subtract what is on hand from the amount needed and add 5 percent as a safety measure.

4. Use the result of this calculation as the amount to purchase.

By following this method, the operation is assured of having the right amount of the freshest product available for service to the customer.

THINK ABOUT IT . . .

Restaurant and foodservice operations use hundreds of products in food preparation. Many of these products have different packaging, reordering levels, and ordering frequency. Why?

Exhibit 5.6

As purchased (AP) amount and edible portion (EP) amount also come into play when determining how much to purchase. These are covered in depth in chapter 3. Because most products will lose volume when cooked, for some managers EP becomes as served (AS), which is the amount available to serve to the customer. In this book, the term *EP* is used and it includes cooking loss.

ESTABLISHING PAR LEVEL

Today in the restaurant and foodservice industry, the most common method used for determining the quantity of nonperishables to purchase is the par stock method. **Par level** means an operation has enough stock on hand to get the kitchen through until the next order is delivered. This method works well in operations that have a relatively steady flow of business and a menu that does not change frequently. The key to this method is assigning a level that should be constantly on hand to every item in the storeroom. When it is time to order, inventory the item as shown in *Exhibit 5.6* and subtract that count from the par level. The resulting number is the amount to order. Par levels are normally created using the counting unit for the product, such as 100 pounds of onions or two cases of frozen green beans.

For example, an establishment famous for its fried chicken serves green beans seasoned with smoked ham chunks and onion as one of its side dishes. It uses 1 case of canned green beans each day, except on Saturdays and Sundays when it uses 2 cases per day. Therefore, its usage is 9 cases a week. The manager has decided to add a safety factor of three cases. Consequently, its par stock for green beans is 12 cases. The operation receives a grocery delivery weekly. When taking inventory of the green beans, the manager finds 4 cases on the shelf. She subtracts 4 cases (stock on hand) from 12 cases (par level) and orders 8 cases of green beans:

$$
\underset{\textbf{Cases par level}}{12} \quad - \quad \underset{\textbf{Cases in stock}}{4} \quad = \quad \underset{\textbf{Cases to order}}{8}
$$

To determine a par level, follow these steps:

1. Determine the amount of time between deliveries—for example, daily, weekly, bimonthly, or monthly.

2. Determine the estimated amount used during this period. This should be done for each item in the storeroom.

3. Add a safety factor to cover any unexpected sharp increases in business or to cover the possibility of shortages from the supplier.

4. Add the estimated amount of product used and the safety factor together to get the par stock.

5. Set par levels for all ingredients and supplies so that they can be easily tracked and nothing is overlooked. Adjust pars by season, and order enough to get through the next delivery, not just until the next delivery.

6. Include the par level numbers on the order guide and place a label with the amount on that item's shelf in the storeroom.

In larger operations, such as a hotel food and beverage department, requisitions are used to retrieve items from the storeroom. In this case, the storeroom manager has a spreadsheet called par sheet for every item in the storeroom and subtracts the requisitioned amount from the inventory on the spreadsheet. When placing an order, the manager looks on the par sheet to determine the quantity currently on hand. This is known as a **perpetual inventory** and is used rather than taking a physical inventory. Then the manager looks at the par sheet, which shows the quantity the operation currently has in inventory and the quantity the operation wants to have on hand to get it through until the next order. A sample par sheet for twice-weekly orders is shown in *Exhibit 5.7.*

Exhibit 5.7

SAMPLE PAR SHEET

Meat	Unit	Supplier	Monday			Thursday			Monday			Thursday		
			Par	Inv.	Buy	Par	Inv.	Buy	Par	Inv.	Buy	Par	Inv.	Buy
1. Prime Rib	Each	Chef Meat	4	2	**2**	6	2	**4**	4	3	**1**	6	0	**6**
2. Duck	Each	Betty Poultry	4	2	**2**	8	2	**6**	4	3	**1**	8	1	**7**
3. New York Strip Steak	Each	Chef Meat	24	6	**18**	48	12	**36**	24	4	**20**	48	8	**40**
4. Beef Patties	Case	Chef Meat	2	1	**1**	4	1	**3**	2	1	**1**	4	1	**3**
5. WOG Chicken	Each	Betty Poultry	36	4	**32**	48	8	**40**	36	6	**30**	48	7	**41**

There are also software programs available that use the perpetual inventory approach to the par level method of ordering. These programs can be used for large and small operations alike. Some of the more sophisticated programs are tied into an operation's point-of-sale (POS) system. When a customer orders a menu item, the software calculates the food used in preparing that menu item. The relevant product is automatically taken out of the inventory. When the inventory drops to a predetermined level, the software subtracts the amount on hand from the par level quantity and generates a **purchase order (PO)** for

Exhibit 5.8

that item. A purchase order is a form issued by the buyer and sent to the vendor that indicates the items and quantities to be purchased.

For example, when a customer orders a hamburger (*Exhibit 5.8*) and the server enters the order into the POS system, one hamburger bun, four ounces of ground beef, three pickle slices, and one-quarter ounce of ketchup are subtracted from inventory. As more hamburgers are ordered, more of these ingredients are subtracted from inventory. When the inventory for ground beef drops to a predetermined level of 50 pounds, the program subtracts the available 50 pounds from the par level of 150 pounds, and generates a purchase order for 100 pounds of ground beef.

Unfortunately, fully automated systems have one real drawback: Someone has to enter the information, and keep it up to date. This has a time and labor cost associated with it, sometimes a significant one. Either the programmers or the server must account for menu substitutions, which are products that are different from those that are ordered regularly, or the numbers will be off. For instance, if a customer substitutes a side order of baked potatoes with coleslaw, the server needs to reflect this substitution in the POS system. Any changes in the menu will also need to be programmed, including daily specials. Many large chains do use their POS system to generate order replenishment; however, the majority of those are quick-service restaurant chains with limited menus that do not change often.

How to Purchase

Once an operation knows what to purchase, managers need to know how to purchase those items. Step 4 of the purchasing process is choosing purchasing methods based on organizational needs. There are various ways to purchase products, and some are more economical than others, which contributes to a lower food cost. However, some are misused and end up costing the organization money. Effective purchasing procedures should include a consideration of purchasing methods required by the vendor and the effect of these methods on the organization. Employees responsible for ordering should be trained about several aspects such as deadlines when purchase requests need to be submitted, ordering frequency, and order minimums required by each vendor.

DEFINING ORGANIZATIONAL NEEDS

Before managers decide on the purchasing method, it is best to define the organization's needs. This allows vendors to customize a purchasing program that makes sense for the specific business. For example, some operations may choose to use a **prime vendor**, which will provide most of the operation's goods. Managers should examine:

- **Level of service needs:** Does the sales representative need to meet with the buyer each week to take an order? Or can the buyer order online, via fax, or by a phone call? Based on space and storage limitations, does the operation need frequent deliveries or will one delivery per week work? If the operation requires a high level of service, is there an additional cost associated with that level?

- **Quality specifications needs:** Will the operation's concept allow the buyer to purchase the majority of meat, seafood, produce, and so on from a broadline distributor that provides multiple products such as meat, produce, food supplies, and utensils? Or does the operation need a dedicated supplier for specific products?

- **Prime vendor relationship needs:** Does the operation do enough volume to increase the primary vendor's drop size—minimum amount that a supplier can deliver—for the establishment, thereby making the operation a more profitable stop for the vendor? Will the efficiencies the vendor gains be passed along to the operation in the form of lower prices?

PURCHASING METHODS

Once the organizational purchasing needs have been defined, managers can determine which purchasing method will work best for their operation. Most operations will use one or more of the methods shown in *Exhibit 5.9*.

Exhibit 5.9

PURCHASING METHODS

	Competitive Quotes	Standing Order	Prime Vendor	Cost-Plus	Sealed Bids	Commissary
Primary Use	Independent establishments, smaller operations	Bakery, coffee, dairy products	Independents and chains	Chain operations	Large foodservice units such as schools, hospitals, government agencies	Chains and franchised operations
Requirements	Detailed specs	Par level; must show manager what is removed and brought in	Operation specs; par level	Purchase 100% of product line from one purveyor	Amount needed for a period of time, usually a year	Paper supplies printed with company logo; purchase 100% of supplies
Pros	Lowest price	Keeps stock levels even	Delivery costs reduced with one truck stopping; purchasing online	Lowest possible price	Lowest bid	Efficient; customized supplies
Cons	Lack of specs could lead to lesser-value shipments	Abuse by delivery person; food cost goes up	If supplier is out of item, no backup purveyor; supplier may not offer lowest prices	No competition between bidders	Delivery times need to be negotiated	Often owned by parent company of restaurant chain; conflict of interest

COMPETITIVE QUOTES   This is a common purchasing method used by independent establishments and smaller operations. The buyer completes a market quotation sheet with the items and item specifications that the operation needs. This sheet is a standardized form that is given to two or more suppliers who are then asked to provide a price quote for the items needed. The quotes are analyzed, and the order is then placed with the chosen supplier. For this method to be successful, specifications must be established. If they are not, then anything could be shipped and not necessarily be the best value for the restaurant or foodservice operation. If specifications are used, the lowest price would be the best value because all suppliers are bidding on an identical product.

STANDING ORDER   This method is used primarily for bakery, coffee, and dairy products, and particularly for perishable items and for linens. In this purchasing method, the vendor works closely with the establishment to replenish stock on a regular basis. This method is quite satisfactory as long as the supplier removes the unused stock and gives proper credit. If proper stock rotation does not occur, the operation is using product that is not as fresh as it should be, which could result in substandard product. For the standing order method to be successful, the delivery person needs to show the manager the items being removed and those being brought in.

PRIME VENDOR   This method, also called the one-stop shop, is becoming the most popular in purchasing goods today. It involves purchasing most, if not all, of an operation's goods from one supplier. Independent managers and chains both use this method. It came about when restaurant and foodservice suppliers began merging with meatpackers, produce houses, bakeries, and dairies to form giant super-suppliers. In theory, it works well. Delivery costs are reduced with one truck stopping instead of several. Purchasing can be done online with the operation's specifications and par levels loaded into the program. The downside of this method is that if the supplier is out of something, the operation may not have a backup supplier for that item. Also, because the buyer relies on a single supplier's pricing rather than getting price quotes, the pricing might not be the most competitive for the restaurant or foodservice organization. Managers should make sure that audit privileges are included in any prime vendor agreement. This will serve as the compliance check. Managers should clearly understand how a distributor defines costs, and must be aware if there are additional charges incurred for splitting cases or for stocking proprietary products. Finally, managers should make sure there is an "escape" clause in the agreement.

COST-PLUS   This method is used primarily by chain operations, as independents do not have enough volume for suppliers to offer it to them. In this method, the chain purchases 100 percent of a particular product line, like meat for example, from one supplier. That vendor sells the product at the vendor's invoice price plus an agreed-upon percentage for handling, delivery, and the vendor's profit. Although this system could be used in conjunction with a one-stop shop, it most often is used with several sources; for example, one source for meat, one for produce, one for dairy, one for groceries, and so on. Chains that use the cost-plus method of purchasing are normally paying the lowest possible price for their goods even though the vendors do not bid against each other.

SEALED BIDS Large foodservice units such as schools, colleges, hospitals, and government agencies primarily use sealed bids. In this method, foodservice operations calculate the amount of a product such as dairy that they will need over a period of time, normally a year. Then suppliers will bid on that amount. Usually, the lowest bidder is selected as the supplier for that product. The supplier delivers the entire order amount at one time, or spreads out the deliveries over a specific time period at the agreed-upon price for the duration of the contract. If the price of the product goes up, the vendor must sell at the lower agreed-upon price.

COMMISSARY This method is used almost exclusively by chains and franchised units. Quite often 100 percent of that operation's supplies will come from the commissary. In the commissary method, orders from individual units are consolidated. The commissary then purchases the consolidated quantity from the preferred suppliers. Normally these products include refrigerated, frozen, or packaged premade items that are produced to the company's standards. For instance, some chains may have a commissary where dough is prepared and then distributed to individual stores. Any paper supplies printed with the company's logo will also come from the commissary. Frequently, the commissary is owned by the parent company of the chain or franchise.

Vendor Selection

The fifth and final step in the purchase process is selecting vendors. The chef or purchasing manager knows what to buy, when to buy it, and in what size and packaging. The manager has decided on the method used for purchasing. Once these variables are known, the purchasing manager must decide from whom to buy the product. This begins by compiling a list of all of the reasonable potential suppliers that meet the operation's needs. Management may then begin to shorten it into an approved-supplier list by reviewing each supplier's quality, consistency, variety, and price. These will then be ranked according to the type of establishment being run, the menu being served, and customer expectations. Consistency in quality, delivery time, and labeling are also important factors when choosing a vendor. And finally, managers should consider using Hazard Analysis Critical Control Point (HACCP)–engaged vendors. HACCP is a system used to control risks and hazards. If a customer has an issue with an operation's food, having only HACCP-approved vendors that can share liability is critical. The best suppliers work as partners to reduce costs, maintain quality, and ensure guest satisfaction. It is in their best interest to help their customers' businesses grow.

CHOOSING A VENDOR

The criteria for vendor selection should always include quality, price, and service. Managers should ask for references and check them out by talking to other restaurant and foodservice operations. Managers need to treat the supplier like a prospective employee. Is the vendor rep motivated? Is he or she passionate about the work? Is the vendor rep conscientious and dedicated to making the partnership work?

Managers should meet with the sales manager and the **sales representative**, the supplier's salesperson who would be assigned to the operation. If possible, visit the prospective vendor's business. Tour the warehouse. Look for an organized, clean storage space, free of debris and litter. If it is a seafood, meat, or poultry vendor, check out the cutting and packing room. Walk through the coolers and freezers. These vendors should meet all regulatory requirements, and the area should be clean and sanitary. The best suppliers will welcome interest in what they are selling and how they are handling the product. Often vendors believe that their high operating standards are a point of difference from their competitors.

Once vendors have been identified, it is essential to establish operational ground rules, such as the company's delivery days, drop size, minimum order amount, payment terms, and the cutoff times for ordering for the next day. Buyers need to establish a delivery window, such as 8 a.m. to 10 a.m. or 2 p.m. to 4 p.m., with no deliveries during peak times such as lunch service. Managers will need to review ordering specifications and any other key information that needs to be shared with vendors. Once both parties have agreed to terms, it is very important to keep to the bargain.

MAINTAINING POSITIVE VENDOR RELATIONSHIPS

Restaurant and foodservice operations and their suppliers are critically dependent on each other. However, too often one party has little empathy for the other. Managers deal with a continuous stream of changing prices, quantity and quality, late deliveries, or drivers showing up at peak times. On the other hand, some managers treat suppliers very poorly. They may be rude to delivery drivers, or abuse the sales representatives and run them ragged with last-minute, high-priority demands. Or managers may ignore the invoice terms and pay when they feel like paying.

Building a positive relationship with vendors is more important now than ever. As companies merge into larger distributors, the selection of vendors continues to shrink, making it very hard to find new options if a manager is not happy with a current vendor. Consequently, it is important to view suppliers as partners in the business. However, vendors should also remember that a given restaurant or foodservice operation is their customer. That is, if management of an operation is not happy with a vendor, they may pursue another vendor that better serves the company's needs.

IMPLEMENTING THE ORDERING SYSTEM

Every restaurant and foodservice operation needs an effective ordering system. Proper ordering procedures help keep fresh product in stock. Ordering too much of a product simply because the kitchen keeps running out may result in product that is past its prime. Management does not want excess inventory, which may increase waste, allow for product theft, and encourage overproduction. A proper ordering system helps ensure that the amounts purchased make culinary and financial sense.

Better ordering control can also keep cash from being tied up in excessive inventory levels. Too much physical product kept in storage means less cash available for the operation as a whole. That is, operations with lighter inventory may have available cash to spend on other things such as new menus, laundering linens, and so forth. It is recommended that inventory levels for food products turn over from four to six times a month. For example, if an operation spends $25,000 per month in food purchases, then the food inventory value should range from a low of $4,166 to a high of $6,250 at any given moment within that month. These formulas show the calculations:

$25,000	÷	6	=	$4,167
Food cost		Turnovers per month (high)		Inventory value (low range)

$25,000	÷	4	=	$6,250
Food cost		Turnovers per month (low)		Inventory value (high range)

Compare that with an inventory that turns over only three times a month because the operation has purchased too much:

$25,000	÷	3	=	$8,333
Food cost		Turnovers per month		Inventory value (excessive)

This would result in an inventory value of about $8,333 and a negative cash-on-hand difference of $2,083 to $4,167:

$8,333	−	$6,250	=	$2,083
Inventory value (excessive)		**Inventory value (high range)**		**Cash-on-hand difference (low range)**

$8,333	−	$4,166	=	$4,176
Inventory value (excessive)		**Inventory value (low range)**		**Cash-on-hand difference (high range)**

The Order Guide

It is critical in tough economic times to combat rising costs. One tool for this is the consolidation of purchasing. Consolidation results in greater buying power with suppliers, which results in lower overall costs. Reducing the number of delivery trucks arriving will also result in staff spending less time ordering and receiving products.

To facilitate this process, an order guide should be used by all employees involved in ordering products for an operation. The **order guide** form is a tool for counting and tracking all the products an operation uses and must reorder. It should contain all or some of the following information:

- **Item description:** The description should be brief but identifiable. The pack and size may also be shown in the description. It is recommended that managers use the description that is on the vendor's invoice. For example, the order guide might say only "Beef Cubes for Stewing." But the specifications have already been established as "USDA inspected select or better. 1–1 ¼″ cubes, fairly uniform in size and shape; fat trimmed, fat not to exceed ½″, all gristle and connective tissue removed. Packed 5/10 lb or 4/5 lb, poly packages, inside NSF approved boxes."

- **Pack and size:** The pack means the number of units in the case, box, or carton. The size describes the type of container or weight of the product. In the previous example, it shows that the stew meat is delivered in either five 10-pound poly packages (50 pounds) or in four 5-pound poly packages (20 pounds).

- **Purchase unit:** The purchase unit represents the unit of measure that the price is based on. Some items are sold and delivered by the case. Items like meat, seafood, and some produce can be priced by the pound but delivered in cases. The stew meat would be priced by the pound but sold either in 50- or 20-pound cases.

- **Count unit:** It is not always feasible to use the delivery or purchase unit when counting product for inventory and reorders. Canned goods, for example, are often sold in a case of six #10 cans. The cases are opened and the cans stored on shelves (*Exhibit 5.10*). So counting the number of cans makes more sense than calculating the number of cases.

Exhibit 5.10

- **Price:** The price column is used to show the current purchase price of items. The price should be updated as often as necessary.

- **Vendor:** This column shows the preferred vendor for each product.

- **Vendor item code:** If possible include the vendor's item code. This helps ensure the correct product is ordered and reduces mistakes.

- **Par level:** As noted earlier in this chapter, par level indicates the quantity the operation wants to have on hand to get it through until the next order so that it can be checked against inventory. It is important to note that when products are ordered weekly, managers need to place an order that will carry the operation through the next delivery, even if current inventory is above established par level.

- **Order history:** Include as much order history as the form will allow. This allows managers to adjust the pars if necessary. At least three weeks of history is recommended to get an accurate product usage.

- **Usage rate:** As an alternative or a supplement to order history, some operations may prefer to establish a usage rate, which is a number or amount of items used in a given period, in order to ease the ordering process. This is because historical usage rate may sometimes prove more reliable than order history.

- **On-hand count:** Before an order quantity can be determined, an actual count must be taken to know how much product is on hand.

THINK ABOUT IT . . .

The order guide is a critical document in purchasing. What if restaurant and foodservice operations had no order guide and tried to simply purchase products as needed? What would the consequences for such an approach be?

It is essential that the order guide show par levels, on-hand count (beginning inventory), and amount that needs to be purchased. As noted, when ordering frequency is weekly or biweekly, managers need to carefully analyze both order history and sales history in order to determine the amount that needs to be ordered.

As can be seen in *Exhibit 5.11*, duck is normally ordered on Wednesdays. Even though the establishment has established *daily* par levels, the manager still needs to estimate *weekly* sales of duck for the establishment. This is because the operation places its order once per week. After analyzing weekly sales for duck, the manager finds that the operation goes through 30 to 35 cases a week. As a result, on Wednesday the manager places an order of 36 cases. On the other hand, when products are ordered daily, weekly sales history may be less critical. This is because if the establishment runs out of prime rib, say on Thursday, the manager needs to order six pieces of prime rib on Friday.

Exhibit 5.11

SAMPLE ORDER GUIDE

Department: Meat   Month_____

Item	Purchase Unit	Supplier Price	Count Unit	Ordering Frequency	Date:	1 Mon	2 Tue	3 Wed	4 Thu	5 Fri	6 Sat
Prime Rib, Oven Ready		Chef Meat			PAR	2	2	2	6	6	6
					INVENTORY	1	2	1	2	0	2
	Each	$48.00	1 each	Daily	BUY	1		1	4	6	4
Duck: 4 ct, 1 cs		Betty Poultry			PAR	4	4	4	4	10	10
					INVENTORY	16	10	6	35	24	15
	Each	$24.00	1 each	Weekly	BUY			36			
New York Strip Steak: 12 oz each		Chef Meat			PAR	24	24	24	24	48	48
					INVENTORY	12	6	6	6	24	12
	Each	$8.50	1 each	Daily	BUY	12	18	18	18	24	36
Beef Patties: 10 lb ground 80/20: ¼ lb		Chef Meat			PAR	1	1	1	1	3	3
					INVENTORY	6	5	4	12	9	6
	Case	$48.00	1 case	Weekly	BUY			10			
WOG Chicken: 2 ½ lb		Betty Poultry			PAR	12	12	12	12	36	36
					INVENTORY	12	0	3	2	2	6
	Each	$3.75	1 each	Daily	BUY		12	9	10	34	6

The Purchase Order

The order guide informs managers when a certain item needs to be ordered and the amount that needs to be ordered. As a next step, managers prepare a purchase order (PO), which is sent to the vendor (see *Exhibit 5.12*). Purchase orders are legal documents that communicate the buyer's intention. Because a purchase order clearly spells out the conditions for the sale, it protects both the seller and the buyer. If the buyer refuses to pay, the seller can sue for the amount of the payment due using the PO as evidence. If it is a large or complicated purchase, a seller may request that a buyer create a PO so that both parties understand the transaction. An **invoice**, which is the receipt for the items delivered, is another legal document that will reinforce the terms of the purchase order. The buyer can match the purchase order to the invoice to make sure that all of the items were delivered and prices are correct.

Exhibit 5.12

SAMPLE PURCHASE ORDER

6023 W. Pratt
Chicago, IL 60601
Phone: 773-555-5555

Hawaiian Dream Restaurant

PO: 56789-00

Charge Account: 304-6395

Date of Order: 11/16

Ship to: PO address

Date Required: 11/23

Quantity	Unit	Item	Price	Per	Amount
3	Case	Pineapple chunks, fancy	16.39	Case	49.17
3	Case	Pineapple slice mini, fancy heavy syrup	18.62	Case	55.86

Purchaser signature _____ Manager signature _____

The purchase order is a primary control used throughout the purchasing, receiving, and payment process. Even small operations should consider using some form of purchase order. One of the benefits of ordering products electronically, which is becoming increasingly common, is that after submitting an order, the manager can automatically print out the PO or receiving report to use at the back door. Managers can compare the prices quoted on the PO with the prices actually charged on the invoice. Without a purchase order system it is virtually impossible to verify prices, which means a manager is at risk of losing money if the invoice price is higher than the quoted price because of a mistake or oversight.

In other words, without a PO, many things can, and usually do, go wrong, as shown in *Exhibit 5.13*. Here, the buyer ordered 100 pounds of beef tenderloin at $9.50 per pound. The supplier shipped 200 pounds. The receiver, not knowing what the buyer ordered, signed for 200 pounds, which was the quantity on the invoice. Without a purchase order, accounting paid the supplier's invoice for 200 pounds of tenderloin at $11.00 per pound. What do you think happened to this operation's standard food cost for this month? It is important that the receiving person always checks in orders using the PO and not the invoice.

Exhibit 5.13

PROBLEMS WITH LACK OF PURCHASING CONTROL

100 lb of beef tenderloin are wasted.

| Buyer orders 100 lb of beef tenderloin at $9.50/lb. | Shipper sends 200 lb of beef tenderloin. | Receiver signs for 200 lb, which is on invoice at $11.00/lb. | Accountant pays $11.00/lb instead of $9.50/lb. |

Preparing the Purchase Order

A purchase order specifies the products to be purchased, their price, their delivery date, and other important information. It includes the following features:

- Unique number to identify the purchase order
- Name of the ordering restaurant or foodservice operation, with address and phone number
- Date of the order
- Signature of the person placing the order
- Supplier's name, address, phone number, and contact name
- Date of delivery, terms of payment, and any special instructions
- Each item to be purchased, the quantity and unit of the item, the item's unit cost, and the extended cost of the item
- Total cost of the order

A standard purchase order is usually used for companies with whom the buyer does infrequent business. If buyers plan to frequently purchase products or services from a seller over time, they often establish a **blanket purchase order**. This type of PO allows the buyer to purchase a certain amount of goods, usually indicated by a dollar amount, at the stated terms within a given time period. This approach speeds up the purchasing process since a separate PO is not needed for each transaction. The buyer merely needs to call the supplier on the phone, send an electronic order, or submit a formal bid request to place an order with the company. As items are purchased, the seller will invoice the buyer for goods received. Blanket purchase orders are very common among restaurant and foodservice managers and allow for the immediate request and delivery of goods or services.

SUBMITTING THE PURCHASE ORDER

Advances in technology mean that today most orders are submitted electronically. However, there may still be some suppliers that require phone or fax orders. When placing phone orders, it is important to ask the supplier to verbally confirm the items and quantity ordered. That way, misunderstandings between buyer and supplier will be minimized. In addition, the buyer will get confirmation of product availability. In some situations, the buyer may ask the supplier to send an e-mail confirmation of the order. When ordering by fax, the buyer should call or e-mail the buyer and request an acknowledgment of order receipt. In some rare cases, the fax machine of the supplier may run out of paper, which can cause order delays.

More and more suppliers use online ordering systems that show real-time inventory availability. This is a great benefit for buyers because they can immediately verify the availability of product. In addition, when an operation places multiple orders with the same supplier online, the operation does not have to deal with multiple paper copies of these orders. Also, when orders are received electronically, the supplier does not have to manually record these orders into its inventory system. By submitting online purchase orders, both the buyer and the seller reduce the amount of paperwork and also save time and labor.

IMPROVING THE ORDERING SYSTEM

The ordering system should be taken very seriously because incorrect ordering can result in food-production delays, excess inventory, or lower-quality meals and dissatisfied guests. One of the main considerations in ordering is to designate a person or position responsible for ordering. The responsible person needs to review order sheets for different vendors periodically. He or she needs to identify any past ordering problems and work with involved parties to resolve them. The final step in the ordering system is to evaluate the success level of remedies to ordering problems. Generally, there are three key areas that can help improve the ordering system: record keeping, security, and training. Each of the areas is discussed here in more detail.

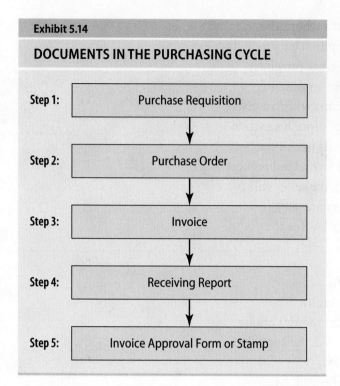

Exhibit 5.14

DOCUMENTS IN THE PURCHASING CYCLE

Step 1:   Purchase Requisition

Step 2:   Purchase Order

Step 3:   Invoice

Step 4:   Receiving Report

Step 5:   Invoice Approval Form or Stamp

Record-Keeping Basics

In all but the smallest restaurant and foodservice operations, purchasing responsibilities are divided up to gain stronger control. Coordination of the various purchasing tasks is achieved using five basic documents, as shown in *Exhibit 5.14*:

1. **Purchase requisition:** A par sheet or order guide is used to assemble a purchase requisition for each department or category.

2. **Purchase order:** A PO is created for each vendor.

3. **Invoice:** An invoice is prepared by the supplier and is simply an itemized listing of the goods or service delivered. Generally, a completed invoice with prices and totals accompanies the shipped goods to the receiving department. Often the supplier will periodically send a statement of invoices to the accounting department.

4. **Receiving report:** Since an operation may have multiple deliveries, a receiving report is used to verify that the goods being received are the goods that were ordered. The receiving report resembles a combination of several purchase orders. The receiving report is used to check every ordered item against the invoice for quality, quantity, weight, counts, and so on. The vendor should issue a credit memo for any shorts or returns. This should be stapled to the original invoice. This report should be completed and sent at the end of each day to the accounting office with accompanying invoices.

5. **Invoice approval form or stamp:** The accounting department will match the receiving report with a copy of the original purchase requisition, a copy of the purchase order, and the related invoice. Everything is then compared and verified. The invoice prices should be compared to the prices quoted and recorded on the purchase order. It is recommended that this be done when the product is delivered as well. The accounting department will also check the math on each invoice. If everything is correct, the invoice is approved for payment. Some organizations stamp the invoice or attach an approval form.

Security Concerns

Security begins with hiring trustworthy employees. In addition, by following the five-step record-keeping basics, an operation can eliminate many security concerns. Typical security issues may include paying a fictitious company, reprocessing and paying an invoice more than once, making math errors on the delivery invoice, or suppliers not issuing credit memos at the time of delivery.

It is a fairly common practice for suppliers in this industry to give "gifts" to managers, owners, and customers that make purchasing decisions on their products. As buyers build a positive relationship with suppliers, they may offer items of their appreciation, such as tickets to a ballgame, free boxes of ribs for the company cookout, or golf outings. It is important that buyers and managers have honest and transparent relationships with all sales representatives (*Exhibit 5.15*). Smart managers understand that the sales representatives are not their friends and that getting too close to suppliers can be dangerous. This does not mean managers should treat suppliers in an unfriendly manner; however, it does mean that they always need to respect the importance of keeping a business relationship first.

Exhibit 5.15

Every operation should have a straightforward and well-communicated policy regarding what's appropriate and not appropriate to receive from suppliers in the form of gifts. For example, some large retail stores bar employees from accepting anything from a supplier, even a free cup of coffee. If they do, and the company finds out, the employee can be terminated. If a manager suspects someone is receiving kickbacks, he or she should check prices for any excessive increases. Another control is having someone outside of purchasing do some competitive bidding.

Another security issue managers face surrounds substitutions in orders. Lower-quality substitutions can cost an establishment serious money if they are not monitored at the time of delivery. Lower-quality substitutions could reduce both product yield and customer satisfaction.

Theft is also a real issue for managers. To combat purchaser theft, managers may want to rotate people out of the purchasing function occasionally. Doing so can prevent buyers or people working in the purchasing department from becoming so comfortable that they begin to engage in questionable behavior. There can be a benefit to not having the same people control purchasing decisions year after year. Additionally, buyers should place orders only with vendors on an approved list, and the same person should not do purchasing and receiving, since this eliminates any checks and balances.

Finally, the purchasing process should be evaluated on a regular basis in order to:

1. Measure the extent to which current purchasing goals are being met
2. Improve the system to more effectively achieve future purchasing goals and enhance performance

Employee Training

Managers should always provide new employees with complete and thorough training and an orientation to the departmental policy and procedures. An organization may want to consider using an order schedule, as shown in *Exhibit 5.16*. The order schedule lists the vendor's contract information and emergency phone numbers. The order schedule can be organized by the number of days each week that products are ordered and should result in a more organized and thorough purchasing process. Information to prepare an ordering schedule comes from the order guide. Use of this tool will quickly get any new employees up to speed with the current ordering frequency of an organization.

Exhibit 5.16

SAMPLE ORDER SCHEDULE

Supplier Information		Mon	Tue	Wed	Thu	Fri	Sat
PRODUCE COMPANY	Sales Rep Name						
	Phone #						
Order method:	Fax #						
	Other	ORDER/ DELIVERY	ORDER/ DELIVERY	ORDER/ DELIVERY	ORDER/ DELIVERY	ORDER/ DELIVERY	ORDER/ DELIVERY
Order due by:	6:00 p.m.						
• **Emergency phone:**	555-495-9000						
MEAT SUPPLIER	Sales Rep Name						
	Phone #						
Order method:	Fax #						
	Other	ORDER	DELIVERY		ORDER	DELIVERY	
Order due by:	Midnight						
Emergency phone:	555-445-2145						
SUPPLIER NAME							
Order method:							
Order due by:							
Emergency phone:							

SUMMARY

1. **Explain the purchase process and determine who should make purchasing decisions.**

   The purchase process involves five steps. First, the manager must designate a purchasing person or buyer. The buyer is the sole person responsible for purchasing goods for an operation. Taking this approach eliminates any confusion about what was purchased and when. Then the organization must identify what is needed to produce the menu and develop product specifications. Order guides and par sheets tell buyers when and how much to order. Purchase methods are chosen based on the specific needs of a given operation. Finally, vendors and suppliers are identified and a preferred vendors list is established.

2. **Describe the importance of par levels and how to establish them.**

   A par level is the amount of stock necessary to get the kitchen through until the next order is delivered. Establishing par levels is of critical importance to restaurant and foodservice managers. This is because they have limited storage space, some products have a short shelf life, and other products need to be served fresh. In addition, by determining the amount that needs to be on hand at all times, operation managers prevent customer dissatisfaction. When determining par levels, managers need to consider factors such as historical sales of a given item and the time it will take from placing the order until the delivery of goods.

3. **Explain different types of purchasing methods and their uses.**

   There are different purchasing methods, and selecting a particular method depends on the size and type of an organization and the intend use of a product. For example, the competitive bidding method is the most appropriate method for small independent operations. On the other hand, chains prefer the cost-plus purchasing method. The commissary method works best for franchised chains, whereas for perishable items such as dairy and fresh seafood, operations use the standing order method.

4. **Describe the parts of a purchase specification and of a purchase order.**

   Managers write the specifications for the food needed to produce the standardized recipes, with input from the chef or production manager. Product specifications should be appropriate for the desired use. Large operations typically write formal specifications; smaller operations might use verbal specifications. A purchase order (PO) is a form listing the products to be purchased, their price, their delivery date, and other important information. It will also show the total cost of the order.

5. **Explain the importance of maintaining an ordering system.**

   A proper ordering system helps ensure that the amounts purchased make culinary and financial sense. In addition to determining par levels and preparing order guides, operations need to adhere to record-keeping guidelines that consist of five key purchasing and ordering documents. Developing strict rules about receiving gifts from suppliers also should alleviate security concerns pertaining to purchasing and ordering. Employees should be properly trained about the ordering schedule. Excess inventory may increase waste, allow for product theft or pilferage, and encourage overproduction.

APPLICATION EXERCISE

Stormy's Steaks and Seafood uses the following par sheet. The manager needs to prepare an order guide for next month, but first a par sheet for the next two weeks needs to be completed. Lobster tails are ordered weekly on Mondays, while rib-eye steaks and asparagus are ordered twice a week.

1. Par level for rib-eye steaks is 4 on Mondays. Par stock doubles on Thursdays. Calculate purchases for Mondays and Thursdays for rib-eye steaks.

2. The par stock for lobster tails is 14. How many lobster tails need to be ordered each week?

3. The par stock for asparagus is 24 cases for Mondays and 48 for Thursdays. Calculate the purchase amount for both weeks.

PAR SHEET FOR STORMY'S STEAKS AND SEAFOOD

Meat	Unit	Supplier	Monday (Week 1)			Thursday (Week 1)			Monday (Week 2)			Thursday (Week 2)		
			Par	Inv.	Buy	Par	Inv.	Buy	Par	Inv.	Buy	Par	Inv.	Buy
1. Rib-Eye Steaks	Each	Steakology	4	2	2	8	3	5	4	1	3	8	1	7
2. Lobster Tails	Each	Betty Fisheries	14	3	11	28		9	14	5	9	28		
3. Asparagus	Case	Produce Products	24	9	15	48	14	34	24	6	18	48	11	37

REVIEW YOUR LEARNING

Select the best answer for each question.

1. **Proper purchasing involves**
   A. purchasing the highest quality available.
   B. purchasing according to the specification at the lowest price.
   C. purchasing as much product as possible in any given time period.
   D. purchasing all goods from only one vendor.

2. **When should perishable goods be purchased?**
   A. Every one, two, or three days
   B. Every one or two weeks
   C. Every day, no matter what
   D. Twice a week

3. What is par level?

   A. The amount of an item ordered each week

   B. An item that an operation has on hand at all times

   C. The level that must be continually in inventory from one delivery to another

   D. A purchasing method where each item has a level at which it is reordered

4. An operation uses one case of tomato sauce per day and has a par level of three cases. Orders are made once a week. Today is order day, and there are three cases left. How many should be ordered?

   A. Three

   B. Four

   C. Seven

   D. Eight

5. To whom is a purchase order sent?

   A. The supplier

   B. The front-of-house manager

   C. The chef

   D. New employees

6. The standing order purchasing method is best suited for which product?

   A. Lettuce and tomatoes

   B. Fresh shrimp

   C. Heavy cream

   D. Ground beef

7. Which purchasing method is used primarily by franchised chains?

   A. Competitive bidding

   B. Prime vendor

   C. Commissary

   D. Cost-plus

8. Which document is used before preparing a purchase order?

   A. Order schedule

   B. Order guide

   C. Order approval form

   D. Standing order

9. An ordering system can be improved by

   A. increasing storage space and par stock.

   B. providing staff training about the order schedule.

   C. paying cash for orders.

   D. using fax orders only.

10. To bring new employees up to speed on the existing purchasing process, an operation should use which tool?

    A. A point-of-sales (POS) system

    B. An order schedule

    C. A par sheet

    D. An invoice

6

Controlling Food Costs in Receiving, Storing, and Issuing

INSIDE THIS CHAPTER

- **The Receiving Process**
- **Storage of Inventory**
- **Issuing of Inventory**

CHAPTER LEARNING OBJECTIVES

After completing this chapter, you should be able to:

- Explain the process for managing vendor delivery schedules.

- Describe the proper procedures for receiving goods.

- Discuss food storage techniques and the FIFO method of stock rotation.

- Identify and describe the proper methods of taking inventory and the various methods of inventory pricing.

- Describe the issuing process, including issuing beverages.

KEY TERMS

CASE STUDY

Chef Culpepper's first week on the job at Beck's Grille had been interesting, to say the least. Beck's Grille had very few systems or policies in place. When the fish vendor made a delivery on Tuesday, it was right in the middle of lunch service. Chef Culpepper had to break away for almost 15 minutes to check in the delivery and make sure it was correct. Plus, he found that the scale used to weigh deliveries did not seem to be accurate.

"We normally deliver between 11:30 a.m. and 1:00 p.m. to this stop," the driver said. "This is the first time anyone ever weighed anything. Don't you trust us?"

Chef Culpepper just looked at the guy and said he would talk to the salesperson. Then the chef made a mental note to drop by and tour the vendor's fish house.

1. How might a lack of policies and procedures contribute to higher restaurant or foodservice costs?

2. Should the chef be checking in orders? Is that the most productive use of his time?

THE RECEIVING PROCESS

Receiving is an area in many restaurant or foodservice operations that gets little, if any, consideration. Inaccurate deliveries and invoices, spoilage, and theft can all contribute to an operation's food cost deviating from the standard. While it is important to ensure that the business receives the correct food products at the correct price, the manager's responsibility for controlling food costs during the receiving process does not end there. An operations manager must also prevent additional food costs due to out-of-control inventory. Luckily, there are many ways a manager can properly control food storage and inventory, using pricing and inventory turnover to his or her advantage.

Once the manager has examined the purchasing costs, another area to review is the receiving procedure. It is one of the simplest controls in the restaurant and foodservice industry, yet many managers take an apathetic approach to it. This is unfortunate since the potential for loss in this area is extremely high. Consider this typical scenario:

> It is midmorning in the busy kitchen of a large establishment. A delivery truck arrives. The driver unloads the order and puts it in the receiving area of the kitchen, and looks for the chef. He finds the chef adding ingredients to the steam kettle in the back of the kitchen and stirring the contents. The driver says, "I've got your order in the back of the kitchen; here's the invoice." The chef says, "I'm busy—hey, Joe, sign this guy's invoice. I don't have time to deal with this now." Joe signs the invoice and the driver leaves.

Exhibit 6.1

RECEIVING PROCEDURES AND CONTROLS

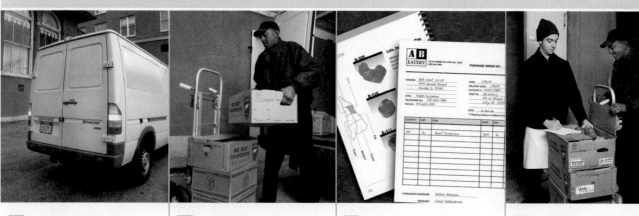

1. Items purchased are delivered.

2. Items purchased are unloaded at receiving area.

3. Be sure to have the PO and purchase specs handy.

4. Check quantity and quality against specs, invoice, and PO.

The order sits in the back of the kitchen until after the noon rush. The meat and produce have been at room temperature for four hours. The frozen goods are partially thawed. The chef tells Joe to put up the order. Nobody knows that part of the order is missing.

Unfortunately, this scenario is more common than not. Without anyone realizing it, the food cost in this operation has just increased and the quality of ingredients that the staff has to work with has diminished.

The receiving function in most operations will vary depending on the size of the organization. In larger operations, there may be a dedicated receiving clerk who is responsible for receiving products. In smaller operations, it may be the manager who performs this function. In either situation, to ensure that you are getting what you are paying for, follow these receiving procedures (see *Exhibit 6.1*):

1. **Have the delivery person put the order in the receiving area of the operation.**

2. **Obtain a copy of the purchase order:** Remember, a purchase order (PO) is a form used to document what was ordered, how much was ordered, and the price quoted. If a manager or receiving clerk does not have this information when the products are checked in, the operation is vulnerable to loss. In addition to verifying ordered items via PO, the receiving person should keep a receiving log as a hardcopy book or electronic software. This way, the receiving log can be matched against the invoice for quantity. It is also recommended to record temperatures of received food items in the log and any corrective action taken.

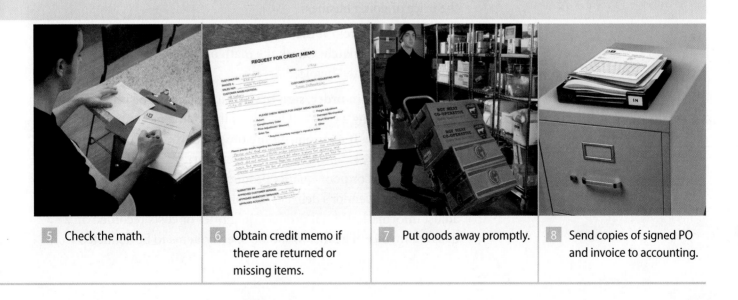

5 Check the math.

6 Obtain credit memo if there are returned or missing items.

7 Put goods away promptly.

8 Send copies of signed PO and invoice to accounting.

3. **Have a copy of the purchasing specifications available:** Inspect the goods and compare them to the specifications to make sure the operation is getting exactly what was ordered in terms of quality, grade, and condition. Open the boxes. Look at the produce. Is it fresh, the right color, the correct size, the precise degree of ripeness, and not bruised? Is the meat fresh, the flesh and fat the right color, and is it USDA stamped? Is the fish fresh, with clear eyes, tight scales, and firm to the touch? Is the fresh poultry properly iced? Check the temperature of all meat, fresh poultry, fish, dairy, and frozen goods. Suppliers do not like to deal with returns and they know which operations check specifications. Operations that accept only the freshest, highest-quality products and reject damaged, bruised, or otherwise below-standard items tend to get what they order.

4. **Check the delivery quantity against both the invoice and the purchase order:** This is the only way to know if any unauthorized items were added to the order or ordered items left out. If the items are purchased by count, then count them. If purchased by weight, then the manager should weigh them, particularly meat and produce. Running out of products lowers staff morale and disappoints guests. This is one reason why an operation should make sure it receives all the items that were ordered. The manager needs to compare the purchase order with the delivery. The sooner an operation is aware of any items that were not delivered or missing, the sooner the manager can correct the situation.

   Delivery drivers notice what the receiving process is at each operation and they know which customers do not follow proper protocol—check weights, count boxes, inspect condition, and so on. Following proper procedures does take extra time, but paying for ice that the fish or chicken are packed with is no way to control costs. Often the driver will not want to wait while a manager weighs everything; however, that is the price of doing business.

5. **Compare the prices on the invoice to those on the purchase order to make sure they match:** Check the math on the invoice, even if it is a computer-generated invoice.

6. **If everything is in order, sign the invoice:** Signing the vendor's invoice is just like signing a check. It legally obligates the receiving company to pay that invoice. If no problems are observed, the delivery invoice can be signed. However, if there are product shortages or other problems, such as expired or poor-quality products, a credit memo should be written by the vendor's delivery person. A **credit memo** is used to adjust information about product quantities or costs recorded on a delivery invoice. The memo should specify items to be deducted from

the amount owed as well as explain the reason why the credit is being granted. Once the credit memo is written, the signature of the vendor's delivery person confirms that the products noted in the credit memo were not received or accepted and that their value should be deducted from the amount owed. The receiving employee should also sign the credit memo to confirm that a copy was received. Use the same procedure if an item is missing. The driver may wish to rush through this procedure. However, it is highly recommended that a credit memo be prepared on the spot, dated, and signed by both parties. Each party should have a copy of the credit memo. The objective here is to make sure that the operation has the correct products, quality, and quantity at the correct price. If any of these elements are missing, the food costs will likely increase and the profit will subsequently decrease.

7. **Put away the goods promptly:** Dairy, meat, fresh poultry, and fresh fish should be put away first, then frozen food, produce, and dry goods. This order is very important to protect against product deterioration and possible theft. When the goods have been put away, secure the storage area.

8. **Process the paperwork:** This final step involves sending copies of the signed purchase order and the signed invoice to the accounting department.

The receiving control process is not difficult to follow and, if done consistently, can ensure that costs are in line with standards. For many restaurant and foodservice operations, as much as half of the food losses occur because of what is happening, or not happening, on the receiving dock or at the back door. Receiving is an area where the combination of poor systems, carelessness, mistakes, and theft can result in large losses. What the manager does or does not do during the receiving process is very closely observed by employees and delivery personnel. To prevent receiving losses, an operation needs a system and a set of procedures that are followed consistently.

Required Tools

The receiving area will need adequate space to collect all the deliveries, plus do the necessary counting or weighing of products. Normally space for a desk, file cabinet, and other basic equipment is needed. The desk will most likely hold a computer, so the space will need to be wired for Internet access. Other useful tools include thermometers to determine temperatures of perishable products, carts, hand trucks, and plastic tote boxes or other storage containers.

Specific guidelines for checking temperatures must be followed:

- Insert the thermometer stem or probe into the thickest part (usually the center) of meat, poultry, and fish. Receiving staff may also check the surface temperature with an appropriate thermometer because it can be a better indicator of potential temperature abuse.

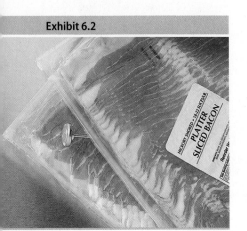

Exhibit 6.2

- For **reduced oxygen packaged (ROP) bulk food**, insert the thermometer stem or probe between two packages (*Exhibit 6.2*). ROP food is contained in a package in which (a) oxygen has been removed, (b) oxygen has been displaced with another gas or combination of gases, or (c) something else has been done to reduce the oxygen content to a level below that which is normally found in air; it is sometimes referred to as "vacuum packed food." It may also be possible to check product temperature by folding the packaging of refrigerated products around the thermometer stem or probe. Be careful not to puncture the packaging.

- For other packaged food, open the package and insert the thermometer stem or probe into the product. The sensing area must be fully immersed into the product, and the stem or probe must not touch the package.

For specific information about the inspection of incoming products, see chapter 6 of the *National Restaurant Association ServSafe Course Book*.

For large operations such as a hotel or hospital, the receiving area should be accessible to the loading dock and storerooms wherever possible to facilitate a smooth flow of food products from the receiving area to storage. Any refrigerated or frozen food items must move from receiving to storage as quickly as possible. Also, fresh produce needs to move quickly through the process to reduce the risk of bugs and other contaminants. If possible, the floors should be smooth so carts and hand trucks can move around easily. Smooth surfaces are also easy to clean and maintain. The area should have plenty of lighting to make it easier to inspect items on arrival.

As mentioned, receiving scales are most important. It is also critical that all equipment including the receiving scales be maintained in sanitary condition. Dirt, grease, and grime accumulating on the moving parts of a scale can add friction, which alters the precision of the scale. Thus, when considering purchasing a receiving scale, look for one that can be washed to save time and money.

Weighing items may sound like overkill, but not using a scale means losing money. Depending on the type of operation and amount of products, it may be big money. In most states, short weighting is commercial fraud, and a criminal offense. **Short weight** is the amount a shipment actually weighs subtracted from the weight given on its label. There are also common types of seafood fraud, such as adding excess amounts of water or ice to the seafood to increase its weight (overtreating). **Slack-out seafood** is another type of fraud where frozen seafood is thawed to appear fresh. Seafood should be removed from any packing ice before weighing. Managers also need to be aware of the possibility that the seafood vendor may attempt to substitute a different species of seafood for the species listed on the label (species substitution); for example, lemon sole for Dover sole fillets.

Employee Training

Receiving and storage is important, and the people who have these responsibilities should be qualified and properly trained. However, it is also basically a repetitive, almost clerical function. The process should be regimented and methodical. It does not make financial sense to have a decision maker or highly paid staff person performing clerical functions if an operation has capable staff members who could get the job done if they were properly trained.

In addition, three separate individuals should execute the procedures for purchasing, receiving, and bill paying. This is to prevent theft and embezzlement. Even in a small operation, assigning separate individuals for purchasing, receiving, and bill paying should be followed to the extent possible. Receiving is very important to the overall control system of an operation and it is vital for managers to ensure that receiving procedures are followed.

Another reason to have an hourly staff person do the receiving is that often managers and chefs are doing the purchasing. It is best not to have the same person do the purchasing "and" receiving, unless an operation has no other choice. There are too many opportunities for unscrupulous people to manipulate the system and obscure their tracks when they do both.

Receiving personnel should be trained along with the buyer. They also need the ability to assess product and make sure all incoming items meet operational product specifications. This is very important for products that are not brand specific, such as fresh produce and fresh seafood. These need to be properly inspected to make sure they meet product standards. Receiving includes observation and inspection; these skills will take time and experience to develop. For example, if the menu includes a lot of exotic produce, high-end fresh seafood, or local farm-to-market products, then the chef or an assistant may need to be involved with examining certain items, at least in the beginning. For the majority of items, however, a well-trained hourly employee can do a consistently better job of receiving than a time-stressed manager.

Successful storeroom staff and receiving personnel need the following skill set:

- Knowledge of and familiarity with appropriate technology
- Commitment to maintain safety and sanitation standards
- Ability to make critical decisions and resolve problems
- A consistent positive attitude, which includes a sense of urgency
- Required physical strength for their respective duties. (Note: *The Americans with Disabilities Act prohibits discrimination against persons with disabilities.*)

Managing Vendor Delivery Schedules

Every operation should establish restricted delivery hours with each vendor. During the vendor selection process, delivery hours should be negotiated and established. Delivery schedules for each vendor should be listed to identify any conflicts. Then, delivery schedules for all vendors need to be organized by dates and times that fit the establishment's operations. For example, deliveries should not be scheduled at peak times, such as the lunch rush. Set hours make it possible to schedule receiving and storeroom staff more efficiently. Managers should convey delivery schedules to vendors so that vendors maximize their truck routes and the operation staff correctly.

All delivery schedules should be posted internally in a prominent location. Also, each order form should clearly state delivery date and time. Managers should check for timeliness of deliveries and identify any deliveries that are off-schedule. Next, managers should promptly contact a vendor to report deliveries that are late. Finally, managers should follow up with the vendor to make sure the corrective course of action is taken to ensure future timely deliveries.

Managing PO–Delivery Discrepancies

It can be aggravating and awkward to deal with deliveries of food or beverages that are either damaged, spoiled, or not what was ordered. The **Uniform Commercial Code (UCC)** explains what to do if a shipment of goods "fails in any respect to conform" to what the buyer agreed to purchase. The UCC contains sets of guidelines established to harmonize business transactions law across states. A given product may be manufactured in state A, warehoused in state B, sold from state C, and delivered to an operation in state D. The UCC helps achieve substantial uniformity in commercial laws across states and, at the same time, allowed the states the flexibility to meet local circumstances by modifying the UCC's text as enacted in each state. The UCC has rules that should be followed when rejecting a delivery that was spoiled, damaged, or not what was ordered. First, the buyer must reject the goods in "a timely fashion," which is why an operation should inspect the product as it is delivered. The buyer can keep any portion that is considered conforming, and return the rest of the order. The UCC allows buyers to get the rest of the shipment or its value refunded to them. Most states have incorporated the UCC into their own laws and statutes.

The UCC also requires all contracts for the purchase of goods in the amount of $500 or more to be in writing in order to be enforceable. It is a smart practice to have all orders in writing, regardless of the amount. Written orders should specify the agreed quantity, pricing, and description of goods. This helps managers make their case in a dispute. It also helps clarify any possible miscommunications or misunderstanding. In addition, it is important to remember that the seller has the opportunity to replace the damaged or nonconforming food or beverage products within a reasonable time period.

However, the UCC does not allow the buyer to reject goods just because they do not meet personal satisfaction. For example, "these tomatoes don't taste like the tomatoes I had in Hawaii" would not be a good enough reason to reject a shipment. The UCC allows for delivery if the goods are of at least average quality and are fit for use.

CREDIT MEMO FORM

As we discussed previously, credit memos are a common practice to make adjustments to a supplier's invoice for a variety of reasons. For whatever the reason, the person doing the receiving needs a process to track returned products or corrected invoices. How does an operation know it actually received credit for those returns and adjustments? The most common way this is handled is to note the change on the invoice and adjust the total invoice amount. This is normally done by hand on the original invoice that the manager keeps and also on the duplicate invoice that goes back with the driver. However, this process can be an accounting challenge. For example, if the adjusted invoice does not make it to the supplier's accounts receivable clerk and the account is not give proper credit for the adjustments, the vendor's books will show that an operation still owes for the adjustments.

Using a simple credit memo system will increase the odds of receiving the proper credit for each invoice adjustment. Managers should keep credit memo forms available in the receiving area and train the receiving clerk on the process. Basically, when the receiving clerk returns products or does not receive what is listed on the invoice, he or she immediately fills out a credit memo form indicating the issue. The price adjustment should also be included on the memo. It is also extremely important to obtain the driver's signature. This shows that the vendor's representative acknowledged the credit as valid at the time of delivery. The original credit memo should be retained for the operation's accountant and a copy should be given to the driver. The operation's accountant should enter the original invoice amount into the accounts payable system and then enter the credit memo as a separate transaction. This process creates an audit trail of credit memos, signed by both companies' employees, which prove a valid credit for returned goods or any other adjustments on an original invoice. A sample credit memo is show in *Exhibit 6.3*.

Exhibit 6.3

CREDIT MEMO

Date: _____   Credit memo no.: _____

Vendor: _____

_____

_____

_____

_____

Issued to: _____

_____

_____

_____

_____

Account no.: _____

For invoice no.: _____

Item	Purchase Unit	Number of Purchase Units	Price per Purchase Unit	Total Price
			Total	$

Reason for credit (check):

☐ Backorder   ☐ Incorrect quality   ☐ Incorrect item

☐ Short count/weight   ☐ Incorrect price   ☐ Not ordered

Other:

_____

_____

_____

Authorized signatures:

_____   _____
        Vendor's representative   Purchaser's representative

STORAGE OF INVENTORY

Managers need to realize that food inventory is the equivalent of money to their operation. A filet mignon in the walk-in freezer represents both an investment in food cost to the operation and an amount that can be counted as revenue when sold to a customer. If for some reason that filet spoils or disappears from the walk-in freezer, both the investment and the potential revenue are lost. The savvy manager quickly learns that product integrity and security are critical components to a successful operation.

Exhibit 6.4

AN ORGANIZED STOREROOM

Inventory Cost Control

Given that product spoilage and lack of security can reduce the profits of an operation, it is critical to implement processes that minimize or eliminate the potential for these two factors to occur. A well-organized storeroom is an asset to any restaurant or foodservice operation and can help with reducing spoilage and theft (see *Exhibit 6.4*). Every item in storage should have a specific place and it should always be in that place.

The shelves should be labeled with the name of the item and its par stock amount. This labeling not only facilitates taking inventory, but also saves labor because kitchen personnel know exactly where each item is and do not have to waste time searching. To manage freshness, all products should also be labeled with use by or expiration dates.

Access to storage areas should be limited to authorized personnel only. Limiting access helps control loss from theft and maintains order. People in a hurry have a tendency to throw items around carelessly, open cases unnecessarily, and generally cause havoc.

INTERNAL SECURITY THREATS

Theft is one of the greatest threats to food while it is in storage. The National Restaurant Association estimates that the typical independent establishment loses up to 4 or 5 percent of its sales each year to fraud and theft, most of which is committed by employees. For an operation to be the target of theft, two sets of circumstances are usually present. First, an individual is motivated to steal and second, he or she perceives an opportunity to get away with it. The motivation factor may be difficult for managers to influence, but they can definitely influence the perception of opportunity.

Exhibit 6.5

THEFT

Employees will be much less likely to steal if they believe they will be caught. Consequently, food must be securely kept. Deciding exactly how to oversee secure food storage, however, can be tough. If the storeroom is wide open, allowing staff to come and go and remove products as they please, these conditions encourage rampant theft. Products can be removed from the storage area in backpacks, trashcans, "empty" boxes, and other concealed ways (see *Exhibit 6.5*). On the other hand, if the storeroom is securely locked at all times, whenever cooks run out of an item or need an ingredient for a customer request, they will have to locate the manager to unlock the storeroom. This extreme control can cause significant delays in preparing a customer's order and could also cause other orders on the line to back up. It is clear that neither of these options is desirable.

While the storeroom should be secure at all times, there are two other possible ways to solve this dilemma. In the first method, a par stock should be established for each area in the operation. Recall that par stock is the average use of an item for a given period plus a safety margin, in case sales for that item spike.

For food storage control, the given period of time is a shift. First determine the average use of the item plus a safety margin for that shift. Prior to the rush, all of the ingredients necessary for that shift should be in the correct area and up to their par stock level. This is done under the supervision of the person responsible for that particular area. For example, the head chef or lead cook would supervise the procurement of supplies for the line, while the bar manager or head bartender would obtain or supervise the fulfillment of bar supplies. This is the same theory covered in chapter 5 for purchasing control, except that instead of buying from an outside source, the item is being "purchased" from the storeroom (see *Exhibit 6.6*).

Exhibit 6.6

CONTROLLING INVENTORY USING PAR STOCK LEVELS

The method of controlling food storage using par stock levels is similar to that used in purchasing supplies from an outside source, except in this case, employees are "purchasing" supplies from their own storeroom.

A second way to keep inventory secure is by giving trusted employees keys to only the storage for the area for which they are responsible. For example, the bar manager or head bartender would have keys to the liquor storeroom but not the meat cooler, while the chef or lead cook would have the keys to the meat cooler but not the liquor storeroom. In this way, should a bartender or line cook need an item, the person with the keys would already be in the area and could retrieve the items quickly. The person supplying the materials follows a process of **issuing**, or taking the food or beverage products from storage.

Another control tool to reduce theft is to keep a running inventory of key products. It may sound like extra work but it is no different than counting the cash, which is done each shift. Managers should choose products that are either high cost or high use. High-use products may have a low unit cost but often make up a large portion of an operation's overall food cost and may be abused. Often, high-use products are well-stocked products, which lead thieves to assume that no one will notice that it is gone. Well-stocked products can also lead to overportioning and misuse. Employees may become careless, since there is always a sufficient supply and very little perceived risk of "running out."

When managers track certain inventory items daily, it has a psychological and behavioral effect on employees. For example, if someone was contemplating walking out the back door with a case of lobsters, the fact that the manager counts the lobsters ever day will have an influence on the decision whether to steal or not.

Running inventory works extremely well when partnered with a point-of-sale (POS) system. For example, suppose that 50 New York steaks were received in the morning meat delivery. At the end of the shift, the POS system tells the manager that 20 were sold and there should be 30 steaks left in inventory. If the next shift manager does a quick physical count of steaks and comes up with 25, then there are 5 steaks missing (see *Exhibit 6.7*). Does the manager have a problem? Maybe, but at least he or she is aware of the potential issue. The key is that the manager knows. If managers do not track high-cost items, they may not know something is missing.

Manager's Memo

While it is important to keep the inventory secure, remember that certain items are more susceptible to theft than others. Fifty-pound sacks of flour or sugar, #10 cans of corn, or five-gallon boxes of cola syrup are probably not going to be stolen. They are large, bulky, of little value, and hard to conceal and remove from the operation.

Managers need to concentrate on items that are more likely to be stolen. These items include those that are easy to conceal or those that are high in value, such as liquor, wine, steaks, and coffee packs. These items must be under lock and key at all times. Some restaurant and foodservice operations have these areas under video surveillance.

Exhibit 6.7

RUNNING INVENTORY

New York Steaks

Formula:

| Opening inventory | + | Items received | + | Items sold | + | Adjustments (returns, soiled, burned items) | = | Ideal ending inventory |

| Ideal ending inventory | − | Actual ending inventory | = | Difference (over or short) |

Example:

| 0 | + | 50 | + | (20) | + | 0 | = | 30 |
| Opening inventory | | Items received | | Items sold | | Adjustments (returns, soiled, burned items) | | Ideal ending inventory |

| 30 | − | 25 | = | (5) **short** |
| Ideal ending inventory | | Actual ending inventory | | Difference (over or short) |

EXTERNAL SECURITY THREATS

Rule number one to protect an organization from external security threats is: Keep the back door locked! Leaving the back door unlocked is practically an invitation for theft. An unlocked back door makes it easier for dishonest employees or delivery drivers to get products out of the operation. From a safety and liability standpoint, an unlocked back door also makes it easy for the wrong people to get into the building. For these reasons, only the managers should have keys. Anytime someone needs to receive a delivery or take out the trash, a manager should be called to unlock the door and supervise the activity. Many operations use a peephole or surveillance camera system at the back door to identify anyone needing access. Surveillance cameras can also be a great deterrent to crime. And a back door should have an emergency bar installed so employees have an exit to get out of the building if necessary.

DELIVERY DRIVERS

As mentioned, delivery drivers should not have access to an operation's storage area or walk-ins. Imagine this scenario: The driver offers to tote the chilled products into the walk-in and someone points in that direction. The driver takes the product into the cooler. However, now there is a nonemployee in the storage room and walk-in, the "safe" where an organization keeps the "money" it has tied up in its food. There is nothing to stop the driver from unloading delivery boxes and then reloading with an operation's high-cost product.

There are some exceptions when delivery drivers can enter establishment premises. For example, some operations need to receive food items and goods after hours when the establishment is closed for business. This is referred to as **key drop delivery**. Generally, drivers may be authorized to make only "inside back door" deliveries. In other words, delivery drivers can move products only from their delivery vehicle to just inside the building. However, this may not be practical when perishable or frozen products are delivered. Consequently, some delivery drivers may have access to a limited area where they will drop products. Operations may provide a special access code to the delivery person so that he or she can enter the premises. In cases when a key is needed to enter, a keybox with access code may be placed in the receiving area. It may be a wise idea to change access codes regularly to prevent any abuse by unauthorized parties. It should be noted that operations should inform the delivery person about new access codes prior to after-hours delivery.

There may be some other exceptions to deliveries, such as with keg beer deliveries. However, if a manager allows the driver to take the keg to the beer cooler, he or she should supervise the driver. Overall, delivery drivers are just like your employees—good, hardworking individuals. However, there may be exceptions, so the best protection is to be prepared.

Inventory Quality Control Procedures

After theft, spoilage is the second biggest cause of loss in the storeroom. While theft is difficult to control, spoilage is fairly easy to manage. Consider that spoilage is most often caused by carelessness and by not following correct procedures to protect the integrity of the product. The three main causes of spoilage are:

- Time and temperature abuse
- Improper stock rotation
- Inadequate sanitation practices

STORAGE TEMPERATURES

Time is not on the side of food products. Fruits and vegetables begin to deteriorate the moment they are harvested. As soon as meat and poultry are processed and fish and seafood are harvested from the water, they too begin to decline. Even among perishable goods, some products deteriorate more quickly than others, and these products must be given special attention. During storage, some products will shrink, while remaining perfectly usable in taste and texture. This shrinkage causes yield loss, however, which increases food cost. While there are methods to slow the deterioration process, eventually all food products deteriorate to the point at which they are no longer good for consumption. Proper purchasing, promptly putting away stock after receiving, and correct stock rotation all go a long way in slowing the deterioration process. However, perhaps nothing is more important in holding food than proper time and temperature control.

Time and temperature control means having policies and procedures in place to monitor the amount of time and the ongoing temperature of food products in the flow of food. Different food products have different temperature requirements. Food items left in the **temperature danger zone** of 41°F to 135°F (5°C to 57°C) for a total of more than four hours are an unacceptable risk and must be disposed of. Time and temperature control is not just for perishables. Dry goods also benefit from storage at the proper temperature. *Exhibit 6.8* identifies the recommended holding temperatures for a variety of food items. The

Exhibit 6.8

FOOD HOLDING TEMPERATURES

Dry storage
50°F to 70°F (10°C to 21°C)

Fresh fruit and vegetables
Vary depending on product

Eggs and dairy
41°F (5°C) or below
Eggs at 45°F (7°C) or below

Meat and poultry
41°F (5°C) or below

Fish
41°F (5°C) or below

manager or staff member responsible for the storage area should check the temperature of the refrigerators, freezers, and other storage areas on a regular basis to be sure the temperatures are in the correct range. Keeping storage facilities in the proper temperature range helps ensure the longest possible usable life of the food products within. It is important to monitor the internal temperature of food items to ensure they are at the right temperature.

Managers need to monitor how well the inventory is holding up to the environment in coolers, freezers, and dry storage areas. Items deteriorate quickly in the warm air of most receiving areas, when product is not stored away immediately. The bacteria count doubles every six days on food that is cooled to a few degrees above freezing. It doubles every six minutes on food at room temperature. A head of lettuce loses a day of shelf life for every hour held at room temperature. Reducing product shelf life increases waste and spoilage and the risk of serving unsafe food.

STOCK ROTATION

The restaurant and foodservice industry generally uses the **first in, first out (FIFO)** method of rotating stock. The FIFO method is commonly used to ensure that refrigerated, frozen, and dry products are properly rotated during storage. Using FIFO helps guarantee that the inventory is turned over in a proper manner. In the FIFO method, an older product is used before a more recently purchased product.

The success of the FIFO method relies on two people: the receiving clerk and the person using the product. After the food item has been properly received, the receiving clerk writes the date received on the package, and puts the goods on the shelf by placing the newest product at the back of the shelf and moving the oldest product forward. Some food products have "use by" or "sell by" dates assigned by the processor. These should be stocked by the processor's supplied date. The person using the product should take the oldest product at the front of the shelf. For processor-dated product, it is extremely important for the staff member using these products to check the date prior to using the product. FIFO should ensure that the oldest product is used before the new, which is very important when rotating inventory of perishable food items such as fresh produce, fresh seafood, dairy products, and ground beef.

Sometimes, however, the receiving clerk may decide that it is easier to simply put the goods on the shelf without rotating them. Or cooks will hunt for fresh ingredients rather than use something a little older. Managers need to keep constant vigil in the storeroom, coolers, and freezers to ensure that proper rotation is being followed. If proper rotation does not occur, eventually the older items—perishables in particular—will have to be thrown out because their quality no longer meets company standards. When this happens, food cost increases and profit decreases.

The other method of rotating stock is **last in, first out (LIFO)**. The LIFO method is used when an establishment intends to use the most recently delivered product before they use any part of that same product previously on hand. By using the most recently received product, the manager ensures that guests receive the freshest product possible. While the LIFO system may be chosen when the use of freshest products is necessary, in general operations do not recommend the use of the LIFO storage system because such a method would result in food spoilage and increased food cost.

Exhibit 6.9

Many health departments mandate that all stored food be labeled (*Exhibit 6.9*). Even if labels are not required, they help reduce waste. A food dating labeling system helps increase the accountability of the back-of-the-house staff following food safety and inventory control standards. Labeling helps reduce the "mistaken identity" syndrome. Once the manager has determined what information is required on food labels, the staff must be trained on how to use the food dating labeling system. Employees need a consistent pattern to follow. For example, should they write May 5 or May 05 or 5/5 or 05/05? Whichever one it is, everyone from the manager on down must know to do it the same way every time. Ongoing training is important. Suppliers may offer ongoing training materials and curriculum to educate staff on food rotation techniques and safety.

Food dating systems may also be used with processed food items and leftovers. The dates on containers will not be sufficient to ensure that the oldest product will be used first. Managers need a system for rotating the inventory on the shelves. Finding soured dairy products is most likely because someone failed to rotate the stock after the last deliveries. However, if after following up and making sure the stock rotation system is in place and working, it is possible that the operation's par levels may need to be adjusted. Remember, sales for most restaurant and foodservice organizations do not stay the same all year long. Most operations have a peak season and a slow season. Inventory needs to be adjusted during these times, especially for expensive and highly perishable items. The amount needed will vary depending on the volume of business and the frequency of deliveries.

SANITATION PRACTICES

High levels of sanitation should always be practiced in all areas of the restaurant or foodservice operation. The storage areas are no exception. In the storeroom, food should be stored away from the walls and six inches off the floor to allow for sweeping and mopping, which should be done daily. Shelving should be washable and durable. Purchase shelving based on the type of environment it will be used in—for example, dry or wet storage. Dry goods such as beans, rice, flour, and sugar should be stored in airtight containers. The walls and floor of the storeroom should be made of a nonporous material that is easy to clean. Insect and rodent control should be performed on a regular basis, preferably monthly, or more often if needed.

Walk-in and reach-in refrigerators and freezers should be wiped down on a daily basis and deep cleaned on a weekly basis. The shelves, walls, floors, and ceilings should be noncorrosive metal, preferably stainless steel. The shelves should be slatted to allow for air circulation. Products should be distributed evenly and not crowded, which also allows for air to circulate freely. This prevents the formation of odors that can be absorbed by other food items, thus rendering them useless and causing an increase in food cost. It is particularly important that the refrigerated storage areas be kept clean and sanitized and that proper food rotation is enforced. Remember to separate raw food items from ready-to-eat products in refrigeration and storage facilities to reduce the potential for cross-contamination. Keeping a clean, secure storage area with properly rotated contents at the correct temperature will result in safer food storage and minimal food spoilage.

Physical Inventory Control

Keeping the storerooms organized and labeled properly is important not only for spoilage and theft prevention but also for the inventory process. An **inventory** is an itemized list of goods and products, their on-hand quantity, and their dollar value. The restaurant or foodservice manager needs to know how much product is on hand to support the operation's menu offerings. In other words, the manager needs to know the operation's inventory. With a known inventory, a manager can calculate the cost of food sold as well as the inventory turnover rate. The total value of the operation's inventory is important since it is part of the assets on the balance sheet.

It is essential for a manager to understand the principles of inventory control and to be able to conduct an inventory. Physical inventory and perpetual inventory are two principles of inventory control that are particularly important. A **physical inventory** is an actual physical count and valuation of all items on hand. It usually is taken at the end of an accounting period. Any system of internal control requires a periodic physical inventory of goods on hand to be done on a consistent basis. Consistency is the key to good record keeping. It helps provide valid comparisons of operating results from one period to another. The basic reason for taking a physical inventory is to verify that an operation has on hand what it is supposed to have. The best technological control system will not verify the physical presence of items on hand.

Perpetual Inventory

A **perpetual inventory** is a theoretical count based on goods received and issued. That is, it exists on paper only. A perpetual inventory is an excellent storeroom control, but because of the high cost of maintaining a perpetual inventory, its use is limited to larger operations, usually ones with multiple outlets. A large hotel with several restaurants and a banquet department or a large employee foodservice complex with several dining rooms or cafeterias would use perpetual inventory systems. In such operations, it is important for the manager to know exactly what the food cost is in each of its units. The perpetual inventory system provides this information.

In these operations, products are purchased by a buyer or purchasing agent for all the units. The food items and supplies are delivered to a central storeroom. Each unit then **requisitions** products from the central storeroom for use in its own kitchen. A requisition is a form listing the items and quantities needed from the storeroom (see *Exhibit 6.10*). As a rule, only the products that are needed for that day are requisitioned. The person needing the products fills out the requisition and the department manager or chef approves it. In addition to requisitions, **transfers** are sometimes used. A transfer is a form used to track items going from one foodservice unit to another. For example, the chef may need some wine for cooking and transfer it from the bar. Conversely, the bar may need a jar of olives for martinis and transfer these from the main kitchen.

Exhibit 6.10

GENERAL REQUISITION FORM

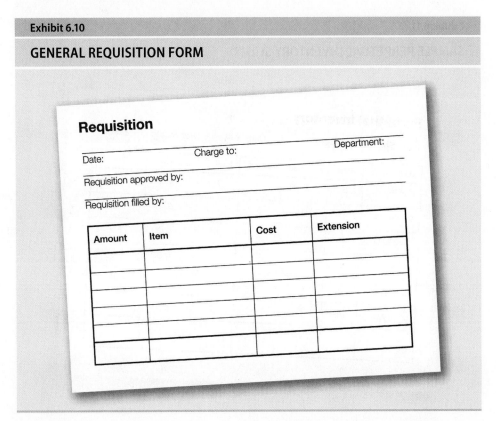

Because the outlying units of an operation carry little or no inventory, a **daily food cost** is needed. Daily food cost is an estimate of cost based on requisitions, transfers, and sales. To determine daily food cost, the daily requisitions for that unit are totaled. Transfers from that unit to another unit are subtracted and transfers into the unit are added to the requisition total to determine the daily food cost for that unit. This total number is divided by the unit's sales to determine a daily food cost percentage.

Requisitions + Transfers in − Transfers out = Daily food cost

Daily food cost ÷ Unit sales = Daily food cost percentage

While this is an estimated food cost, it is usually quite accurate since most, if not all, of the food brought into a unit is used that day, hence there is little, if any, inventory on hand.

In addition to figuring the daily food cost for each of the units, a check and balance can be run on the main storeroom. When product is purchased from suppliers and received into the main storeroom, it is recorded on a perpetual inventory sheet and added to the inventory already on hand in the storeroom (see *Exhibit 6.11*). When product is requested from one of the units on a requisition form, the storeroom manager subtracts the requested product from inventory on the perpetual inventory sheet. The balance that is shown indicates how much product is on the shelf at all times.

Exhibit 6.11

SAMPLE PERPETUAL INVENTORY SHEET

Perpetual Inventory

Item: Sliced peaches   Unit: #10   Par Stock: 12 cans

Date	Start	Received	Issued	Ending	Unit Price	Total
12/05/12	8	0	1	7	$ 5.00	$ 35.00
12/06/12	7	0	0	7	5.00	35.00
12/07/12	7	6	2	11	5.00	55.00
12/08/12	11	0	2	9	5.00	45.00
12/09/12	9	0	1	8	5.00	40.00
12/10/12	8	6	1	13	5.00	65.00

When a physical inventory is taken at the end of the month, it is compared to the perpetual inventory. This comparison is often called actual value versus book value. A variance between the two values means that food is missing from the storeroom. The reason for the missing items could be theft, spoilage, or inaccurate bookkeeping. Whatever the issue, it needs to be found and the inventory needs to be corrected, since food missing from the storeroom means that the food cost for that operation has just increased and profit has decreased.

Perpetual inventory aims to eliminate the need for frequent counting by adding to the inventory when goods are received and subtracting from the inventory when requisitions or issues occur. Perpetual inventory is a popular method to keep track of the changes in a liquor room's inventory. The manager can monitor against internal theft by comparing the last entry on an item's perpetual inventory sheet with the actual number of bottles on hand in the liquor room. It should also be noted that the process of auditing the bar's physical inventory is solely a management function. If an employee is stealing, participation in the physical inventory process will allow him or her to cover up any theft.

Recording the Inventory

Inventory should be taken periodically, corresponding with the frequency of an operation's income statement. In most operations this is monthly or every 28 days. Some quick-service operations and bars take inventory weekly. Still others, while a rare occurrence, do inventory quarterly or annually. Regardless of when an organization takes inventory or whether managers are recording a physical inventory or keeping a perpetual inventory, an important point to remember is to build uniformity into the process by weighing or counting items consistently, using a consistent inventory pricing method, and taking inventory at a consistent time of day.

When the manager sets up a restaurant or foodservice operation's inventory process, he or she will want to consider what **inventory breakdown** to use. An inventory breakdown is a method of categorizing the operation's food and supplies. In some restaurant or foodservice operations, inventory is taken of all goods in the kitchen without regard to breakdown. In other operations, inventories are broken down into food and supplies. This breakdown is particularly important if food and supplies are separated on the income statement. Some operations further break down food into meat, dairy, bakery, produce, frozen goods, canned, and dry goods. Establishments may use all of these categories, or some of them, or may even need to use different ones. The determining factor is what food items an operation wants to track. For example, a steakhouse may want to track meat cost and would therefore categorize and inventory meat items separately from all other products in the

THINK ABOUT IT . . .

Keeping a perpetual inventory record is costly and time-consuming, so managers may opt to control only those items that are expensive and susceptible to theft. What items might managers control in this way?

kitchen. A quick-service operation may want to track paper supplies and will inventory these separately from the other supplies. Inventory is instrumental in figuring the cost of goods sold.

When taking inventory, use two people. One person counts or weighs the items and the other person records it on the inventory sheet like the one shown in *Exhibit 6.12*. This makes the process move more quickly, and more important, it reduces the possibility of "**padding**" or inflating the inventory for the purpose of reducing the food cost.

Exhibit 6.12

SAMPLE INVENTORY SHEET

Inventory						
Category: _____ Date: _____ Counted by: _____ Recorded by: _____						
Item	Count/ Weight	Unit	Price	Unit	Total	
TOTAL						
				Page _____ of _____		

To take inventory, start in one place and progress through the establishment in a logical manner. For example, start in the storeroom in the upper left-hand corner. Move through the storeroom going down every shelf from left to right. When the storeroom is inventoried, move on to the walk-in refrigerator and inventory it in the same manner as the storeroom, then inventory the walk-in freezer. In the kitchen, start in the left-hand corner and progress through the kitchen. Do not forget to inventory food and supplies, such as coffee, condiments, paper napkins, placemats, and straws in the service areas and dining room.

Some operations count everything in the kitchen, while some may estimate the amount for a few items. An example of estimating the amount might be in the use of spices. If the spice inventory is fairly consistent from period to period, a price is applied to all spices and recorded as "spices, one lot." Another example is the steam table or the pickup line, which would be recorded as "goods in transit."

When the physical inventory is complete, the counts are turned over to the manager. At this point, if the operation uses a perpetual inventory system, the manager will compare the physical inventory to the perpetual inventory. Because restaurant and foodservice operations are dynamic in nature, the physical inventory and perpetual inventory will most likely not match completely. The manager will request a recount of any areas with large discrepancies. Having an accurate physical inventory is a critical preparatory step to inventory pricing.

Calculating Inventory Values

Although recording an inventory will tell the manager what products are in stock and in what quantities, it will not tell him or her how much an operation's inventory is worth. Determining the worth of the inventory is an important step because the dollar value of the inventory is reported on the operation's income statement. Remember, the formula for cost of goods sold is as follows:

$$\left(\begin{array}{c} \text{Opening} \\ \text{inventory} \end{array} + \text{Purchases} \right) - \begin{array}{c} \text{Closing} \\ \text{inventory} \end{array} = \begin{array}{c} \text{Cost of} \\ \text{goods sold} \end{array}$$

Inventory is an integral part of this formula. Only with an accurate inventory can the true cost of goods sold be known. Remember that the opening inventory is the same figure as the closing inventory from the previous period. Note that when closing inventory goes up, cost of goods sold goes down. Conversely, when closing inventory goes down, cost of goods sold goes up.

Some managers will use this fact for an illegitimate gain, particularly if there is a bonus connected to meeting a standard food cost. If the cost of goods sold on the income statement is not up to standard, they will add dollars to the closing inventory to bring the cost of goods sold down to the company standard. This highly unethical activity is known as padding the inventory. Padding is the inappropriate activity of adding a value for nonexistent inventory items to the value of total inventory in an effort to understate actual costs. Padding is illegal in many states and, in some cases, is against federal law. It is also easy to catch. If the closing inventory is padded, then the opening inventory of the following month is also inflated. This means that for the food cost to meet standard for the next month, the closing inventory must be padded again even more. It will not take the establishment owner long to discover the deception and terminate the dishonest manager, who will then have a hard time finding other employment.

COMPARISON CHART OF PRICING METHODS

FIFO

The latest price paid for the item is recorded.

LIFO

The oldest price paid for the item is used.

Averaged Price

A composite of all prices paid is averaged and used.

Actual Price

The actual price is listed on the inventory for all items.

To calculate the value of inventory, an operation must first find the value of the items it is storing. There are several methods of valuing items, as shown in *Exhibit 6.13*. Whichever method is chosen, the manager will achieve the best results by using it consistently. Consistency in inventory pricing takes two forms. First, the price used for the item must be in the same unit as the count for the item. For example, if Kadota figs are counted by the can, then the pricing unit is per can. If the invoice price for Kadota figs is per case, then the price per case must be converted to price per can. Second, the manager must use the chosen pricing method throughout every period. Not only is this important for providing reliable reports to the operation's owner, but also for reporting income to the Internal Revenue Service.

There are a variety of pricing methods used:

- FIFO (first in, first out), also known as the **latest price method**, uses the latest price paid for a product to value an inventory. This method assumes that the oldest product is used first and that the most recent product, purchased at the most recent price, represents the majority of product on the shelf when inventory is taken. This is the most widely used pricing method in the restaurant and foodservice industry for two reasons. First, it is the easiest and quickest way to cost an inventory because managers will use the latest invoices to research prices. Second, it tells managers what the product in storage is worth in today's market. FIFO results in a higher inventory valuation and lower cost of goods sold. The lower cost of goods sold results in higher net income. In this method, the latest price paid for the product is the one that is recorded in the price column on the inventory sheet (see *Exhibit 6.14*).

Exhibit 6.14

FIFO PERPETUAL INVENTORY CONTROL RECORD

Item Description:			Balance Available
June	Purchases Received	Issued Sales	Units × Cost = Total Cost
01	Opening Inventory		2 @ $20 = $40
05	6 @ $19 = $114		2 @ $20 = $40 6 @ $19 = $114
12		2 @ $20 = $40 2 @ $19 = $38	4 @ $19 = $76
19	10 @ $22 = $220	4 @ $19 = $76 2 @ $22 = $44	8 @ $22 = $176
28	6 @ $21 = $126	6 @ $22 = $132	2 @ $22 = $44 6 @ $21 = $126
Ending	Purchases = $460	Cost of Sales = $330	Ending Inventory = $170

The first column of the inventory shows the transaction date. The second column shows purchases received and price paid. The next column shows issued sales from storage, again including the value of each item. The last column indicates the balance of goods available at each respective date (e.g., on June 19 balance available is $176).

As can be seen in *Exhibit 6.14*, opening inventory was $40 (2 units $\times$ $20 each). On June 5, six units are purchased at $19 each. Since no issues are made on June 5, the available balance consists of two units at $20 each and six units at $19 each. The last row of the inventory sheet shows ending purchases, ending cost of sales, and ending inventory. The value of ending inventory, cost of sales, and purchases can be verified as follows:

$$\underset{\textbf{Opening inventory}}{\$40} \quad + \quad \underset{\textbf{Purchases}}{\$460} \quad = \quad \underset{\textbf{Goods available}}{\$500}$$

$$\underset{\textbf{Goods available}}{\$500} \quad - \quad \underset{\textbf{Ending inventory}}{\$170} \quad = \quad \underset{\textbf{Cost of goods sold}}{\$330}$$

- LIFO (last in, first out) is the opposite of the FIFO pricing method. LIFO is a method of inventory pricing in which the oldest price is the one used for valuing the inventory. This method assumes that the most recently purchased product is used first and that the product that is on the shelf, when inventoried, is the oldest. Therefore, the oldest price paid for that product is used to value the inventory. This method is not widely used in the foodservice industry because the typical practice is to use the oldest product first (FIFO) due to spoilage.

- **Averaged price method** uses a composite of all prices paid for an item during the inventory period to evaluate the inventory. The first step is to determine the total cost of food available by adding purchases during the period to the opening inventory of the item. Then the averaged price is calculated by dividing the cost of food available for sale by the number of units available for sale. For example, assume that 5 cases of green beans were on hand at the beginning of the period at a cost of $19 per case (opening inventory), and that 5 cases were purchased at $20 per case and 5 cases at $21 per case. The average price would be $20 per unit. This is calculated as follows:

1. Calculate the cost of food available in inventory.

Opening inventory		
5 cases at $19		$ 95
Purchases		
5 cases at $20	$100	
5 cases at $21	$105	
	$205	$205
Cost of food available		$300

2. Calculate number of units available.

Number of units available for sale:

5 cases	+	10 cases	=	15 cases
Opening inventory		Purchases		Units available for sale

3. Calculate inventory price per unit.

Inventory price per unit:

$300	÷	15 cases	=	$20
Cost of food available		Number of units available		Inventory price per unit

It should be readily apparent why this method is not widely used in the restaurant and foodservice industry. Because of the sheer number of items in inventory, this method is too time-consuming to be practical. It is mentioned here solely because it is a recognized method of inventory valuation.

• Actual price method is also known as the specific unit cost method. In the **actual price method**, the actual price paid for the product is the cost that is listed on the closing inventory sheet. Thus in the green bean example, there would be two lines—one line for the number of cases of green beans remaining at $20 per case, and another line for the number of cases in inventory at $21 per case. The actual price method takes discipline on the part of the manager. Every item that is received must be marked with its per unit cost. In the green bean example, the first cases received would be marked $20.00 since the inventory is by the case. If the green beans were inventoried by can, each can would have $3.33 written on it:

$20.00	÷	6	=	$3.33
Cost per case		Cans per case		Cost per can

The cost must be written on each and every unit in inventory for this method to be used. If the item is not marked, the manager will waste valuable time researching the cost of that item. The actual price method is the most accurate method of pricing inventory since the real cost of each item is reflected in the value of the closing inventory. Restaurant and foodservice organizations that use computerized inventory systems most often use the actual price method of inventory valuation.

EXTENDING AND TOTALING

After the inventory has been counted, recorded, and priced, it is then extended and totaled. **Extending** the inventory means multiplying the number of units of each item by the item's unit price. For example, 8 cases of cherry pie filling priced at $34 per case would be $272:

8	×	$34	×	$272
Number of units		**Unit price**		**Total cost of inventoried item**

When each line has been extended, the page is totaled. When each page has been totaled, then all pages are totaled to give the complete inventory figure. In cases where the inventory is categorized, then a total is calculated for each category. *Exhibit 6.15* shows an extended inventory for the dairy category.

Exhibit 6.15

SAMPLE DAIRY INVENTORY

Inventory

Counted by: G.B.
Recorded by: M.K.

Category: Dairy   Date: 12-12

Item	Count	Unit	Price	Unit	Total
Milk, Homogenized	2	5 gal	15.75	5 gal	$ 31.50
Milk, Homogenized	20	gal	3.25	gal	65.00
Milk, Homogenized	125	½ pt	0.21	½ pt	26.25
Milk, 2%	140	½ pt	0.19	½ pt	26.60
Cream, heavy	8	qt	6.75	qt	54.00
Cream, half & half	15	qt	4.15	qt	62.25
Cream, sour	20	qt	3.55	qt	71.00
Butter	79	lb	2.69	lb	212.51
Butter pats	4	case	14.55	case	58.20
					$607.31
TOTAL					

Page 1 of 1

The totals for all categories are then totaled to arrive at the entire inventory figure. Notice in the following example that the extended inventory value for dairy is added to the totals for the other categories:

Meat	$ 4,375
Dairy	607
Produce	780
Bakery	250
Groceries	3,770
Supplies	1,435
Total	**$11,217**

Bar code scanners are used to automate data collection by translating patterns into information. They also make it easier to track inventory. How would you convince your operation to invest in this type of application?

RESTAURANT TECHNOLOGY

Historically, there was a general perception that only large restaurant and foodservice operations could use technology devices and software in receiving and inventorying food and beverage items. However, managers of small operations have discovered how technology can assist with their management, control, and accounting responsibilities. Over the years, systems became more affordable for small-volume operations. Now, it is not uncommon for a small establishment to use bar code systems for receiving and issuing food items. By using more technology in receiving, storing, and issuing, managers can devote their attention to other aspects of operations.

This number is the ending inventory for the operation for that period. It is used in figuring the cost of food sold and inventory turnover. It is also the beginning inventory for the next period.

SOFTWARE APPLICATIONS

There is software available for taking, pricing, and extending inventory. The inventory portion of the software is tied into the general accounting process so when goods are received and entered into the system, the price of those goods is transferred to the inventory software. In those operations with inventory software, the person taking inventory passes a handheld bar code scanner over the bar code of the product and enters the count on a keypad. The software recognizes the product by its bar code and retrieves the product's price. The software then takes the count entered on the keypad, extends the price for that product, and totals the inventory. The software can be programmed to use any of the pricing methods previously discussed. Smaller operations may use a set of spreadsheets to calculate the math.

Calculating Inventory Turnover

Inventory turnover is a measure of how quickly an item in storage is used. It is an important number for managers to monitor. Remember, an operation should have adequate supplies on hand to serve the customer yet not so much as to tie up cash in inventory. An operation with a high inventory turnover rate may not have adequate supplies on hand to produce all of the items listed on the menu at all times. However, an operation with a low inventory turnover rate will have excess cash tied up and will also have a higher spoilage rate, which will contribute to a high food cost.

Knowing the inventory turnover is also important for the independent restaurateur who wants to borrow money from a bank. Inventory turnover is the number one consideration that banks use in their evaluation of a business when making loans.

Figuring inventory turnover is a two-step process. If an operation has an opening inventory of $8,500, a closing inventory of $10,750, and a cost of food sold of $10,200, the inventory turnover rate can be determined as follows:

1. First, determine average inventory:

$$(\$8,500 + \$10,750) \div 2 = \$9,625$$

Opening inventory	Closing inventory	Average inventory

2. Then, use the average inventory to get the inventory turnover rate:

$$\$10,200 \div \$9,625 = 1.06$$

Cost of food sold	Average inventory	Inventory turnover rate

An inventory turnover rate of 1.06 means that the inventory turned over once during this period. Remember, this is the total inventory. As discussed earlier, perishables should be purchased daily or at least every two or three days, while food staples should be purchased weekly. Therefore, perishables may have turned over several times during a given week, while nonperishables may have sat on the shelf for a month or more. Inventory turnover rate is an average. An operation that uses more perishables than nonperishables should have a higher turnover rate than an operation with a menu concentrating on nonperishables.

Inventory turnover rate can be calculated for any period: weekly, monthly, or annually. For comparison purposes, it is normally calculated on a weekly basis. But if an operation took inventory on a monthly basis, it would figure the inventory turnover rate on a monthly basis and divide the results by 4.3 (the average number of weeks in a month) to get its weekly turnover rate.

The general rule of thumb in the restaurant and foodservice industry is that inventory should turn over one to two times per week. Another rule of thumb is that food inventory should equal one and one-half times the weekly food cost. Thus, if an operation has a weekly food cost of $5,000, its average food inventory should be $7,500. As with all guidelines, there can be exceptions. Frequency of delivery, storage and refrigeration space, availability of capital, and specific menu items all influence how much inventory should be on hand. For example, an establishment in a metropolitan area that specializes in fresh salads would have a higher inventory turnover rate than a hospital foodservice operation located in a rural area. However, for the most part, inventory turnover should be maintained within the one to two times per week range.

Another gauge is to calculate "number of days of inventory on hand." This calculation will let a manager know how many days the existing inventory will last. Of course it assumes that an operation is carrying the right mix of products. The calculation is based on how much food the operation is using in an average day, which translates to the average daily food cost.

Steps to calculating "number of days of inventory" on hand:

1. Calculate average daily food cost:

Food cost ÷ Number of days in period = Average daily food cost

2. Calculate days sales in inventory:

$$\text{Ending food inventory} \div \text{Average daily food cost} = \text{Days sales in inventory}$$

Example:

Number of days in the period = 30

Food cost for the period (from P&L statement) = $30,000

Ending food inventory (from the balance sheet) = $10,000

$30,000	÷	30 days	=	$1,000
Food cost		**Number of days in period**		**Average daily food cost**

$10,000	÷	$1,000	=	10 days
Ending food inventory		**Average daily food cost**		**Days sales in inventory**

So, based on the previous calculations, the operation had about 10 days of food on hand. For most operations that would be too high of an inventory. In full-service restaurants, most managers would like to run at about six or seven days of food on hand. Virtually all the major chain restaurants calculate food cost each week, which would allow for better inventory controls.

ISSUING OF INVENTORY

If the manager decides the storeroom should be secure at all times, then a general requisition form must be filled out, approved, and turned over to a steward or storeroom clerk. The clerk fills the order and sees to the delivery. However, if the operation does not have full-time storeroom staff, then the cook may simply go into the storeroom and grab whatever he or she needs. While there is no universal practice, normally the tighter the controls, the better the food cost. In general, small operations tend to follow more informal practices. Larger operations may have larger staffs, with specific procedures requiring a paper trail.

Issue Requisitions

Issued items fall under two basic headings: directs and stores. **Directs** are charged to food cost as they are received by the operation, on the assumption that these perishable items will be used immediately. The assumption is that directs will be used that day. In reality, there is likely to be leftover product used the next day. When determining daily food costs, the total dollar for directs is used, again on the assumption that all product will be used that day. Unfortunately, because that is not strictly accurate, daily costs can be artificially high on days when the entire product inventory is not consumed and artificially low on days when products charged the previous day are actually used.

For record keeping, directs are generally listed as being issued the moment they are received, and no further paperwork is kept of the items. The other option is to follow an issuing procedure similar to that described below for stores, which would require significantly more time and labor. This is why most small operations handle all products as directs. Once products arrive at the back door, they are considered put to use and no more tracking is done except when inventory is taken.

Stores are considered part of the inventory until issued for use in an establishment and are not included in food cost until they are issued. It is necessary to establish policy and procedures for issuing items and tracking costs. The process starts with filling out a requisition form that lists the items and quantities needed from stores. Each requisition should be reviewed and approved by either the chef or a manager. The requisition is then given to the storeroom, which fills the order (see *Exhibit 6.16*). It is recommended that the manager require requisitions to be submitted in advance, at a minimum of one day for the main requisition and during set hours for any supplemental requisitions. Most operations have set hours of operations for the storeroom.

After orders have been issued, the clerk or bookkeeper must list on each requisition the cost of each item and to determine the total value of the requisition. At the end of each day, all requisitions are sent to the accounting office or bookkeeper.

Exhibit 6.16

Issuing Food

Issuing food is critical in many organizations. When an operation issues food, it allows managers to equate food taken from inventory with the actual product sales without taking physical inventory. In a formal food issuing system, the person in charge of the storeroom checks to determine that each order has been properly authorized via issue requisition, removes product storage tags and labels that show the name of an item and its storage date, and proceeds to fill the order. The storeroom staff then costs out each item ordered and totals the costs. A copy of the completed issue requisition form is sent to the operation's accounting office along with any storage tags removed from the items. This system prevents personnel from helping themselves to whatever they want, whenever they want it.

While putting orders together, the storeroom staff should note any items in short supply and direct this information to the operation's purchasing person so the items can be reordered. Careful inspection of written requests for inventory items and accuracy are important during food issuing. In some establishments, the storeroom staff not only assembles the order for a department, but also delivers it to that area. Prearranged issuing times for each department can eliminate confusion and enable the storeroom person to work more efficiently.

Generally, the same kinds of equipment are used during the receiving and issuing of inventory. Products issued on the basis of weight should be weighed before they are released to the production department. Calculators are useful to determine the dollar amount of each department's order and the total of all issues for the day. Handcarts and dollies are used to transport the products from storage facilities to production areas.

Issues should be properly costed to facilitate the calculation of daily food cost. Requisitions must be subtracted from perpetual inventory records to maintain accuracy. Daily issues help establish usage rates and future reorder points.

Storeroom facilities should not be left unattended if the issuing control system is to remain intact. For maximum security, storeroom facilities should be kept locked with access limited to the storeroom person and the manager. Staff members in other departments need to be organized and request in advance the items they need for the day rather than running in and out of the storage areas all shift. Restricting unauthorized access to storage areas helps eliminate losses due to thefts and pilferage.

It is the manager's responsibility to establish policies and standards for issuing. Although some operations do not find it necessary to use a formalized issuing system, managers who view their inventory as a form of money realize the importance of carefully controlling the issuing function. It is the manager's job to follow up on the issuing control point to determine that standards are being maintained.

Issuing Beverages

Managing liquor, beer, and wine may be challenging but it is absolutely essential for the profitability of any restaurant or foodservice operation that sells them. Managing beverage inventory involves knowing precisely what is on hand, how much was paid for it, where it is, and when it was sold. Just like food or other items, beverage management starts with the purchase order. The PO provides a way to verify the delivery of the stock. After the product has been correctly received, the perpetual inventory system is used to track the flow of inventory in and out of the liquor and wine storerooms. This process provides an accounting of each product's rate of turnover.

The third element of the beverage inventory management system, the requisition form, is used to record the movement of inventory from the storeroom to an outlet. Bartenders also use the requisition form to log every product emptied (sometimes called "breakage") during a shift. A replacement bottle is then issued for the product being requisitioned (based on emptied bottles) and noted in the perpetual inventory book or spreadsheet.

A bar should have a par level that is used to control the quantity of items. Many bars also use a depletion allowance form to track the amount of inventory spilled, transferred to another outlet, or given away in complimentary drinks. Establishing and maintaining par levels is an effective tool in controlling internal theft. Any product not accounted for on the shelves or backups can be noted quickly and reported immediately.

To complete the inventory cycle, the manager would do a physical audit of the inventory. A physical audit determines the dollar value of the liquor, beer, and wine inventory on hand. The higher the volume, the more control the manager

---

THINK ABOUT IT . . .

Many operations do not require requisition forms for small items such as condiments, sugar, hot sauces, and so forth. However, access to unlocked storage areas exposes expensive items to theft. How can operations protect their expensive items?

needs, so the more often he or she should take inventory. Taking liquor inventory requires determining the amount of product in each opened bottle behind the bar. The most frequently used method of determining the amount of product remaining in a bottle is the "tenthing method," which estimates the content to the nearest tenth of a bottle. For example, if the content of a bottle is a little less than half full, it is recorded as 0.4. The cost is then multiplied by 0.4 to determine the inventory value. Some managers audit their bar inventory daily, so if there is a problem the managers will know about it and will be able to take timely and appropriate action. Remember, managers must perform the physical audit of the inventory. Staff personnel should not be involved.

SUMMARY

1. **Explain the process for managing vendor deliveries.**

   When an operation selects a vendor, the manager needs to negotiate and establish delivery hours that fit restaurant and foodservice operations. Then, delivery dates and times need to be organized and posted internally within the establishment. The manager should note the time and date of a delivery, and identify any off-schedule deliveries and contact the vendor about late deliveries promptly. If necessary, the manager should ensure that a corrective course of action is taken by the vendor.

2. **Describe the proper procedures for receiving goods.**

   The receiving process has several steps that start with items being purchased and delivered. Then items are unloaded in the receiving area. The receiving person checks quantity and quality against specifications, invoice, PO, and the total invoice amount. If there are any missing, broken, spoiled, or returned items, a credit memo should be obtained. Last, goods should be put away promptly and the signed PO and invoices should be sent to accounting.

3. **Discuss food storage techniques and the FIFO method of stock rotation.**

   Storerooms need to be secured to prevent theft. Managers must decide on the control processes that will work best for their establishment, but all managers should control products during storage as they would control money in a bank vault. Storage areas must be physically secure, and a running inventory system that tracks the quantities of expensive and theft-prone items is important.

   After theft, spoilage is the second biggest cause of loss in the storeroom. To prevent spoilage, dry, refrigerated, and frozen storage areas must be maintained at the proper temperatures. Cleanliness is important, and several food safety practices must be implemented to help maintain product quality during storage.

   The restaurant and foodservice industry generally uses the first in, first out (FIFO) method of rotating stock. In the FIFO method, an older product is used prior to a more recently purchased product.

4. **Identify and describe the proper method of taking inventory and various methods of inventory pricing.**

   When taking inventory, one person counts or weighs the items and the other person records it on the inventory sheet. Start in one place and progress through the establishment in a logical manner. Some operations count everything in the kitchen, while others estimate the amount for a few items, such as spices. When the physical inventory is complete, the counts are turned over to the manager. Because restaurant and foodservice operations are dynamic in nature, the physical inventory and perpetual inventory will most likely not match completely. The manager will request a recount of any areas with large discrepancies. FIFO calculates the value of inventory using the latest price paid for the item. LIFO calculates the value of inventory using the oldest price paid for the item. Averaged price is a composite of all prices paid averaged and the average price used to calculate the value of the inventory. Actual price calculates the value of the inventory based on the actual price listed on the inventory of all items.

5. **Describe the issuing process, including issuing beverages.**

Direct issue items are placed directly into product and are charged to food cost as they are received by the operations. Items that are placed in stores are considered part of the inventory until issued for use. The process starts with filling out a requisition, a form which lists the items and quantities needed from the stores area. Each requisition should be reviewed and approved by a manager. The requisition is then given to the storeroom and filled. Bartenders also log every product emptied (aka "breakage") on the requisition form and normally issue a replacement bottle based on the bar par.

APPLICATION EXERCISE

Part 1

The following are inventory figures for the White Pearl restaurant:

Physical inventory, March 1	$ 2,900
Physical inventory, March 31	$ 3,000
Total invoices dated March 1–31	$16,000

1. What was the monthly cost of food sold in dollars for this operation?

2. What was the inventory turnover rate for March?

Part 2

Bruce was recently hired as a receiving clerk for the White Pearl restaurant. He has a PO for three bags (40 pounds each) of Russet potatoes, 9 boxes of "Perry" brand napkins (1,000 napkins per box), and three packs of beef loins (50 pounds per pack). Bruce went to the receiving dock excited about the first receiving task at his new job. He weighed one of the bags of potatoes and the weight was correct. He decided that all bags looked alike and did not

weigh the other two bags. He also did not check the label of potatoes, which read "Yukon Gold Yellow Potatoes."

Then Bruce moved to the meat. He did not remove the meat packs from their boxes. Instead, he weighed all three packs and the boxes together and recorded the weight as net product weight. There was also a bloody leak under one of the boxes but the pack looked intact to him. The delivery driver was in a hurry to make another delivery, so Bruce let the driver help with moving items into the storage area. The invoice indicated six boxes of "Curly" napkins (at 1,500 napkins per box). Bruce signed the invoice and waved goodbye to the driver. Content with his first receiving job, Bruce recorded the items into the system and sent a copy of the invoice to accounting.

1. Identify and discuss in detail at least three mistakes Bruce made during the receiving process.

2. What are some of the corrective actions that Bruce could have undertaken during the delivery of items? Explain.

REVIEW YOUR LEARNING

Select the best answer for each question.

1. **What is FIFO?**
   A. A method of stock rotation
   B. The same as closing inventory
   C. Part of an approved vendor sheet
   D. A way to issue product

2. **What is the formula used to extend an inventory?**
   A. Dividing ending inventory by purchases
   B. Multiplying the unit cost by the number of units
   C. Obtaining the total cost of the inventory
   D. Combining the cost of a product located in the kitchen and the storeroom

3. **Which two key documents should be compared during receiving by the receiving agent?**
   A. Purchase order and delivery invoice
   B. Product specification and purchase order
   C. Purchase order and credit memo
   D. Product specification and product requisition

4. **What does a food dating labeling system do?**
   A. Applies only to perishable products, but is optional for nonperishables
   B. Ensures that the proper storage temperatures are maintained
   C. Helps increase the accountability for food safety and inventory control standards
   D. Satisfies requirements for local health departments

5. **If the hotel lobby coffee and pastry bar had requisitions of $565, transferred in goods of $25, and transferred out goods of $50, what would its daily food cost be?**
   A. $490
   B. $540
   C. $565
   D. $640

6. **Given an opening inventory of $9,000, a closing inventory of $12,000, and a cost of food sold of $22,000, what would the inventory turnover for this establishment be?**
   A. 1.0
   B. 2.1
   C. 2.8
   D. 3.8

7. **What type of inventory is counted, recorded, priced, extended, and totaled?**
   A. Perpetual inventory
   B. Theoretical inventory
   C. Closing inventory
   D. Physical inventory

8. **How is a credit memo form used?**
   A. It is used only on food returns from guests.
   B. It is used to issue credits to restaurant or foodservice departments.
   C. It is used to account for missing, returned, or spoiled items.
   D. It is used when products are paid by credit card.

9. **What is the key provision of the Uniform Commercial Code?**
   A. Allows the buyer to reject goods for any reason
   B. Requires the buyer to reject the goods in "a timely fashion"
   C. Excludes some food and beverage purchases
   D. Disallows replacement of damaged goods

10. **Which document should employees present to have products issued?**
    A. Issue requisition
    B. Issue removal claim
    C. Issue authorization form
    D. Issue adjustment record

7 Controlling Food Costs during Production

INSIDE THIS CHAPTER

- Estimating Food-Production Levels
- Monitoring Food Production
- Monitoring Beverage Production

CHAPTER LEARNING OBJECTIVES

After completing this chapter, you should be able to:

- Describe the tools managers use to estimate food-production levels.

- Explain how managers monitor food quality.

- Detail how managers monitor the food-production process.

- Detail how managers monitor the beverage-production process.

- Explain how managers monitor beverage quality.

KEY TERMS

CASE STUDY

The management team for the Graze Buffet meets each Monday at 9:00 a.m. to discuss the previous week's outcomes, including budget actual numbers compared to forecast numbers, production standards, equipment issues, employee challenges, and any other management concerns. For the last three weeks, one of the major topics has been lack of consistency from the kitchen. The new chef, Gina joined the team a short time ago and there is an expectation that the numbers will improve.

1. What information or feedback should the manager share with the new chef about "lack of consistency" from the kitchen? What do you think that means?

2. How might lack of consistency from the kitchen impact food cost?

Exhibit 7.1

THINK ABOUT IT . . .

Forecasting how many of a given menu item need to be produced every day is more complicated than estimating futures sales and guest counts. What can managers do to improve the accuracy of daily menu item production forecasts?

ESTIMATING FOOD-PRODUCTION LEVELS

Like the other segments of an operation, the production area can contribute to increased food costs. One principal cause for this is overproduction by the kitchen. It is a manager's job to apply the correct controls to counteract this issue. No manager can predict the future, but there are tools the manager can use to limit waste by the production staff. By developing sales forecasts, using historical data, and creating detailed production schedules, managers can minimize the amount of overproduction.

Developing Sales Forecasts

The most basic tool for controlling production costs is the sales forecast. It is not only critical to estimate the number of covers for the next period (i.e., week or month) but it is also important to forecast the menu mix for the next period. A sales forecast is the total customer count multiplied by the average check per person. The sales forecast allows managers to estimate the total amount of revenue coming in for a given period. This figure gives the manager an anticipated budget to work within for a given period. The average check estimate consists of several items such as an appetizer, an entrée, a beverage (or beverages), and a dessert (*Exhibit 7.1*). Therefore, managers need to forecast how many entrées, appetizers, beverages, and desserts will be sold.

Exhibit 7.2 details how average check counts are calculated. This chart assumes that all guests will order an entrée. The average price of that

Exhibit 7.2

ESTIMATING AVERAGE DINNER CHECK (PER CUSTOMER)

Dinner	Average Price Point	Percentage Ordered	# per Order	Average Check Food	Average Check Beverage	Average Check
Food						
Entrée	$15.25	100%	1.0	$15.25		
Appetizer	6.45	20	1.0	1.29		
Dessert	6.00	20	1.0	1.20		
Beverages						
Non-alcoholic	$ 3.00	20%	1.0		$0.60	
Tap water	0.00	20	1.0			
Liquor	8.00	10	1.5		1.20	
Beer	6.50	20	1.5		1.95	
Wine	7.00	30	2.0		4.20	
TOTALS				$17.74	$7.95	$25.69

entrée is $15.25. It also assumes that 20 percent of guests will order appetizers and desserts. The assumptions about percentage of items ordered are based on sales history. To calculate the average contribution of an appetizer to total average, the manager multiples the average price point of the appetizer by 20 percent to arrive at the average check figure for that line item:

$$\underset{\substack{\textbf{Average} \\ \textbf{appetizer price}}}{\textbf{\$6.45}} \quad \times \quad \underset{\substack{\textbf{Percentage} \\ \textbf{ordered}}}{\textbf{20\%}} \quad = \quad \underset{\substack{\textbf{Average check} \\ \textbf{appetizer}}}{\textbf{\$1.29}}$$

Repeating that calculation for desserts gives a dessert check total of $1.20 per check. The average food check total is the sum of all these figures:

$$\underset{\substack{\textbf{Average check} \\ \textbf{entrée}}}{\textbf{\$15.25}} \; + \; \underset{\substack{\textbf{Average check} \\ \textbf{appetizer}}}{\textbf{\$1.29}} \; + \; \underset{\substack{\textbf{Average check} \\ \textbf{dessert}}}{\textbf{\$1.20}} \; = \; \underset{\substack{\textbf{Average check} \\ \textbf{food}}}{\textbf{\$17.74}}$$

Average beverage sales per customer are arrived at by estimating the average selling price of each beverage type, assuming what percentage of the customers will order each type and how many servings the average customer will order. For example, if the average beer is priced at $6.50, the estimate assumes that 20 percent of the customers will order a beer and that the average number ordered will be 1.5:

$$\underset{\substack{\textbf{Average beer} \\ \textbf{price}}}{\textbf{\$6.50}} \; \times \; \underset{\substack{\textbf{Percentage} \\ \textbf{ordered}}}{\textbf{20\%}} \; \times \; \underset{\substack{\textbf{Average number} \\ \textbf{ordered}}}{\textbf{1.5}} \; = \; \underset{\substack{\textbf{Average beer} \\ \textbf{check}}}{\textbf{\$1.95}}$$

Calculating all of the line items in *Exhibit 7.2* shows an average food check of $17.74 and an average beverage check of $7.95. Combined, the total average check would be $25.69. However, the manager still does not know much about customer count per meal period and count of menu items to be produced. In most establishments, the numbers of customers served will vary dramatically by meal period and day of the week. For example, many operations do as much as 50 percent or more of their weekly sales on Friday and Saturday. This is why forecasting expected guest counts for every meal period in a typical week is important. Accurate sales forecasts are essential for efficient food production (see *Exhibit 7.3*). The next step is forecasting food production for the next period by looking at sales history and menu mix, topics that will be discussed in the next section.

Exhibit 7.3

THINK ABOUT IT . . .

Without historical sales information, how might an establishment determine how much of a new menu item to produce? Do you think this would result in higher or lower food costs? Why?

SALES HISTORIES

Sales history is the best predictor of what is likely to happen in the future. The more data a manager can review and analyze, the better he or she can forecast. For example, if a manager knows sales volume for the last two years and breaks that down by days, he or she will have a much better chance of forecasting next Saturday's customer count. A point-of-sale (POS) system will help track revenues, record item sales, and do many of the necessary reports required for forecasting.

A sales forecast by menu item would be similar to a food sales report or menu analysis (see chapter 4). The difference is that both of these reports are based on an actual sales history, while a forecast is an estimate of what is expected to happen.

MENU MIX

When managers compute a popularity index for each item on the menu, it can be a big help in meal planning. A **popularity index** is the percentage share of a given menu item in its respective category (e.g., entrée). A popularity index is derived by dividing the number of portions sold by the total number of items in the same category (entrées, appetizers, salads, etc.) that were sold. Managers determine what percentage of the total sales each menu item provides, and then multiply the percentages by the customer forecast. For example, an establishment runs these items every Monday on its menu:

- Chicken à la King in a puff-pastry shell
- Roast loin of pork with dressing
- Broiled salmon with lemon butter sauce
- Roast sirloin of beef au jus
- Vegetable lasagna

From the sales history, managers know that when this menu runs, the following percentages are sold:

Chicken à la King in a puff-pastry shell	22%
Roast loin of pork with dressing	18
Broiled salmon with lemon butter sauce	15
Roast sirloin of beef au jus	35
Vegetable lasagna	10
Total	**100%**

Managers can then predict how many customers will come in on that Monday. This calculation is based on past sales history. Managers must consider any new competitive establishments that might be opening, as well as special events in the area including major sporting events and concerts, weather, and any other pertinent information that could affect sales. If 180 customers are expected, then the following portions of each item should be produced:

Chicken à la King in a puff-pastry shell	(180 × 0.22) = 40
Roast loin of pork with dressing	(180 × 0.18) = 32
Broiled salmon with lemon butter sauce	(180 × 0.15) = 27
Roast sirloin of beef au jus	(180 × 0.35) = 63
Vegetable lasagna	(180 × 0.10) = 18
Total	**180**

Developing a Production Schedule

A **food-production chart** provides the essential information a staff needs to know exactly what and how much to prepare. *Exhibit 7.4* is an example of a completed production chart, using the previous menu mix information. The production chart is simple and easy to use. These records will help gauge production the next time that certain items or combinations of items are served.

Exhibit 7.4

SAMPLE PRODUCTION CHART

DAILY PRODUCTION CHART

DAY Monday	DATE 1/28/12	WEATHER Hot, Dry, 101°	EVENTS none		CUSTOMER FORECAST 180

Item	Recipe No.	%	Prepare	Sales	Leftover
Chicken à la King	C-33	22%	40	38	2
Roast loin of pork	P-12	18%	32	29	3
Broiled Salmon	F-48	15%	27	Ran out - 1:10pm	0
Roast Sirloin of beef	B-8	85%	63	60	3
Vegetable lasagna	V-14	10%	24	20	4

Notes _____

To use a production chart, follow these steps:

1. Enter the name of the dish to be produced on the production record, and fill out the number of portions that will be needed.

2. Pull the necessary recipes for production. Review recipes to make sure they meet standards and are current. Deliver recipes to the various departments, along with the production chart. If possible, deliver the chart a day ahead and have a short preproduction meeting with the team responsible for the actual production. Review any potential problems, product issues, or equipment challenges.

3. Supervise for compliance and to check that everyone is working to the standards that have been set.

4. Follow through by checking on the number of portions that were yielded by the particular recipe. Discuss and investigate either production shortages or large amounts of leftovers.

Not all recipes lend themselves to producing the exact amount predicted. For example, in the previous forecast, vegetable lasagna is made in either a full steam table pan or a half pan. A full pan will produce 24 portions while a half pan will produce 12 portions. In this case, the manager has to decide whether to make a full pan or a half pan. Since 18 portions were predicted, the manager decided to produce a full pan, which yields 24 portions. This means six portions will be left over, which should also be recorded on the production sheet.

The leftover column on the production chart is important because the number of leftover portions can change over time. Customers' tastes could change or they could react to the latest diet fad and alter their eating habits. Since a production chart is not static, and changes constantly, managers must use good record-keeping to maintain an accurate production schedule.

When the production chart has been completed, it should be posted in the kitchen along with the standardized recipes so that the staff knows exactly how much and which menu items to produce. Managers should periodically conduct **recipe yield** tests to observe how many portions a standardized recipe produces. Then, recipe yield should be checked against the daily production sheet to make sure that the kitchen is producing the proper amount.

Adjusting (Scaling) Standardized Recipe Portions

As evident from the food-production chart in *Exhibit 7.4*, it is important to produce only what is anticipated to sell. This strategy will help prevent product outages and will also help reduce leftovers. In a few cases, such as the lasagna, leftovers cannot be eliminated because of various constraints. However, in most cases it is possible to produce exactly what is called for on the production chart.

Industry recipes are for portions of 25, 50, or 100. However, if an operation is using production charts, managers know it usually does not need portions of exactly 25, 50, or 100. To produce exactly what is needed, the recipe must be converted. **Recipe conversion** is a method used to change the yield of a recipe from its original yield to a desired yield. When converting recipes, use a **conversion factor**, or multiplier, to adjust the quantity of ingredients on the existing recipe to the quantity needed to produce the desired yield. The formulas to do this conversion are:

$$\textbf{Desired yield} \div \textbf{Current recipe yield} = \textbf{Conversion factor}$$

$$\textbf{Conversion factor} \times \textbf{Current ingredient amount} = \textbf{Desired ingredient amount}$$

When multiplying each ingredient amount by the conversion factor, the ingredient amounts must be in an easily converted form. This means that pounds should be converted to ounces, and that cups, pints, and quarts should be converted to fluid ounces. Teaspoons and tablespoons can be left as is.

To see how a recipe conversion works, follow these steps to walk through an example of the Chicken à la King in *Exhibit 7.5* on the next page. In this example, 40 portions are needed. However, the recipe yields 50 portions.

1. Determine the conversion factor by dividing the desired yield by the existing recipe yield:

$$\underset{\textbf{Desired yield}}{40} \div \underset{\textbf{Current recipe yield}}{50} = \underset{\textbf{Conversion factor}}{0.8}$$

2. Change the recipe ingredient amounts to ounces (weight) and fluid ounces. The new amounts are listed in their own column in the chart.

3. Multiply each ingredient by the conversion factor. In this example, the conversion factor is 0.8. This calculation provides the "Converted Amount" column.

4. Convert the ingredient amounts back to the original recipe's amount format. For example, ounces are converted back to pounds and fluid ounces to quarts.

Looking at the converted amount column, it is obvious that there can be some unusual numbers. When converting these numbers back to the original units, a manager must use common sense. For example, the result of converting 12.8 ounces of butter to pounds is 0.8 pound. Since 0.75 pound equals ¾ of a pound, 0.8 pound could be rounded to ¾ of a pound. However, do not make the mistake of converting 0.8 pound to 8 ounces, or ½ pound. Remember that 0.5 pound is ½ pound, or 8 ounces.

THINK ABOUT IT . . .

Various software solutions can automate recipe conversions and other kitchen functions. What criteria might you use to determine which software to purchase?

Exhibit 7.5

SAMPLE CONVERSION CHART

CONVERSION CHART

ITEM
Chicken á la King

Ingredient	Recipe amount	New amount	Conversion factor	Converted amount	Recipe amount
			0.8	102.4 oz	6.25 lb
Chicken, diced	8 lb	128 oz	0.8	12.8 oz	0.75 lb
Butter	1 lb	16 oz	0.8	9.6 oz	10 oz
Green pepper, chopped	12 oz		0.8	12.8 oz	0.75 lb
Mushrooms, sliced	1 lb	16 oz	0.8	11.2 oz	0.75 lb
Pimentos, sliced	14 oz		0.8	76.8 oz	2.5 qt
Heavy cream	3 qt	96 oz	0.8	9.6 each	10 each
Egg yolks	1 doz	12 each	0.8	3.2 tsp	3 tsp
Salt	4 tsp		0.8	25.6 oz	0.75 qt
Sherry	1 qt	32 oz	0.8	to taste	to taste
White pepper	to taste		0.8		

Notes _____

_____

With all of the converting and rounding, it is possible that the recipe may be changed slightly. When converting recipes, a manager must use good judgment. For example, hold back some of the spices and taste the product when it is finished, since the spices can always be added later if needed. When converting recipes to smaller yields, such as converting a recipe with a yield of 50 portions to one with 40 portions, there will be little variation in the final outcome. However, problems can arise when converting a small-yield recipe, such as one that produces 50 portions, to a large-yield recipe, such as one that produces 400 portions. In this situation, judgment and experience come into play. For example, one of the reasons that "home" recipes do not always work in a commercial setting is due to the extreme conversion factor needed to produce large quantities. For example, a home recipe for two servings may be difficult to produce for 400 customers. This is because multiplying each ingredient by 200 may not produce a standardized recipe. Whether converting an existing recipe to a smaller yield or a larger one, a manager will use the same conversion process. In the case of converting to a larger yield, the conversion factor will be greater than 1.0, while in converting to a smaller yield it will be less than 1.0. For example, if 75 portions of Chicken à la King were needed instead of 40, the conversion factor would be 1.5:

$$75 \div 50 = 1.5$$

Desired yield	Recipe yield	Conversion factor

BAKER'S PERCENTAGE

Professional bakers do not use "recipes"; they use "formulas." Formulas show basic proportions of ingredients, calculated and expressed as percentages. A **baker's percentage** is not the same as true percentage. In true percentage, the total of the ingredients always add up to 100 percent. In baker's percentage, the weight of the flour in the formula equals 100 percent. All the other ingredients are calculated in proportion to the weight of flour. The mathematical equation is as follows:

$$\left(\frac{\text{Weight of ingredient}} {\text{Weight of total flour}}\right) \times 100 = \frac{\text{Ingredient}}{\text{percentage}}$$

Not only does baker's percentage give bakers an uncomplicated way to compare formulas, it also gives them a clear-cut way to resize or scale a formula. Once the percentages are known, the calculations are straightforward.

Calculating Recipe Yield

Working with recipes means understanding yields. Does the recipe yield 3 quarts or 1 gallon? More important, what does the recipe need to yield? A key component in managing food cost is managing recipes and their yields. Recipes that produce more than the recipe card states can easily end up creating food waste and increasing food cost. Or a recipe made often when it could be made once a week is wasting labor. Tracking what the operation needs and managing the correct production keeps food fresh and costs in line. It is very important that butcher test or yield test be done on all items butchered in-house and any fresh produce processed. Each item has a price per pound, yet that price changes after the product is preparation-ready. To create accurate recipe and plate costs, the correct raw product costs have to be established and kept current.

MANAGER'S MATH

Calculating Baker's Percentage

Baker's percentage enables managers to work with precision using only one unit of measure. It is also easy to scale a formula up or down since ingredients are measured as a proportion to flour. This is an example for a white bread recipe:

Ingredient	Weight	Percentage
Flour	50 lb	100%
Water	33 lb	?
Salt	1 lb	?
Yeast	0.6 lb	?

What is the proportion of each ingredient to flour?

(Answer: By using the previous formula we find the water, salt, and yeast percentages:

Water percentage = (33 lb ÷ 50 lb) × 100 = 66%

Salt percentage = (1 lb ÷ 50 lb) × 100 = 2%

Yeast percentage = (0.6 lb ÷ 50 lb) × 100 = 1.2%

Ingredient	Weight	Percentage
Flour	50 lb	100%
Water	33 lb	66
Salt	1 lb	2
Yeast	0.6 lb	1.2

These percentages show that the bread has 66 percent hydration, or percentage of liquid in a dough. In addition, one can say that the bread has 2 percent salt.)

Occasionally, a recipe will not yield the number of portions that it is supposed to or an establishment will opt to serve a different portion size than what is listed on the recipe card. Although managers may have determined the standard portion cost for various items on the menu, if the operation identifies that the recipes are not producing the number of portions listed, managers will need to determine exactly what kind of yield the recipe is generating. Recall that a recipe yield is the process of determining the number of portions that a recipe will produce. To determine how many portions a recipe yields, first calculate the total volume of the recipe either by weight or by volume, depending on how the portion size is calculated. Weigh or measure only the major ingredients. Remember to take cooking loss into account, especially for meat, vegetables, and fruit.

For example, to determine the total number of eight-ounce portions available from a macaroni and cheese recipe, first look at the recipe's list of ingredients and their volume:

3 lb raw macaroni

2 qt white sauce

2 c grated cheese

4 oz butter

1 tbsp salt

1 tsp paprika

4 oz breadcrumbs

In this particular recipe, only the volume of the macaroni and the white sauce must be calculated. The cheese is not calculated since it is absorbed into the white sauce. Butter, salt, paprika, and breadcrumbs are negligible and also are not counted. Three pounds of raw macaroni yields nine pounds when cooked. Then convert both into the same measure, in this case into ounces. Nine pounds converts to 144 ounces ($9 \times 16 = 144$). Two quarts converts to 64 ounces ($2 \times 32 = 64$).

The total volume of the macaroni and cheese recipe is:

$$
\begin{array}{ccccc}
\textbf{144 oz} & \textbf{+} & \textbf{64 oz} & \textbf{=} & \textbf{208 oz} \\
\textbf{Macaroni} & & \textbf{White sauce} & & \textbf{Product}
\end{array}
$$

The total volume is then divided by the portion size to provide the yield of the recipe:

$$
\begin{array}{ccccc}
\textbf{208 oz} & \textbf{÷} & \textbf{8 oz} & \textbf{=} & \textbf{26 oz} \\
\textbf{Product} & & \textbf{Portion} & & \textbf{Servings}
\end{array}
$$

MONITORING FOOD PRODUCTION

An essential area of competence and consistent execution in any restaurant or foodservice operation is the preparation stage of food production. Not having standards and proper systems has a direct effect not only on food cost but, even more important, on the guest dining experience. To be consistent and prepare food that looks and tastes the same every time, an operation must not only have standardized recipes, but it must use them. Remember, use of standardized recipes has a direct bearing on customer satisfaction.

Maintaining Quality Standards

There are certain steps that managers must take to ensure that the kitchen prepares the appropriate production levels of menu items. One of the primary duties of managers is to make sure that the standards and standardized recipes of the operation are being followed. Recall from chapter 3 that standardized recipes are formalized, consistent guides to preparing menu items, and are essential for any establishment to be consistent and prepare food that looks and tastes the same every time, day after day, week after week, and year after year.

Exhibit 7.6

A well-written recipe with accurate yields will not only help a manager figure out an operation's costs for a particular dish, but it will also be a big help to the chef in his or her ordering and preparations (*Exhibit 7.6*). While occasionally running out of an item or having too much of something left at the end of a shift is to be expected, the less this happens, the better. Recipes should be updated as needed, and all weights indicated should be as accurate as possible to ensure that the recipes and the production charts work together.

Remember that the restaurant and foodservice industry is often a fast-paced environment, which makes it impractical to use standardized recipe cards for every menu item. Cooks are normally required to memorize the proper portions and steps for preparing each item on their station. The recipe would then be used as a reference if necessary to maintain standards. Many operations also use a photo of the finished product as a recipe reference. Proper portioning and adherence to recipes, along with a visual reference of the correctly prepared item, help ensure production consistency in both taste and presentation.

Ensuring that the kitchen production staff is adhering to established standards and standardized recipes should be part of the manager's daily monitoring. Cooks often stray from the standard, sometimes out of carelessness and sometimes because they are trying to improve the product. In either case, it is not in the operation's best interest to have inconsistent products. Therefore, it is critical that managers monitor adherence to standardized recipes.

Exhibit 7.7

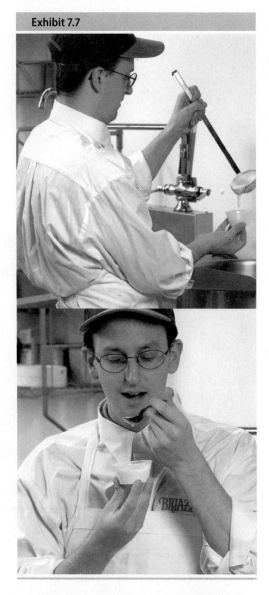

Exhibit 7.8

Quality-control line check, a system that encompasses tasting tests and checking standards, is one of the most effective tools for ensuring product freshness and sufficient quantities. It also aids an organization in meeting standards and correct holding temperatures. Quality control should include **taste tests**, which are done prior to the start of a meal period to determine if products meet the establishment's standards (see *Exhibit 7.7*). It should be a daily ritual of managers to taste everything on the hot food line as well as all pantry items. When tasting, remember to practice good sanitation by using a different tasting spoon for each item to prevent cross-contamination.

If a product does not meet the standard, it should be pulled from the line and not be served to customers. However, sometimes these items can be salvaged. For example, if some seasonings or a crucial ingredient was not included, sometimes the recipe can be brought up to the standard by adding those ingredients. At other times, the product is a total loss. It could be that the sauce "broke" or that too much of a spice was added and the food item cannot be corrected. In this case, the item should be discarded, which forces managers to choose the lesser of two evils. By throwing out the item, food cost goes up and profit goes down. However, while wasting food is serious, it is much worse to sell the inferior product and lose customers.

When a product does not meet the operation's standard, managers must immediately determine the reason and take corrective action. There are several questions that a manager should ask:

- Is the recipe written clearly?
- Did the cook understand the recipe?
- Are the spices, ingredient bins, packages, and cans clearly labeled?
- Are the appropriate ingredients in the proper containers?

Even something as seemingly small as correct labeling can make a big difference. For example, imagine how a chocolate cake might taste if salt were inadvertently put into the sugar bin. After the manager has determined the cause of the problem, he or she must take corrective action to avoid having the problem recur.

Managing the Production Process

Managers must constantly monitor food production, not only for quality and quantity but also for waste and other practices that may impact cost (*Exhibit 7.8*). In addition to conducting quality-control line checks and monitoring adherence to standardized recipes, managers should also observe customers' food consumption in the dining room. Are customers consistently leaving large portions of their meals on their plates? If so, there may be a quality issue. It may also be that the portion sizes are too large. Portion size may also be the issue if many customers are consistently requesting take-home boxes for their unused portions. Also remember that the servers act as representatives to the customers, and as such, servers often have insights into customer quality concerns. Managers should confer with the service staff regularly.

If an issue is found, managers should work quickly to find a resolution to the problem. Once a problem has been identified, managers must work to determine the cause of the issue. Effective managers consider all possible causes. Once the cause is known, managers weigh a variety of alternatives to determine the most appropriate solution. It is not enough to prescribe a change, however. Managers must also oversee the resolution process to ensure that it has been implemented correctly. It may be that recipe cards need to change, that a process needs to be revised, or a staff member needs additional training. In any case, once the problem is resolved, managers should train all affected staff appropriately so that the issue does not recur.

WORKER OUTPUT

In addition to monitoring the food products themselves, managers should observe the production levels of their kitchen staff. One of the best ways to increase worker production is to develop and use prep (*Exhibit 7.9*) lists and station diagrams. For an establishment to serve hundreds of meals in a timely fashion, workstations must provide cooks with the correct equipment, utensils, and sufficient product close at hand. The prep list ensures that proper quantities are available for serving during both slow and peak hours. In particular, having the availability during peak periods is paramount to an establishment's success. Having a diagram of how each station should be set up ensures that the cooks are properly prepared to handle meal production. Plus, a station diagram helps ensure that all cooks set the station the same, which can be helpful if anyone needs to step in and help.

Exhibit 7.9

SAMPLE PREP LIST

Item	Slow Par	Busy Par
Onion Rings	3 pans	6 pans
Cilantro-Lime Ranch		1 gal
Prep BBQ Chix	8 ea	16 ea
BBQ Marinade		1 gal
Blackberry Gastrique		1/2 gal
Heavenly BBQ Sauce		1/2 gal
Potato Croquettes	16 ea	32 ea
Smoked Salmon		1 ea
Smoked Salmon Brine		2 gal
Smoked Coho Salmon		1 ea
Smoked Sockeye Salmon		1 ea
Smoked King Salmon		1 ea
Crab Cakes (2/order)	18	35
Clam Fritters		3 1/6 pans
Wild Rice Strudel	10	20
Scallop Potato Pies	25	60
Scallop Potato Pans	4	7
Scallop Potato Hash	2 pans	4 pans
Minced Garlic		1/6 pan
Minced Shallots		1/6 pan
Ched Horseradish Butter		10 #
Onion-Bleu Butter		10 #
Sweet Butter		10 #
Lobster Stock		10 gal
Beef Demi		2 gal
Chicken Stock		10 gal
Fumet		3 gal
Lobster Bisque		3 gal
Salmon-Corn Chowder		3 gal

There are also ways to minimize the negative impact production staff may have on food cost. It is not unusual for managers to remove all trash cans out of the kitchens and replace them with clear plastic food boxes. This way, the manager can briefly inspect the content at the end of each shift. When good product is discovered in the waste, managers can bring it to the appropriate employee's attention, which may result in some on-the-spot training.

Another way that staff can negatively impact food cost is through employees "snacking" (*Exhibit 7.10*). Many managers underestimate the cost of this. For example, suppose 10 employees have two pieces of shrimp and one dessert each during their shift. If each food item has a cost of $0.45, then each of the 10 employees cost the operation an extra $1.35 or $13.50 per shift. If the operation is open 360 days per year, this employee nibbling costs $4,860 per year. It is recommended that managers have a "no nibbling" policy to reduce the amount of unauthorized employee snacking. That means no snacking, except during line checks or testing the quality of a product. This policy makes good business sense, not to mention that the health inspectors do not like to see employees eating in production areas.

It should be mentioned along with no snacking that employees should not be allowed to consume kitchen "mistakes." If employees are able to consume products that cannot be served to customers for cosmetic or preparation reasons, managers may be providing incentive for those mistakes.

Exhibit 7.10

Ensuring Proper Holding Temperatures

There is nothing more basic in the restaurant and foodservice industry than the fact that hot food should be served hot and cold food should be served cold. The same principle applies to food holding. When food is held, cooled, and reheated there is an increased risk from contamination. Products that are not held at the proper temperature have the opportunity to grow harmful bacteria. Keeping food products at 135°F (57°C) or above during hot holding and keeping food products at or below 41°F (5°C) during cold holding is effective in preventing microbial growth. How often managers should monitor the temperature of food during hot holding determines what type of corrective action they are able to take when 135°F (57°C) is not met. Options for corrective action may include evaluating the time the food is out of temperature to determine the likelihood of hazards and reheating or discarding the food based on that evaluation. Frequency of monitoring during this operational step can mean the difference between reheating the food to 165°F (74°C) and discarding it.

There are some guidelines for holding cold food:

1. Prechill ingredients for items to be served cold.

2. Schedule food production to minimize the time that food is maintained on the serving line.

3. Use batch preparation for cold items to minimize the time that ingredients and completed food products are at room temperature.

There are a few systems or policies that managers should consider to make serving hot food a priority:

1. Make hot food in the window a top priority for everyone on the service staff. A ticket system shows each order's table number and who, at each table, gets what. The manager or server, whoever is closest, should take the order to the table.

2. Use a server paging system. This system notifies servers that their orders are coming up.

3. Put hot food on hot plates. Plates should be 180°F to 200°F (82°C to 93°C). Servers will need something to protect their hands, such as small serving towels.

Using Carry-Overs

Smart managers know not to throw away quality food if there is a good way to use it in another recipe or as employee meals. Many operations have been very creative when using **carry-over production**, food that has been previously produced but not served to customers. One chain introduced a potato skins appetizer primarily as a way to use leftover baked potatoes. Another fast-food chain added chili as a way to use leftover burger meat. Day-old bread and rolls become croutons for salads or bread pudding. Managers must identify which products can and cannot be safely used the next shift or the next day. It is recommended that one staff person be assigned to collect carry-over product. That person should evaluate, properly store, and label any usable products.

MONITORING BEVERAGE PRODUCTION

The beverage or bar area of an operation should be extremely profitable. Managers must maintain the same standards in this operational area as they do in the food-production area. Managers must create and monitor budgets and sales goals, as well as train, supervise, and coach the service staff and bartenders. An operation should create standardized recipes or use industry standardized recipes. Recipes should be costed out and selling prices should be set based on the cost to create the beverage plus the established beverage markup.

One method to effectively measure bar employee productivity is to calculate sales per hour. This is computed by dividing the shift's gross sales by the number of hours the bartender worked. For instance, if a bar sold $1,000 in a four-hour shift, and one employee worked four hours during that shift, the bartender's productivity would be $250 per hour. Using this approach, managers can determine if all employees are meeting sales standards. A bar employee that consistently has low sales numbers could indicate a serious problem. There are a number of possibilities when bartenders do not reach normal sales per hour standards. It is possible that they could not meet demand due to a lack of urgency. Or perhaps they made drinks that did not meet quality standards, so guests did not order more than one. Or they may lack the people or sales skills that a good bartender needs. Finally, they could be stealing money, giving away free drinks, or not recording certain purchases.

Maintaining Beverage Quality Standards

Beverage quality standards follow the same steps as other areas of the operation:

Exhibit 7.11

1. Set standards and describe them in detail and in writing.

2. Establish policies and procedures for meeting these standards. Remember, a procedure is the way in which the plan is implemented.

3. Provide the required facilities, equipment, and environment to be able to deliver the standards.

4. Train and educate the bartending staff on the operational standards managers have established (*Exhibit 7.11*).

5. Review and monitor employees periodically. Provide feedback so they know if they are meeting the quality standards and how they can improve.

6. Coach bartenders and service staff on how to perform specific tasks in order to meet quality standards. Consider creating checklists, station diagrams, prep sheets, side work lists, and job descriptions.

Bar menus often fail to deliver on their promise. Too often, drinks fall short of their descriptions or how they are graphically illustrated. The consequence of delivering a poor beverage is a guest who is underwhelmed and disappointed.

Ensuring that bartenders consistently deliver a high-quality beverage is a training issue. However, serving only high-quality brands and products may not be the best strategy for many operations. Beverages should meet the following standards: great taste, good food presentation, good production value, and perceived value. Remember, perceived value comes down to providing quality at a fair price.

Establishing quality standards is not where the hard work comes in. It is the training and daily follow-up that managers often struggle with. Standards will vary from operation to operation. The key to success is consistency.

Maintaining Beverage Cost Controls

In the beverage business, there are a number of areas that must be managed for success. Because the beverage area requires significant investment in inventory that can quickly "evaporate," tight controls are required. To remain profitable, an operation absolutely must have the capability of tracking what it has on hand, what was paid for it, at what rate product is used, and where it is at any point in time.

Managers should establish a process to determine if they have a liquor cost problem. Knowing that there is a liquor problem sooner rather than later allows an operation to react quickly. The first step is to determine "actual" liquor use and cost for the period, which should be no longer than one week. Managers need to know the beginning and ending liquor inventory and any liquor purchases for the period. This means that managers must do a physical inventory, estimating the quantity of opened bottles to the closest tenth, as shown in *Exhibit 7.12*. If possible, have the same person each week do the counting to maintain consistency. Liquor quantity is normally initially calculated in liters and then converted to ounces.

Exhibit 7.12

ACTUAL LIQUOR USE AND COST

	Quantity	$ Amount	Reference/Calculation
Beginning inventory (L*)	735.2	$13,456	Liquor inventory worksheet
Purchases (L)	288.0	5,364	Liquor invoices
Ending inventory (L)	(728.3)	(12,859)	Liquor inventory worksheet
Actual usage	= 294.9		
Actual usage (oz)	9,967.6		294.9 L × 33.8 oz per L
Actual cost		= $5,961	
Actual cost per oz		= $0.598	$5,961 liquor cost per 9,967.6 oz

*L = liter.

The example in *Exhibit 7.12* shows that 294.9 liters or 9,967.6 ounces of liquor were actually used at a cost of $5,961. Calculate this figure by adding the beginning inventory and purchases, and subtracting the final inventory:

$$(753.2 \quad + \quad 288.0) \quad - \quad 728.3 \quad = \quad 294.9$$

| Beginning inventory | Purchases | Ending inventory | Actual usage (liters) |

Then convert liters to ounces. There are 33.8 ounces per liter:

$$294.9 \quad \times \quad 33.8 \quad = \quad 9,967.6$$

| Liters | Ounces per liter | Total ounces |

The total liquor cost was $5,961. The average liquor cost per ounce for the week was $0.598.

The second step is to calculate the "ideal" liquor use and cost. The ideal numbers are how much liquor should have been used if everything went perfectly. To calculate ideal use, managers must have the liquor sales mix categorized by drinks sold that call for the same quantity of liquor. In the following example, the operation sells drinks with 1.5 ounces, 2.0 ounces, and 2.5 ounces of liquor, as shown in *Exhibit 7.13*. A POS system can easily handle this task.

Exhibit 7.13

CALCULATE IDEAL LIQUOR USE AND COST

	Quantity	$ Amount	Reference/Calculation
Liquor sales			
1.5-oz drinks	2,455	$ 9,820	POS system
2.0-oz drinks	1,650	9,900	POS system
2.5-oz drinks	856	5,992	POS system
Total liquor sales		$25,712	
Ideal quantity used (oz)	9,122.5		$(2{,}455 \times 1.5) + (1{,}650 \times 2) + (856 \times 2.5)$
Ideal cost ($)		$ 5,455.25	9,122.5 oz × $0.598

The cost of the 9,122.5 ounces of liquor is $5,455.25, which is the number of ideal ounces multiplied by the average cost per ounce of $0.598 calculated previously.

The third and final step is for managers to calculate the difference between the actual and ideal liquor costs, as shown in *Exhibit 7.14*.

Exhibit 7.14

DIFFERENCE BETWEEN ACTUAL AND IDEAL LIQUOR COSTS

Quantity	$ Amount	Percentage	Reference/Calculation
Liquor usage			
Ideal quantity	9,122.5 oz		from step 2 above
Actual quantity	−9,967.6 oz		from step 1 above
Difference	= (845.1) oz	(8.5%)	
$ Cost			
Ideal cost	$5,455.25	21.2%	from step 2 above
Actual cost	−$5,961.00	23.2%	from step 1 above
Difference	= ($505.75)	(2.0%)	

Based on the previous example, managers should investigate because there appears to be a problem. The bar used 845 ounces more than it should have. There will always be differences between actual and ideal; the question is what is reasonable and what is excessive. The difference of 845 ounces is 9 percent more than it should have been. If the operation lost $505.75 in liquor each week, the annual loss would be $26,299.

To control beverage cost, managers must monitor **pour cost percentages**, which are the proportion of beverage cost to sales price. The bar's pour cost or cost percentage indicates the level of profitability. The sales price of a beverage is based on a standard portion of alcohol or ingredients. A lax or nonexistent portioning control on drinks will reduce beverage profits. For example, if the bartender overpours an ounce portion of liquor by as little as ¼ ounce, the cost percentage will increase by 25 percent. So, for every four drinks that are overportioned, the establishment loses one full drink's worth of product and revenue. Managers must also be aware of the customer overconsuming alcohol. If a person believes there is only 1 ounce in each drink he might set his limit at three drinks. But if in reality he is consuming almost four, this increases the property's liability.

Underportioning is also a problem. If, for example, the standard is 1 ¼ ounces of liquor in a drink, the bartender could short pour four drinks and then after the fourth he or she could pour one and pocket the proceeds. The pour cost will not be affected and the theft is unlikely to be detected. The guests and the operation's reputation are the real victims.

Technology has made significant improvements in helping managers control the dispensing of liquor and reducing theft. There are several versions of liquor control systems on the market, including towers, undercounter systems, and freestanding counter configurations.

However, not all customers find liquor control systems acceptable. These systems are often considered inhospitable and guests sitting at a bar may be put off. Before installing a system, consider whether it goes with the establishment's concept. An all-bottle system, which does not require complicated installations or pressurized lines, may be an appropriate compromise for many smaller operations. This system uses either a hand-measuring jigger (*Exhibit 7.15*) or a bottle-attached pour spout control device capable of delivering precise measurements.

Managing inventory appropriately also reduces cost. As mentioned in chapter 6, do not allow bartenders to participate in the physical inventory process. The process of auditing the bar's physical inventory is a managerial function. Managers should also create a perpetual inventory system for liquor. This system tracks the changes in the liquor room inventory. That way, managers can control internal theft by comparing the last entry on a product's perpetual inventory sheet with the actual number of bottles on hand.

Two final policies can help control beverage costs. First, it is good business to not allow anyone but managers to approve complimentary drinks. This policy prevents someone from selling a drink and then pocketing the money, claiming it was a complimentary drink. Second, do not allow anyone but managers to use the "no-sale" feature on the register. The no-sale feature is normally used to make change. Once the register is open, however, the cash will be there for the taking.

SUMMARY

1. **Describe the tools managers use to estimate food-production levels.**

Managers develop sales forecasts to project revenue and costs for given time periods. Managers use historical data, as well as menu mix analyses based on those data, to estimate the number of menu items needed for a given shift or day. Managers populate the food-production chart to communicate to the staff the estimated levels of each food item to prepare. When needed, managers scale recipes to the appropriate yields, as indicated on the food-production chart. Managers also know how to calculate yields for all recipes.

2. **Explain how managers monitor food quality.**

Managers first monitor adherence to standardized recipes. Managers also conduct quality-control line checks, including taste tests, to ensure that products are of the appropriate quality and are meeting other established standards, including portion sizes. When there are quality issues, managers investigate and implement solutions.

Exhibit 7.15

RESTAURANT TECHNOLOGY

OPEN FOR BUSINESS

Liquor control systems dispense any type of beverage through a computerized main controller. The systems can track inventory from delivery to sale, compute beverage cost percentages, and determine gross profit. Using liquor control systems also prevents overpouring, ensures serving consistent drinks, and helps pricing accuracy. The majority of these liquor control systems can interface with a POS system so that every drink poured is registered on the spot, which makes the bartender accountable for the sale. At the end of a shift the data are downloaded into reports showing what was poured and at what price.

3. **Detail how managers monitor the food-production process.**

Monitoring food production process consists of several aspects such as controlling, minimizing food waste and increasing worker output. Quality standards are met by implementing quality-control line check. Savvy managers check with the service staff because those staff members generally act as representatives to the customers and hear about issues first. As with quality issues, when a problem is identified, it is the manager's responsibility to implement the solution and ensure that staff members are adequately trained so that the issue does not recur. Worker output can be improved by using prep lists and station diagrams.

4. **Detail how managers monitor the beverage-production process.**

Managers use some of the same principles to manage the beverage-production process as the food process, including the use of standardized recipes. In addition, managers also calculate sales per shift to monitor individual productivity levels. To control costs, managers compare actual to expected liquor sales, looking for areas where the variance is great. A large variance indicates a problem that must be resolved. Managers must also closely manage the inventory process, the number of complimentary drinks, and the use of the "no-sale" cash register feature to ensure that liquor sales are made appropriately.

5. **Explain how managers monitor beverage quality.**

Managers can establish and monitor beverage quality by setting standards that are described in detail in writing. An operation should provide clear procedures and necessary facilities and equipment to meet these standards. Employees should be trained and educated about established operational standards. A periodical review of standards with employees is essential so that employees understand how they meet standards and in what areas they could improve.

APPLICATION EXERCISE

Chef Johnson of Bowman Creek Bistro needs to prepare a production chart for the dinner shift on Saturday. Chef Johnson has sales information from last Saturday and wants to use menu mix numbers from last week.

1. Calculate the actual menu mix percentage for each item for last Saturday.

Item	Number of Items Sold	Menu Mix Percentage
BBQ Ribs	122	34.7%
Parmesan Chicken	46	13.1 %
Coconut Shrimp	35	10 % %
Blackened Redfish	77	21.9 %
Firehouse Spaghetti	71	20.2 %
Total Items Sold	**351**	

122 /351 =

2. The manager expect the covers for next Saturday to be higher than last week. Use the previous information to estimate the number of portions for each item for next Saturday.

Item	Menu Mix Percentage	Items to Prepare
BBQ Ribs	.348	139.2
Parmesan Chicken	.131	52.4
Coconut Shrimp	.10	40
Blackened Redfish	.21	82.6
Firehouse Spaghetti	.20	80.8
Expected Number of Covers	**400**	

REVIEW YOUR LEARNING

Select the best answer for each question.

1. A production schedule is based on
   A. knowing the percentage of each item's sales.
   B. the number of servers working that day.
   C. recipe yield tests.
   D. knowing each item's food cost.

2. Quiche Lorraine will be served on tomorrow's menu. Each quiche will produce 6 servings. The production chart shows that the anticipated sales are 40 servings. How many quiches should be produced?
   A. 5
   B. 6
   C. 7
   D. 8

3. The primary reason for using a production chart is to
   A. control employee snacking.
   B. better track inventory.
   C. meet customer demand.
   D. schedule staff appropriately.

Use these data to answer questions 4 and 5:

A standardized recipe for lamb stew makes 25 portions. When it runs against other menu items, it accounts for 27% of the sales. The prediction for Tuesday is 450 customers.

4. The number of portions that should be produced is
   A. 25.
   B. 112.
   C. 122.
   D. 450.

5. The conversion factor on the standardized recipe should be
   A. 1.4.
   B. 4.9.
   C. 5.6.
   D. 6.9.

6. If the amount of an ingredient was 0.9 lb after converting a recipe, what would it probably be rounded to?
   A. 8 oz
   B. 9 oz
   C. 16 oz
   D. 20 oz

7. A taste test is part of what managerial function?
   A. Food-production chart test
   B. Quality-control line check
   C. Nightly service staff training
   D. Monthly product profitability evaluation

8. A manager notices that many of the guests are not finishing their meals. When the manager discusses this with the service staff, the manager learns that significant numbers of guests are also requesting take-home boxes. What is the likely issue related to the uneaten portions?
   A. The chef is not monitoring food quality.
   B. Food arriving at the table is too cold.
   C. Portion sizes may be too large.
   D. The recipe yield is off so too many portions are produced.

9. Which step should managers consider to make serving hot food a priority?
   A. Keep food on the grill until it is served.
   B. Put hot food on hot plates.
   C. Reheat food if needed.
   D. Use hot vegetables for meat entrées.

10. What is the purpose of using liquor control systems?
    A. Help develop food-production charts
    B. Help guests make their beverage selection
    C. Help bartenders fill orders more quickly
    D. Help control beverage pour costs

FIELD PROJECT

You want to add two new salads to your salad bar in order to take advantage of seasonal produce. First, it is necessary to research the two recipes—one recipe should have cucumbers as its main ingredient and the other should contain blueberries.

Research the recipes online or in the school library. Look for institutional recipes that are written in larger quantities such as 25, 50, and 100.

When you have selected the two new recipes, convert them to a different amount. In other words, if the recipe you selected serves 25 portions, convert it to serve 50 or 60 portions. Enter your information in the charts below.

Cucumber Salad Recipe					
Ingredient	Recipe Amount	New Amount	Conversion Factor	Converted Amount	Recipe Amount
Recipe name:			Prepared by:		

Blueberry Salad Recipe					
Ingredient	Recipe Amount	New Amount	Conversion Factor	Converted Amount	Recipe Amount
Recipe name:			Prepared by:		

8 Controlling Food Costs during Service and Sales

INSIDE THIS CHAPTER

- Service and Portion Control
- Employee Service Training
- Product Usage and Waste Reports
- Controlling Food Costs in Sales
- Guest Payment

CHAPTER LEARNING OBJECTIVES

After completing this chapter, you should be able to:

- Explain the importance of portion control to food cost.

- Explain the importance of training, monitoring, and follow-through as they relate to the service team.

- Explain the importance of product usage and waste reports to control the cost of high-cost food items.

- List and describe each payment method used by the restaurant and foodservice industry.

- Explain how to complete a daily sales report.

KEY TERMS

CASE STUDY

Enrique, service manager at El Carmen, has been noticing a downward trend in sales during the night shift on weekends. Enrique also noticed that the number of steaks and chicken sold had decreased drastically. Enrique checked the customer count for the past four weekends, and realized that the number of customers actually increased.

El Carmen does not have an electronic system to record orders and instead uses a duplicate check system where one copy remains with the server and the second copy goes to the kitchen for production. Two of the servers are close friends with the cooks and Enrique suspected that cooks prepared food without requiring a copy of the guest check.

1. How would cooks not requiring tickets present an opportunity for the servers to mishandle cash?

2. What are the disadvantages of using a paper duplicate check system?

3. How can Enrique make sure that every guest order is recorded?

SERVICE AND PORTION CONTROL

Because most of the controls in restaurant and foodservice operations are interconnected and dependent on each other, it is critically important for managers to make sure that each individual control works and is enforced. If even one or two controls are missing, there is a strong possibility that food cost will increase. Even in the best operations, mishaps can occur to cause food cost to increase.

Previous chapters addressed controls and processes in purchasing, receiving, storing, issuing, and production. Managers must also implement controls in the service area. The two principal causes of loss in the service area are portion control and theft.

Portion Control

A major cost control in restaurant and foodservice operations is portion control. **Portion control** is the amount of food in a serving as determined by the standardized recipe or the company standard. Portion control starts with the menu listing. Quite often the menu will list items with their corresponding portion size, such as a "fourteen-ounce strip steak," "six jumbo shrimp," or a "quarter-pound hamburger." These are all examples of portion control. Remember, the customer often purchases an item based on its description, and the selling price on the menu is based on the portion being served. If the product is underportioned, the customer may be unhappy and not return. If the product is overportioned, the food cost increases and the operation loses money.

Successful food costing relies on correct portioning by the production staff. The protein in most recipes is typically the most important portion and the one that will most affect food cost. For example, if a Southwestern Chicken Breast with Grilled Vegetables has a food cost of 25 percent, and the chicken breast weight is supposed to be six ounces, the cost increases significantly if the portion served is actually seven or eight ounces. However, be aware that other ingredients may also drive up food costs. It would make sense to weigh and bag the vegetables with the same focus on value as the chicken breast. Assume the cost of the vegetables in the recipe is $1.35 for four ounces, or $0.34 an ounce, and that the establishment sells 308 Southwestern Chicken entrées every 28 days. Overportioning the vegetables by just one ounce costs the operation $104.72 in overages per 28 days:

$$0.34 \times 308 = \$104.72$$

Cost per ounce   **Entrées per 28 days**   **Overages per 28 days**

Over the course of the year, that is approximately $1,365 in overages for one dish alone.

Portioning problems can also arise if the front of the house does not control or portion food as well as it should. To run food costs properly, a system should be in place to track items being used in the front of the house. An

---

THINK ABOUT IT . . .

Portions of food served have been getting bigger and bigger in America. How does portion control affect the profitability in operations?

---

operation may believe it uses only a few lemons and creamer packets. However, a closer look will reveal more product used in this area than the manager might think. For example, the bar normally uses fruit for the garnish tray, such as olives and cherries. Large stuffed olives often cost as much as $0.15 each. Specialty drinks now require exotic fruit and other costly beverage ingredients. Products may be cross-used between departments, so extra care is needed to track what is used and where. Losing track of products leads to losing control of their cost.

In many operations, front-of-the-house staff members are responsible for preparing portions of butter, dressings for salads, and cream and milk for coffee. Managers need to establish systems and standards in this area as much as in the kitchen. Bartenders and servers, much like line cooks, often believe "more is better." Managers need to monitor side work, such as cutting lemons and limes, to prevent overproduction and waste. Having to throw away improperly stored cream, milk, butter, or last week's sliced lemons can quickly add up and increase overall food cost.

Finally, it is important for managers to inspect portions and weights during each shift. Pull one item off the line and weigh the key ingredients. If there is an issue, address it immediately. Take the time to do a little one-on-one coaching.

Portion Control Devices

Portion control is also linked to the cook's line through the use of standardized recipes. The total amount to prepare is based on the day's anticipated sales for that menu item and the number of portions a recipe produces. The proper portion control device should be specified in each recipe's instructions.

There are a variety of tools that can be used to help the portioning process. By using the correct portioning tools, prep cooks, line cooks, and service staff all do their part in controlling food costs, increasing customer satisfaction, and boosting the operation's bottom line. **Portion control devices** assist in the portioning of food items. They include scoops, ladles, serving spoons, serving dishes, and portion scales. Technological advances in scales and slicing equipment continue to make it easier for employees to portion product faster and with greater accuracy. Anything managers can do to help staff do a better job of portioning is a great investment.

- **Scoops:** Also known as dishers, these are used to portion semisolid products such as cottage cheese, ice cream, and chicken salad. Scoops are sized and numbered from 4 to 40, according to how many portions the scoop yields per quart, as shown in *Exhibit 8.1*. A number 4 scoop yields 4 portions

Exhibit 8.1

SCOOPS ARE SIZED BY NUMBER

Number 16 is one-fourth cup. Number 12 is one-third cup. Number 8 is one-half cup.

Exhibit 8.2

LADLES ARE SIZED ON THE HANDLE

per quart, while a number 40 scoop yields 40 portions per quart. The most common scoop sizes are 8, 10, 12, 16, and 20, with a number 8 scoop holding one-half cup (four ounces) and a number 20 scoop holding an eighth of a cup (one ounce). Quite often, scoops are color-coded on the base of the handle for easy identification by line personnel. Product is portioned correctly when it is level with the top of the scoop.

- **Ladles:** These are used to portion liquid products such as sauces, soups, salad dressings, and entrées with a liquid or sauce base, such as beef stew. They range in size from one-half ounce to eight ounces. Ladles, like scoops, are often color-coded. The size of the ladle is embossed on the top of the handle, shown in *Exhibit 8.2*.

- **Serving spoons:** There are two types of serving spoons, solid and slotted. Solid serving spoons are used for semisolid food items, such as macaroni and cheese or mashed potatoes. Slotted spoons are used for products that are in liquid but should be served without the liquid, such as canned vegetables or stewed fruit. A rule of thumb is that one slightly rounded serving spoonful will yield four ounces of product.

- **Serving dishes:** Many serving dishes also are used as portion control devices:

  - Ramekins, which are used for sauces or salad dressings, can vary in size from one to four ounces (*Exhibit 8.3*).

  - Vegetable side dishes, also known as monkey dishes or nappies, can also be used for fruit or sometimes sauces. For vegetables, the rule of thumb is that a vegetable side dish will hold four ounces.

  - Individual casseroles, usually round or oblong in shape, typically hold eight to ten ounces of product. This is an excellent way to portion items such as stews, ragouts, and potpies.

Exhibit 8.3

- Cups and bowls can also be used for portion control. Soup cups and coffee cups usually hold five to six ounces. A bowl normally holds seven to eight ounces. Some bowls are designed to hold the same amount of product as a cup, yet the charge for a bowl of soup is substantially higher than for a cup of soup. This is a deceptive practice that should not be used by any establishment.

- **Portion scale:** This tool is used for items that are portioned by weight, such as roasts, deli meats, and French fries. Portion scales are adjustable so that when a serving plate is placed on the platform, the dial can be adjusted to zero. To adjust the dial to zero, managers need to take into account the weight of a plate. The combined weight of a food item and a plate is called gross weight. The weight of a food item is the net weight. The weight of the plate is the difference between gross and net weight, called tare. When a scale is adjusted for tare, the scale will show the exact weight of the product, that is, its net weight. Always make sure that the setting is at zero prior to weighing a product. Portion scales are normally suitable for products weighing up to 32 ounces.

Portion control is also important in protecting beverage profit margins. Since the sales price of a drink is based on the serving portion of alcohol, if the portion size fluctuates, so does the profit margin. As mentioned in chapter 7, there are a number of different portion control devices for the bar. The most common are handheld measuring devices, such as shot glasses and jiggers. Bottle-attached control devices offer a cost-effective method of ensuring strict portion control and accuracy without interfering with the server–guest relationship. These portion control spouts are designed to deliver only one measurement, thereby restricting a bartender's pouring flexibility. There are also computerized liquor control systems, making the dispensing of liquor more precise and less vulnerable to theft.

Although some people in the kitchen and behind the bar may believe that they have a "feel" for exact portion sizes, it is important that staff use portion control devices rather than guessing. It is the manager's responsibility to coach employees on the proper use of portion control devices and to insist that employees use them. As managers supervise the kitchen and service lines, they need to monitor and insist on the proper means to ensure portion control.

Pre-Portioned Items

A pre-portioned item is food that is measured or weighed prior to going to the service line. There are many ways to pre-portion food, depending on the type of operation. Fine-dining restaurants do not typically pre-portion as much as a busy sandwich shop. But in fast-casual and casual dining, where volume is necessary for success, pre-portioning is a must. Pre-portioning results in true cost control, improved consistency, and speed.

It is important for managers to review the menu ahead of time and identify items that can be pre-portioned. Salads or cold appetizers with ingredients such as smoked salmon, Kalamata olives, cured or deli meats, and upscale cheeses like Parmigiano-Reggiano or blue cheese can add up very fast if overportioned. Items like these can be easily pre-portioned by either weight or volume, helping keep the plate cost in line with the established standard. Other examples of pre-portioned items include lasagna, Swiss steaks, individual potpies, and presliced meatloaf.

Pre-portioning also helps control product freshness. Portions can be easily labeled with food-dating systems and rotated, helping staff and managers monitor prepped food. Fine-dining chefs benefit from pre-portioning high-end items like *foie gras* or expensive cuts of meat. Vacuum-seal machines are very affordable and allow managers and chefs to create pre-portioned, service-ready items without the risk of quality loss or waste. A disadvantage of these machines is that they present food hazard concerns and require a HACCP in most establishments.

PRE-MADE ITEMS

Very few establishments offer 100 percent of their menu items from "scratch" or 100 percent "pre-made." Almost all restaurant and foodservice operations use a mixture of the two approaches. Fine dining tends to create more items from scratch than fast-food operations, but even the most expensive establishment still uses some prepared items. Determining the correct balance between pre-made products and scratch will change over time. Managers need to weigh the advantages and disadvantages of each approach. Customer acceptance, kitchen staff and equipment capabilities, storage space, menu pricing, and food costs will all contribute to the decision.

Pre-prepped, prepared, or precooked items have been around for a very long time and are used by the restaurant and foodservice industry because they save time and money, and are accepted by the customer. The variety and quality of pre-made items has dramatically improved over the last 20 years. For example, an operation can purchase whole chickens and have the chef butcher them, or it can purchase chicken breasts or legs, chicken with or without skin and bones, portioned chicken, cooked chicken, marinated chicken, and many other options. There are three basic categories, based on the level of processing. Of course, the more processing, the more an item will cost. However, it is important to factor in labor, equipment, utilities, and storage to arrive at a true cost.

Exhibit 8.4

The first category is prepared but raw, which includes ingredients that may arrive cleaned, sized, or blanched but basically in their raw state. Examples of this category include washed lettuces, chopped fruit and vegetables (*Exhibit 8.4*), cut portion controlled meats—for example, 10-ounce New York strip steak—and peeled deveined raw shrimp.

The second category includes prepared food items that may be raw, partially cooked, fully cooked, blanched, or combined with one or more ingredients. These items require additional preparation and are not ready to serve. Examples are pre-breaded chicken, frozen dough, spice mix packets, marinated items, soup and sauce mixes, and ready-to-bake desserts. In the bar area, items such as daiquiri or margarita mixes fall into this category.

The third category is fully prepared items, such as salad dressings, cut and serve desserts, deli meats, and fresh breads. This category offers maximum convenience. These ready-to-serve items may or may not be combined with additional prepared or scratch items. This category also includes **speed scratch**, which are pre-made products that are nearly complete but lack finishing touches such as sauces and flavoring.

Managers must still inspect these ingredients, including tasting the product and reading the ingredients label. Knowing the ingredients of any pre-made product helps protect guests and minimizes the operation's exposure to liability. For liability reasons, all employees should have access to a list of the ingredients of menu items, including the ingredients of any prepared items, to avoid causing allergic reactions in guests who are sensitive to certain ingredients. That is, managers should be aware of ingredients of pre-prepared items and communicate these ingredients to serving employees.

Exhibit 8.5

EMPLOYEE SERVICE TRAINING

Managers spend a good deal of time training employees on the issue of portion control. Portion control is not a subject that can be reviewed during employee orientation and then forgotten. Employees have to be constantly trained and retrained to use the portion control devices and give customers exactly what they are paying for (*Exhibit 8.5*).

One important reason for this repeated training is that employees have a tendency to "go the extra mile." They want customers to be happy and may feel that giving customers a little extra will make them happier. In some cases, money is involved—employees might believe that a larger portion will secure a larger tip. Whatever the case, managers need to constantly educate their staff.

Effective service training goes beyond portion control issues, however. Having an established server training program is one of the most important components of a successful restaurant or foodservice operation. Service staff members impact the guests more than food and décor. A successful server training program has several parts and it is necessary to tailor the training to fit the operation's service style and menu. Job duties will vary depending on service style. However, there are basic tools and practices that can be applied to just about any service style.

Every operation should have an employee manual that communicates the operation's policies, work rules, and expectations. Then, prior to the training period, each new server should be given an orientation. During orientation, the operation's culture, mission statement, and purpose should be explained. This is also the time to lay the groundwork for communicating the manager's expectations. The training program should demonstrate how those expectations can be met.

Additional areas of service training should focus on taking guest orders and offering menu suggestions. For example, when asked about ingredients of a given menu item, a thorough explanation would help reduce any misunderstandings. As a consequence, any possibility of food order returns by the guest will be reduced. In addition, when taking steak orders, servers should have a good knowledge of the types of meat cuts. Some meat cuts will taste overcooked when they are cooked "well done." In that case, if a customer orders a well-done New York strip, a server may suggest that a steak that is cooked "medium-well" may be more flavorful and juicy. On the other hand, using an incorrect sauce on a menu item may have negative consequences. Taking an incorrect order not only increases food costs but also increases labor costs and negatively affects customer satisfaction. An effective training manual should reference and include training tools and everyday operational tools. Materials that can be included are as follows:

- **Written job descriptions:** These convey the expectations for every position in the operation.

- **Work assignments:** Managers should include a list of opening, running, and closing side work assignments for each shift as part of the training. Side work is often divided up and assigned to each station.

- **Station diagrams:** These show the dining room divided into stations consisting of groups of three to five tables. Each station is numbered or labeled, as are the tables.

- **Menu training:** This includes a list of all menu items with detailed descriptions. Photos are an excellent way to help servers remember details about the menu. It should also include how items are prepared, what ingredients are in each item, and whether substitutions are allowed. All servers should have an opportunity to sample every menu item that is offered.

- **Customer service standards:** Training should be ongoing and reinforced daily in shift meetings. Topics for service standards might include the following:
  - Handling guest complaints
  - Handling a long ticket time, when it is taking too long to get the food out
  - Fraternization guidelines
  - Making a guest feel welcome
  - Exceeding guests' expectations, also knows as the "wow" factor
  - Reinforcing that the guest is always right
  - Helping customers who are disabled
  - Inviting guests back
  - Handling tips; for example, never pick up a tip before the guest has left

Managers should create and post a "steps of service" chart. This lists the expected order of service for each step of the guest dining experience. It should also include ticket time expectations. This provides a reference for both the front- and back-of-the-house staff.

If the operation uses a **point-of-sale (POS) system**, a system for controlling the operation's cash generation, product usage, and inventory, then the training program should allocate the necessary time to learn how to use it. Operations often rely on the POS system for kitchen timing, menu item sales mix, and proper guest-check tabulation. Entering inaccurate information into the system may lead to operational problems and dissatisfied guests. Service training must also include cash-handling and shift-closing procedures, which will be addressed later in this chapter.

While most training manuals offer a great deal of information, they are merely the first step. Training must be reinforced and refined as employees practice the skills learned from trainers and experience. And for managers, follow-through is just as important as training. For instance, the manager needs to regularly check portions to ensure that they meet specified standards. For example, if while walking through the kitchen, a manager notices a cook cutting steak, the manager should periodically pick up a steak at random and put it on the portion scale to determine if it is the correct weight. The manager should also do things like check the scoop size used by the pantry person for the tuna salad sandwich, and randomly weigh an order of French fries. When employees know that portion control is a priority with the manager, they tend to pay closer attention themselves.

Exhibit 8.6

Table Management

It is important to distribute customers equally among waitstaff and tables to ensure the quality of service. **Table management** is a process of managing customer preferences, seating capacity, and available staff. Many managers underestimate the value of a well-trained, knowledgeable host who can seat guests, manage a waiting list so that customers know they are valued and important, and evenly distribute guests across all dining stations (*Exhibit 8.6*). Table management is one area of operations that has really benefited from technology. Software can help quote more accurate wait times to guests, maximize seating, integrate with most major POS systems, support the most popular mobile devices, and send alerts to managers if ticket or wait times are missed.

RESTAURANT TECHNOLOGY

OPEN FOR BUSINESS

Table management systems help operations manage their seating capacity more efficiently by allowing managers to match the number of guests in a party with available seating. The table management system gives hosts a full view of the operation's seating areas from the host station. It also helps the hosts balance the number of covers evenly among the waitstaff. One of the key benefits of using a table management system is the ability to improve table turnover, the number of times tables are sold. Another major benefit is the increase in guest satisfaction due to accuracy of seating wait times and seating preferences.

Suggestive Selling

Suggestive selling, often called "up-selling" or "add-on selling," uses value-added suggestions from servers to increase the number or type of items customers purchase. This type of selling is one of the easiest, most cost-effective ways to increase revenue, profit, and if done correctly, customer satisfaction. Suggestive selling must be presented in a positive, soft-sell approach. Then guests' perception of having received enhanced value and enjoyment increases because they feel that the server personalized the experience and recommendations for them. This personalized service builds customer loyalty, which increases the chance of repeat business.

For suggestive selling to be successful, servers need training and direction. The benefits to the server and operation must be pointed out and demonstrated as part of a sales training program. Most servers do not realize how much small increases in sales can add up on the check. Servers should be adept and comfortable with suggestive selling, not only to increase check totals and tips, but also to help guests make up their minds and feel pleased with what they have selected. It is an essential part of excellent service.

There are a number of effective suggestive selling techniques. Servers should remember to give customers a choice and should not push a certain food item. Using positive adjectives such as "freshly made" and "slow cooked" can be very effective. Also, servers should mention unique features of a product such as "this milk curd is made in the Swiss Alps using a 400-year-old recipe." If an establishment serves wine or craft beer, recommendations for food and wine or beer pairings should help improve both revenues and profitability. Building sales by increasing the check can backfire, however. Many servers do it poorly because they do not actually believe in suggestive selling. Also, if servers concentrate on how much money a table is spending, it comes across to the guest as insincere, shallow, and manipulative. This creates a distraction that impedes establishing a good rapport with the guests.

The danger of suggestive selling is that it can place the emphasis on the needs of the establishment rather than the needs of the guest. A servers' first job is to make sure the guests are happy, as unhappy guests do not return. Servers may increase the check average but lose the guests' future patronage. It is not easy to create a team of servers that feels comfortable with suggestive selling. Rather than investing in training on how to up-sell, operations may want to invest in training servers how to treat the guest in such a way that they want to come back more often. Getting the guest to come back one more time each month translates to increased sales without having any pressure to increase the average check.

PRODUCT USAGE AND WASTE REPORTS

In addition to controlling costs in the service processes, it is important to track some of the more costly food items. Two reports are helpful in this regard—the product usage report and the waste report. *Exhibit 8.7* shows a sample **product usage report**, which details the number of items issued to the cook's line, the number returned to inventory, and the number sold to customers. The product usage report is often used to track high-cost items such as steak, lobster, and some other seafood items. These items are monitored because they are small and expensive, making them susceptible to theft. High-cost items should be locked in the walk-in and issued by the manager to the cook's line prior to a meal period. The amount issued should correspond to a predetermined par stock—the average amount needed for a

Exhibit 8.7

SAMPLE PRODUCT USAGE REPORT

PRODUCT USAGE REPORT

| DATE: 11/16 | SHIFT: Dinner | ISSUED BY: CO | VERIFIED BY: R.B. | RETURNS VERIFIED BY: |

Item	Issued	Returned	Sold	Comments
Strip steak (12 oz)	35	5	30	
Rib-eye steak (14 oz)	40	2	37	1 ret'd overcooked
Medallions	25	1	24	
Filet mignon	50	6	44	
Lobster tails	40	10	30	

NOTES _____

THINK ABOUT IT . . .

Often usage of high-cost food items such as caviar, aged steaks, and truffles requires careful storage, preparation, and service. Why would an establishment use high-cost food items?

shift, plus a safety factor. At the end of the shift, the manager should tally the number of items left. The amount sold on the product usage report should be compared to the guest checks or the POS printout to determine if any items are missing.

The waste report is also useful in tracking product in the service area. As *Exhibit 8.8* shows, the **waste report** lists any item that had to be discarded and the reason why. Losses, such as meals returned by customers, dropped trays, items left on the steam table too long, and products that were not up to the establishment's quality standards are shown on the waste report. By reviewing the waste report, managers can track breakdowns in the system and determine the root causes of these breakdowns, such as preparing too much product in advance or slippery floors that cause trays to be dropped.

Exhibit 8.8

SAMPLE WASTE REPORT

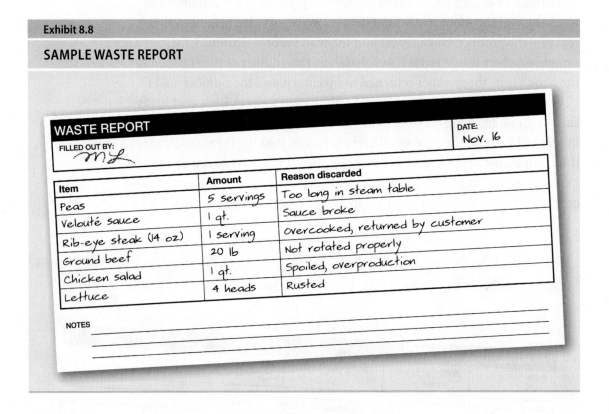

Item	Amount	Reason discarded
Peas	5 servings	Too long in steam table
Velouté sauce	1 qt.	Sauce broke
Rib-eye steak (14 oz)	1 serving	Overcooked, returned by customer
Ground beef	20 lb	Not rotated properly
Chicken salad	1 qt.	Spoiled, overproduction
Lettuce	4 heads	Rusted

WASTE REPORT — DATE: Nov. 16 — FILLED OUT BY: ML — NOTES

Causes of food waste usually fall into two categories: poor training or lack of attention by the manager. In both situations, employees may feel that a little waste is unavoidable. The manager must stress the importance of valuing all products on a daily basis. In addition, the manager must encourage all staff to realize that wasting food not only hurts profits but can ultimately affect their well-being and livelihood through labor cutbacks and other budget cuts that may have to be implemented to bring down overall costs.

CONTROLLING FOOD COSTS IN SALES

So far, the focus has been on controlling product from the time it is purchased to the time it is served. Once customers have received their meals, managers should make sure that what leaves the kitchen is paid for and that the cash is handled properly. Unfortunately, money is the easiest thing to steal in any restaurant or foodservice operation. Consequently, it must be strictly accounted for, and the employees entrusted with money must be held accountable for it through tight controls.

Duplicate Guest-Check and POS Control Systems

The duplicate guest-check system and the point-of-sale (POS) system are the most widely used methods in the restaurant and foodservice industry today. The **duplicate guest-check system** is a procedure that uses written records of what guests purchased and how much they were charged for the items. The POS control system uses a computer to ensure that what leaves the kitchen is billed to and paid for by customers. Although both processes are used to monitor, control, and ensure payment for food, the major difference is that technology takes the place of manually writing a guest check in the POS system, sending a copy of the check to the kitchen, and tracking the inventory of sold items. In addition, the POS system stores historical data that can be easily retrieved when needed. As more restaurant and foodservice operations embrace technology, the POS system is rapidly replacing the duplicate guest-check system.

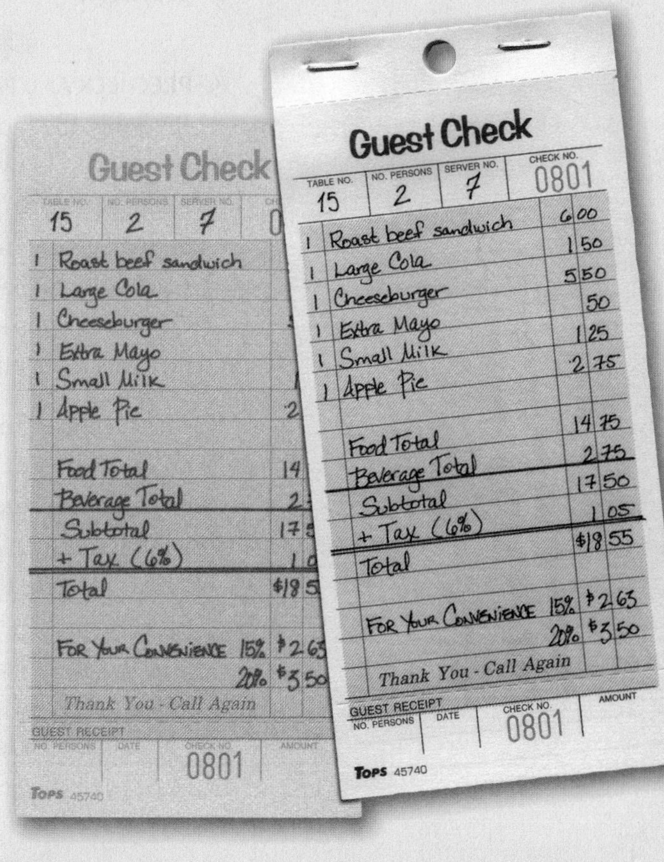

DUPLICATE GUEST-CHECK SYSTEM

Each guest check is prenumbered and has a duplicate; that is, when the customer's order is written on the first copy of a check, it is also written on the second copy, shown in *Exhibit 8.9*. The following process steps detail the use of the duplicate guest-check system:

1. At the start of the shift, a set of guest checks is issued to each server. The numbers on the checks are recorded.

2. The server writes the customer's order on the guest check, which copies the order to the second, or duplicate, copy of the guest check.

Exhibit 8.9

DUPLICATE GUEST-CHECK SYSTEM

3. The second copy is turned in to the kitchen; the kitchen fills the order and keeps the duplicate. No order leaves the kitchen without the duplicate of a guest check.

4. When the customer has finished eating, he or she is presented with the original check that has been totaled.

5. The customer pays the bill.

6. At the end of the shift, the server checks out. All guest checks, used and unused, must be accounted for.

7. At the end of the shift, the manager collects all of the duplicates from the kitchen.

8. The bookkeeper matches the originals with the duplicates to see if there are any discrepancies, alterations, or missing checks.

Policies on how to handle missing checks vary among establishments. Some operations charge the servers a set amount for each missing check. Others do not. When setting this policy, note that the Federal Minimum Wage Law prohibits charging employees for mishaps if the charge brings the employee's wages below minimum wage. There are also state laws governing such practices.

PRECHECK AND POSTCHECK SYSTEMS

Probably the most important aspect of revenue security is matching the products sold by an establishment with the money received from customers. As a result, operations should ensure that all orders are recorded in the system. There may be situations when a server takes an order without recording it, charges the customer, and keeps the money for himself or herself. To prevent this kind of fraud, many managers implement a precheck and postcheck system for guest checks.

The precheck and postcheck process can be described as follows. The server records the order—precheck—on a guest check when the order is given to him or her by the guest. Kitchen and bar personnel are, in this system, prohibited from issuing any products to the server without a prechecked guest check. When the guest is ready to pay his or her bill, the cashier recalls the prechecked total—postcheck—from the system and the guest then pays the bill. In this case, products ordered by the guest, prechecked by the server, and issued by the kitchen or bar should match the items and money collected by the cashier. Today, precheck and postcheck systems are sold as a component of nearly all POS systems.

POS-INITIATED GUEST-CHECK SYSTEMS

In an establishment with a POS system, servers have a unique password to access the system. Thus, the potential for fraudulent access by other individuals is minimized. Operations that use a POS system function similarly to duplicate check systems, except that there are no pre-numbered checks (see *Exhibit 8.10*). Instead, each server is assigned a code. This means that all checks will have a server code and a table number. When the server inputs the customer's order into the system, the order is allocated to that server, who is then responsible for it. The order is simultaneously printed in the kitchen. No order should leave the kitchen without a printed directive. When the customer has finished his or her meal, the server prints the check and presents it to the customer, who then pays it. When the customer receives his or her change or charge slip to sign, the customer is given a copy of the check.

Exhibit 8.10

SIMILARITIES AND DIFFERENCES OF DUPLICATE CHECK AND POS SYSTEMS

Similarities

- If not careful, server can order incorrect meal with either system.
- Both allow for accounting of meals ordered.
- Both allow for reconciliation of meals ordered with meals delivered by the kitchen.
- Both allow for presentation of meal check to customer.

Differences

- POS uses a computer; duplicate check uses paper.
- POS system keeps running tally of sales; with duplicate check, sales must be totaled manually or taken from cash register.
- Order entry in POS system can automatically track food costs and perpetual inventory; food costs and inventory must be calculated manually when using a duplicate check system.
- Employee-level data, such as covers sold or sales per cover, are easily derived from POS systems. Deriving the same information from duplicate checks is largely a manual effort.
- Some POS systems can display more information for kitchen staff about the dish ordered. In the duplicate check system, only the server's notation of the order is displayed.
- In the duplicate check system, kitchen staff must know how to read each server's handwriting and shorthand notes. A POS system displays the order information on a screen or prints out a copy of the order.
- In the duplicate check system, reconciliation of original check and duplicate check must be done by hand. This is done automatically in POS system.

GUEST PAYMENT

Regardless of the guest-check control system used, one of the last steps in either system is for the customer to pay the bill for the food that was served. Restaurant and foodservice operations can accept payment in several forms. Some will use all of these payment options while others will use only some of them. In fact, some operations will accept cash only. The following list details each of the payment options:

- **Cash:** Cash is universally accepted.

- **Credit card:** A **credit card** obligates the card user to pay the credit card company for the products and services charged to the card. There is, however, a cost involved to the establishment. Either the bank that issues the card or the credit card company charges the operation a fee that is usually a percentage of the guest check. When the guest presents a credit card to the person collecting, it is processed for authorization, which completes the transaction. The cash terminal prints two receipts. The customer keeps one receipt and signs the other. The signed receipt is turned in with the cash proceeds at the end of the day.

- **Debit card:** From the operation's point of view, a debit card is processed in the same way as a credit card. However, the main difference is from the customer's standpoint. With a credit card, the cardholder pays for the entire amount due at the end of the billing cycle or extends payments and pays interest, much like taking out a loan. When using a **debit card**, the amount is immediately withdrawn from the cardholder's bank account.

- **Traveler's check:** Traveler's checks are used because of their security, as the issuing company safeguards them against theft. However, traveler's checks are decreasing in popularity and acceptance. There are two signature lines on a traveler's check. One signature line is signed when the check is issued. The second signature line is signed when the check is cashed. The person receiving the check should observe the customer signing the check and then compare the two signatures.

- **Personal check:** Personal checks are no longer accepted in many operations due to the possibility of receiving a bad check. A bad check could be due to **nonsufficient funds (NSF)**, which means the check's bank account did not contain enough money to cover the amount written on the check. A bad check could also be a stolen check. In either case, the check is returned to the operation, which is not paid for the value of the check. Restaurant and foodservice operations that do accept checks often pay for a check approval service that will preapprove checks and cover any losses from bad checks. When checks are submitted for payment, they should be stamped on the back "for deposit only" and deposited to the operation's account at the end of the day.

- **Other methods:** It is becoming more common for organizations to offer other means of payment, such as corporate accounts, house accounts, vouchers, and comps (complimentary meals). Each organization has its own policies on these methods of payment.

Preventing Skips

On occasion a customer will skip, or leave an establishment without paying for his or her meal. To prevent this from occurring, managers should teach their staff the following preventive measures:

- If the operation's procedure is that guests order and consume their food prior to receiving payment, instruct servers to present the bill for the food promptly after the guests have finished their meal.

- If the establishment has a cashier in a central location in the dining area, have that cashier available and visible at all times.

- If each server collects for his or her own guest's charges, instruct the servers to return to the table promptly after presenting the guest's bill to secure a form of payment.

- Train staff to be observant of exit doors near restrooms or other facilities that may provide an unscrupulous guest the opportunity to exit the dining area without being seen.

- Train staff members to notify the manager immediately if they see a guest leave without paying the bill.

- When approaching a guest who has left without paying the bill, the manager should ask the guest if he or she inadvertently "forgot" to pay the bill.

If a guest refuses to pay the bill or flees the scene, the manager should contact the police. He or she should then complete an incident report that notes the time and date of the incident, the name of the server who served the guest, the number of guests involved, the amount of the bill, a physical description of the guest, and a vehicle description. Under no circumstances should staff or managers attempt to physically restrain or detain the guest. The liability that could be involved could far outweigh the value of the unpaid dining bill.

Exhibit 8.11

Cash Handling

Whether a cashier, counter attendant, or server handles the cash transactions in a restaurant or foodservice operation, the procedure is the same (*Exhibit 8.11*). **Cash-handling procedures** are the activities that operations follow to ensure that all cash and charge transactions are accurate and accounted for. For the purposes of this discussion, the term *cashier* will be used to describe the employee handling the transaction.

1. A bank is issued to each cashier. A **bank** consists of coins and dollar bills sufficient to make change. The number of anticipated transactions determines the size of the bank. In some operations, a particular cash register or POS drawer, which holds signed credit card receipts and cash, may be assigned to multiple users.

2. The cashier receiving the bank counts and verifies the amount, since he or she is responsible for it.

3. No person other than the cashier should be allowed in the cash register during the cashier's shift. If the cashier leaves for any reason, the drawer should be locked. When more than one person has access to the same cash drawer, it becomes difficult to assign responsibility.

4. Only managers should be able to void register overrings and mistakes. However, operations that have high volume and where managers are not always available should pay close attention to the POS reports that show voids and overrings by a server.

5. The cashier collects cash, debit and credit charges, and personal checks, if allowed, from the customers.

6. At the end of the shift, the manager runs a sales total for the shift. Servers, cashiers, or bartenders should never take register readings. When an employee can figure out what he or she owes, it is very easy to skim excess cash from unrecorded sales. If a cash register is being used, the readings are locked with only the manager having a key. The readings are continuous; that is, they continue from shift to shift and are not totaled. Thus, the reading from the current shift has to be subtracted from the previous shift to get the sales for the current shift. If the operation uses a POS system, the manager enters a code to obtain a reading.

7. The cashier counts the drawer, sets aside the bank, totals the checks and the charges, and fills out a cash report or check-out sheet. If possible, this report should be completed in the manager's office

with the manager watching. As shown in *Exhibit 8.12*, a **cash report** or check-out sheet is a form filled out by the cashier to report all money, checks, and charge slips collected during the shift.

Coupons should be handled like cash. Each time a coupon is presented, the manager should write void across it. It is recommended that coupons be accounted for in the same way as cash or credit cards. When running the server reports at the end of a shift, make sure there is a corresponding number of coupons stapled to their accompanying order ticket.

8. The manager or a bookkeeper completes a daily sales report from the cash report and the register readings. A **daily sales report** is a form that shows sales, cash, and charges collected, as well as any money over or short for a shift. *Exhibit 8.13* shows an example of this report.

Notice that the cash report and the daily sales report are done separately and by two different people. In most operations, the cashier does not know what the cash register readings are for the shift. The reason for this is to encourage the reporting of actual results and to discourage theft. Another reason is that the cashier's bank may not match sales at the end of the shift. Most times, there will be overages or shortages; however, they should be minor. In fact, the manager should be suspicious if the cashier balances every time, as this may indicate skimming.

In the system where the server collects the payment from the customer, the server's cash report will always balance. The reason for this is that servers turn in the bank and cash and credit or debit slips for the total of their sales. Any monies left over are their tips. Whether the cash control is manual or automated, the manager must respect the importance of implementing procedures like these to ensure that all sales are accounted for.

SAMPLE CASH REPORT

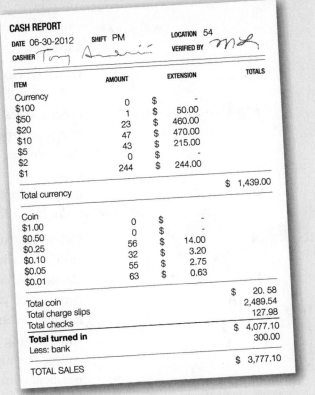

CASH REPORT

DATE 06-30-2012   SHIFT PM   LOCATION 54   VERIFIED BY

CASHIER Tony A_____

ITEM	AMOUNT	EXTENSION	TOTALS
Currency			
$100	0	$ -	
$50	1	$ 50.00	
$20	23	$ 460.00	
$10	47	$ 470.00	
$5	43	$ 215.00	
$2	0	$ -	
$1	244	$ 244.00	
Total currency			$ 1,439.00
Coin			
$1.00	0	$ -	
$0.50	0	$ -	
$0.25	56	$ 14.00	
$0.10	32	$ 3.20	
$0.05	55	$ 2.75	
$0.01	63	$ 0.63	
Total coin			$ 20. 58
Total charge slips			2,489.54
Total checks			127.98
Total turned in			$ 4,077.10
Less: bank			300.00
TOTAL SALES			$ 3,777.10

Exhibit 8.13

SAMPLE DAILY SALES REPORT

DAILY SALES REPORT

DATE 06-30-2012   SHIFT PM   LOCATION 54   VERIFIED BY

CASHIER Tony A_____

Registered reading ending	$	576,382.90
Less: register reading start		572,603.36
= Sales		3,779.54
Currency/coin turned in	$	1,459.58
Checks turned in		127.98
Charges turned in		2,489.54
= Total amount turned in	$	4,077.10
Less: bank		300.00
= Net turned in	$	3,777.10
Sales	$	3,779.54
Less: net turned in		3,777.10
= Difference	$	2.44
Reason: wrong change given		

WHO SHOULD HANDLE THE CASH?

While many operations now do most of their business through credit cards, there is still a large amount of cash that flows through most operations every day. This makes it very important to have a solid cash control process. Each establishment has cash-handling strategies that it uses.

- **Quick service:** In quick-service restaurants, several people could handle cash, depending on business volume. A counterperson takes a customer's order and enters it into the POS system. The order is printed in the kitchen. The counterperson collects money or completes a charge transaction with the customer. In some operations, the same counterperson assembles the order and gives it to the customer. In other operations, a number is printed on the customer's receipt and another counterperson gives the customer his or her order.

- **Cafeteria:** Customers select their own food and then proceed to the cashier's station, where they pay prior to going into the dining room. Cafeterias may be cash only or they may accept charge cards. Some commercial cafeterias have a checker who adds up what the customer has selected and gives him or her a receipt that is then paid to a cashier when leaving the premises. Some noncommercial cafeterias, such as college dorms, have no cashiers but operate on a monthly or semester payment plan.

- **Family style:** These operations include hotel coffee shops and truck stops. The cashier collects money for all transactions in the establishment. These operations normally use the duplicate guest-check or POS control system.

- **Casual and fine dining:** This group of restaurants includes upscale establishments and sports bars as well as bar and grill operations. In these operations, the server normally collects from the customer. Servers are responsible for their own checks and turn money and charge receipts over to the manager at the end of their shift. These operations have no cashier since each server acts as his or her own cashier.

One rule that every operation should follow: Any person who has access to the accounting records should not handle cash. To be able to commit fraud, a person must be in a position of trust. It may seem like it makes sense for the same person to receive the daily receipts and then prepare the daily sales report along with the deposit and take the deposit to the bank. However, the person in this scenario now has access to both records and cash. This makes it very easy for a dishonest person to cover up theft in the account records. The person keeping the account records can receive the daily sales report and the bank deposit slip, but never the cash.

SUMMARY

1. **Explain the importance of portion control to food cost.**

   The major cost control in restaurant and foodservice operations is portion control, or the amount of food in a serving. Successful food costing relies on correct portioning. This starts with the menu listing and is linked to the cook's line via the use of standardized recipes. Portion control devices are implements that assist in the portioning of food items. They include scoops, ladles, serving spoons, serving dishes, and portion scales. Whatever portion is represented on the menu must be translated accurately into the standardized recipes and then monitored in the serving process to ensure that food cost stays in line.

2. **Explain the importance of training, monitoring, and follow-through as they relate to the service team.**

   Employees have to be constantly trained and retrained to use the portion control devices and to give customers exactly what they are paying for. Follow-through is just as important as training. Managers need to constantly check portions to ensure that they are exactly what they should be. In addition, servers need to possess knowledge about menu item ingredients and cooking methods in order to reduce customer food or beverage item returns.

3. **Explain the importance of product usage and waste reports to control the cost of high-cost food items.**

   Use of costly food items such as steak and seafood should be monitored carefully because these food items are more vulnerable to theft and fraudulent sales by some employees. Therefore, par stock and daily usage of expensive items should be monitored regularly. Waste reports for high-cost food items should be analyzed carefully to detect any negative deviations in food waste from predetermined standards.

4. **List and describe each payment method used by the restaurant and foodservice industry.**

   There are many ways for customers to pay for food and beverages. Cash is universally accepted. Credit cards and debit cards involve a cost to the operation. The bank that issues the card and the credit card company charge the operation a fee that is usually a percentage of the guest check. Traveler's checks are decreasing in popularity and acceptance. Not many operations still accept personal checks due to the possibility of receiving a "bad check," in which case the operation is not paid for the value of the bad check. Organizations may also offer other means of payment, such as corporate accounts, house accounts, vouchers, and comps. Each organization has its own policies on these methods of payment.

5. **Explain how to complete a daily sales report.**

   A daily sales report is a form that shows sales, cash, and charges collected, as well as any money over or short for each shift. The manager or a bookkeeper completes a daily sales report from the cash report and the register readings.

APPLICATION EXERCISE

Cathy operates a small, upscale bakery in a quaint resort village in the mountains. She uses a duplicate guest-check system and compares the total daily sales report with guest receipts. Sales figures and guest orders are as follows:

Daily Sales Report
Date: Friday, September 20
Prepared by:
Location:
Shift:
Verified by:

Sales:

Cash sales	$1,111.30
Sales by check	$ 72.78
Credit card charges	$ 944.85

Orders:

Guest food orders: $1,671.90

Guest beverage (alcoholic and non-alcoholic) orders: $577.23

1. Calculate total sales and total guest orders.

2. How much is the discrepancy between total sales and total orders?

3. What are some possible causes for this difference?

4. What solutions would you suggest to eliminate this problem?

REVIEW YOUR LEARNING

Select the best answer for each question.

1. **What is at the center of portion control?**
   A. The inventory
   B. The cashier
   C. The server
   D. The menu

2. **If a portion served is slightly higher than standard, what will happen?**
   A. Guest satisfaction will go down.
   B. Labor costs will decrease.
   C. Food quality will go down.
   D. Food costs will go up.

3. **A food-production cost-control training manual should contain**
   A. standard weights and measures.
   B. customer service standards.
   C. table management reports.
   D. daily sales reports.

4. **Why might an operation use suggestive selling?**
   A. To increase profitability
   B. To decrease server efficiency
   C. To keep front-of-the-house staff engaged
   D. To limit the number of dishes the kitchen has to track

5. Monitoring high-cost items, such as steak and seafood, on the cook's line is best done by

   A. creating a product usage report.

   B. monitoring guest ordering reports.

   C. using a standardized recipe.

   D. installing a POS system.

6. In the duplicate guest-check system, the guest checks turned in by the cashier and the copies from the kitchen are matched by

   A. the chef.

   B. the server.

   C. the customer.

   D. the bookkeeper.

7. The use of POS systems enables managers to

   A. increase sales.

   B. control portions.

   C. handle guest complaints.

   D. match sales with guest orders.

8. To make sure that everything leaving the kitchen gets paid for, the most popular system in use today is

   A. a cash-only system.

   B. the POS control system.

   C. a suggestive selling system.

   D. the duplicate guest-check system.

9. If a guest skips without paying his or her bill, what should a manager do?

   A. Write off the loss.

   B. Pursue the suspect.

   C. File a police report.

   D. Fine the server.

10. Cash register readings at the end of the shift are usually taken by the

   A. server.

   B. cashier.

   C. bookkeeper.

   D. manager.

9

Controlling Labor and Other Costs

INSIDE THIS CHAPTER

- Understanding the Cost of Labor
- The Relationship between Labor Cost and Business Volume
- Measuring Labor Productivity
- Labor Usage Forecasts
- Managing Payroll Records
- Optimizing Labor Productivity

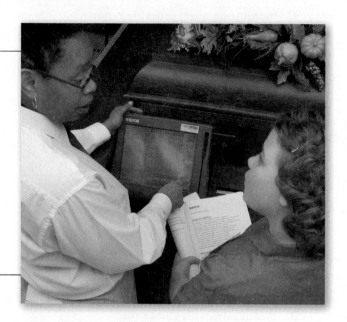

CHAPTER LEARNING OBJECTIVES

After completing this chapter, you should be able to:

- Explain how payroll cost, FICA, Medicare, and employee benefits make up labor cost.

- Explain the methods used to measure labor productivity.

- Outline the steps involved in controlling labor costs.

- Describe the components and factors to consider in the development of a master schedule.

- Describe the methods used for managing payroll records.

- Explain how managers can optimize labor productivity.

KEY TERMS

covers per server, p. 242

crew schedule, p. 245

employee turnover, p. 251

Federal Insurance Contributions Act (FICA), p. 229

fringe benefits, p. 230

labor contract, p. 250

master schedule, p. 242

Medicare, p. 229

overtime, p. 249

payroll dollars, p. 240

productive, p. 232

productivity standard, p. 234

quality standard, p. 234

sales per labor hour, p. 235

standard man-hours (SMH), p. 238

CASE STUDY

Paul is the service manager at Twyla, a fine-dining restaurant. Recently, he has been struggling with his labor costs. The number of guests per server is dropping and guest surveys have not been positive for the last two weeks.

Paul has spent the last two days reviewing standard operating procedures, labor hours, and payroll cost. However, he has lost both of his top-performing servers over the last month and the in-house wine training has had to be postponed. Plus, he has hired a new shift manager and she is still in the "trial" stage of training.

1. If Paul reduces the number of service staff on each shift, what impact, if any, will that have on guest service and employee morale?

2. What can Paul do to reduce the negative effect on sales and customer service due to the departure of the top two servers?

3. What are the consequences of postponing wine training?

UNDERSTANDING THE COST OF LABOR

Labor costs consume the second-largest part of a restaurant or foodservice organization's revenue, after food costs. Because of this, managers must use the available cost controls to the greatest extent possible. However, labor is a very difficult cost to control for three reasons:

- Managers are dealing with people—their personalities, their ability to work with others, their productivity and quality of work, and their individual personal problems. Managers may need to be reminded that the two most important groups affecting business success are customers and employees. An operation must respect and appreciate both.

- Labor costs have a limited range of adjustments. Food and beverage costs may be managed using price adjustments, portion controls, and purchasing strategies. Labor costs, however, cannot be controlled by paying lower wages. The minimum wage sets the floor for the price of labor in the United States. On top of that, supply and demand help create the industry wage scale. An employer who deviates too far from the industry wage scale will find it hard to attract and retain good employees.

- The future is unknowable. When scheduling employees, the manager does not know for certain what future sales will be or how many employees will actually be needed. While every manager strives to make accurate sales projections, unforeseen events can lead to sales increasing or decreasing. Managers must be able to make adjustments quickly so that labor cost does not get out of line.

Payroll Cost

Payroll cost is the amount of money that is spent for employee wages. Recall from chapter 1 that payroll costs—as part of the overall labor cost—can be fixed, variable, or semivariable (see *Exhibit 9.1*). The fixed payroll cost is usually manager salaries. Managers often are paid a salary that remains the same regardless of sales volume. For example, if the general manager's salary is $70,000 per year, that is the amount the general manager would receive, regardless of whether the operation brings in $500,000 or $2 million per year.

The hourly employees needed to staff the operation during the slowest hours, meal periods, and days of the week make up the greatest portion of labor cost. It is the "skeleton crew" needed to open the doors even when there is little or no volume. Unless managers or other employees are doing more than one job, labor cannot be further reduced without jeopardizing quality standards. The remainder of the hourly wage workers—waitstaff, line cooks, and dish washers—are scheduled according to anticipated sales. For example, more staff is scheduled at peak sales times. This means that staff payroll costs are higher during peak sales times than they are at slower sales times. Since staff

Exhibit 9.1

PAYROLL COSTS VERSUS SALES

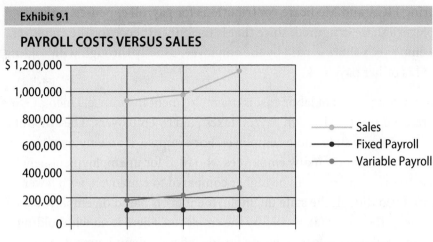

Variable payroll costs change in direct proportion to sales, while fixed payroll costs do not.

payroll costs increase or decrease in proportion to sales, staff payroll cost is a variable cost.

Adding the fixed management payroll cost to the variable staff payroll cost results in a semivariable payroll cost (see *Exhibit 9.2*). This semivariable payroll cost increases as sales increase and decreases when sales decrease but not in direct proportion with sales.

Benefits Costs

Often the terms *labor cost* and *payroll cost* are used interchangeably in the restaurant and foodservice industry. They are, in reality, two different things. As explained, payroll cost is the total of employees' salaries. Labor cost, as expressed on the income statement, is all-inclusive and includes the employer's contribution to FICA and Medicare, workers' compensation insurance, and employee benefits as well as wages. All of these must be calculated into the total labor cost. It is also important to remember that payroll cost is the gross total of the paychecks (pay before taxes are deducted), not net total.

The **Federal Insurance Contributions Act (FICA)** is a program for retirement and medical benefits administered by the federal government and paid for by employers and employees. This program sets aside money for Social Security payments. Both employers and employees pay FICA at a preestablished percentage of wages, up to a certain wage ceiling. These rates can sometimes fluctuate, so savvy managers check with accountants or tax professionals when setting up payroll. Likewise, **Medicare** contributions are money set aside for health benefits for people age 65 or older and for individuals with certain disabilities. Medicare is also paid at a set percentage, but unlike the Social Security tax, there is no cap (ceiling or limit). When

Exhibit 9.2

LABOR IS A SEMIVARIABLE COST

Labor is considered a semivariable cost because it has a fixed component (salaried employees), as well as a variable component (hourly employees).

Manager's Memo

Offering benefits is one way that a business attracts and retains the best employees. These may include paid vacation, health insurance, and other benefits. However, offering employee benefits can make up as much as 50 percent of an employer's payroll costs.

Of the benefits an employer can offer, managers should ask themselves which benefits they find most desirable, which will be most appealing to the staff, and what are some ways that employers can reduce benefit costs but still offer desirable benefits to employees?

figuring FICA and Medicare contributions for payroll expenses, only the employer's share is figured, since that is the only expense for the employer. The employee's share is paid by the employee, usually through withholding from his or her paycheck.

Another component of labor cost is unemployment insurance. Unemployment insurance is funded through payroll taxes paid by employers. The amount of this tax varies by state and by employer. For example, if an employer has terminated or laid off many employees who filed for unemployment benefits, that employer's tax rate will be higher compared to employers with fewer claims. Even though the state unemployment tax is based on employee salaries and wages, the entire tax is paid by the employer. There is no withholding from an employee's salary or wages for the federal unemployment tax.

Fringe benefits, also called employee benefits, vary widely from company to company, but are also part of the overall labor cost. **Fringe benefits** provided by an employer have monetary value but do not affect an employee's basic wage rate. Employers may offer all, some, or none of the following benefits:

- Paid holidays
- Paid vacation
- Paid sick days
- Health insurance
- Life insurance
- Dental insurance
- Company-paid retirement plans
- Paid continuing education

Over the past few decades, the cost of group insurance policies (health, dental, vision, life, disability) has risen significantly. As a result of these escalating costs, most companies now require employees to pay a portion of the premium cost. This amount is usually collected through employee payroll withholding. The employer's net cost (or expense) is simply the total amount of premiums paid to the insurance company minus the portion of the cost the employer collects from its employees.

Adding payroll costs, employer's FICA and Medicare contributions, unemployment tax, and the costs associated with employee benefits gives managers the total labor cost. The example in *Exhibit 9.3* illustrates the difference in the wage rate per hour and the actual labor cost per hour for the operation. Benefit costs normally range from 15 to 30 percent of the base pay per hour for restaurant and foodservice operations. Operations can pay lower wages to employees who receive tips, such as servers. This is why the hourly wage for a server in *Exhibit 9.3* is estimated as $2.13. In the example in *Exhibit 9.3*, the benefit cost percentage is 18.65 percent for all three positions.

The cost of each benefit item is calculated by multiplying the benefit cost percentage of each respective item by hourly wage. For instance, unemployment tax cost per hour for a server earning $2.13 per hour is calculated as follows:

$2.13	×	3%	=	$0.064
Hourly wage		**Benefit cost percentage for unemployment tax**		**Unemployment tax cost per hour**

Exhibit 9.3

LABOR COST PER PRODUCTIVE HOUR

Description	Server	Prep Cook	Shift Supervisor
Hourly wage	$2.13	$7.25	$12.00
Social Security/Medicare (7.65%)	0.16	0.55	0.92
Unemployment tax (3%)	0.06	0.22	0.36
Workers' compensation (2%)	0.04	0.15	0.24
Vacation (2 weeks/year) (4%)	0.09	0.29	0.48
Sick leave (1 week/year) (2%)	0.04	0.15	0.24
Total cost per hour	$2.52	$8.61	$14.24

If the employee received health insurance and the annual premium was $2,985, paid by the company, the total cost per hour would then be higher, as seen in *Exhibit 9.4*. Total annual working hours are estimated at 40 hours over 51 weeks (due to vacation time). As a result, health insurance contributes an additional $1.46 cost per hour ($2,985 divided by 2,040 hours).

Exhibit 9.4

LABOR COST INCLUDING HEALTH INSURANCE

Description	Server	Prep Cook	Shift Supervisor
Hourly wage	$2.13	$ 7.25	$12.00
Total cost per hour (with benefits)	2.52	8.61	14.24
Health insurance ($2,985/2,040 hours)	1.46	1.46	1.46
New total cost per hour	$3.99	$10.09	$15.69

It is important that all costs of labor be considered when determining the actual costs and evaluating the performance of an operation. Labor costs are a significant portion of the expenses for an operation, even when the majority of employees are paid at the minimum wage. To ensure efficiency and profitability, these costs must be controlled.

REAL MANAGER

EMPLOYEE PRODUCTIVITY AND SALES

While operating a concession stand, I noticed that most of the people ordered the burger with the works, a large soda, and a regular fries. The price came to $10.50. If someone paid with a $20.00 bill, the cashier had to give change of a $5 bill, four $1 bills, and two quarters. This process slowed down the line, as the cashiers were bogged down with the transactions.

By changing the price for the bundled meal to $10.00, the transaction time was reduced and the lines were shorter. With shorter lines, we were able to sell to more customers, hence increasing sales.

THE RELATIONSHIP BETWEEN LABOR COST AND BUSINESS VOLUME

As explained in earlier chapters, costs are divided into three categories—fixed, variable, and semivariable. Fixed costs are costs that stay the same regardless of sales volume. Variable costs are costs that increase and decrease as sales increase or decrease and do so in direct proportion. Semivariable costs are costs that increase and decrease as sales increase and decrease, but not in direct proportion. The reason for the lack of a direct relationship with a semivariable cost is that this type of cost is made up of both fixed costs and variable costs. Payroll and labor are good examples of a semivariable cost—both consist of fixed and variable costs. Variable payroll costs change in direct proportion to sales, while fixed payroll costs do not.

MEASURING LABOR PRODUCTIVITY

Productive is defined as producing or capable of producing an effect or result. For a restaurant or foodservice manager, that normally means producing abundant sales, profits, and customer satisfaction. To make this happen, staff members need to be as efficient and productive as possible during the time they are on the clock. Productivity and labor cost efficiency should not be monitored and assessed only by the numbers, however. Managers should not lose sight of the qualitative side of cost control numbers. If customer service is compromised, the initial savings of lower labor costs may be followed by a decrease in sales, caused by customers deciding to go to another establishment for faster or better service.

Labor Cost Percentage

So, how should managers maximize and measure productivity? To look simply at the dollars spent is to see only part of the picture. The traditional productivity measurement is the ratio of labor cost to total sales. This allows managers to compare labor cost to sales volume by converting it into a percentage of sales. This is called labor cost percentage. For example, suppose that an operation spent more labor dollars in July than in June. By merely looking at the dollars spent, it is not easy to determine if this increase indicates a problem or not. However, by converting labor costs in June and July to a percentage of sales, the manager could determine if corrective action is needed. To calculate labor cost percentage, divide the actual labor cost by sales as shown in the following formula:

Labor cost ÷ Sales = Labor cost percentage

For example, if an establishment's sales are $12,000 for a week and the labor cost is $4,000 for the same week, then the labor cost percentage for that week is 33.3 percent:

$$\underset{\text{Labor cost}}{\$4,000} \div \underset{\text{Sales}}{\$12,000} = \underset{\text{Labor cost percentage}}{33.3\%}$$

While most operations look at labor cost percentage monthly, many also analyze it daily by using a calculation for the estimated daily payroll cost percentage. Divide the weekly fixed cost (management salaries) by the number of days that the restaurant is open that week to get the daily fixed payroll cost:

Weekly management salaries ÷ Days open = Daily fixed payroll cost

Add the daily fixed payroll cost to the variable payroll cost for hourly employees to get the total daily payroll cost:

$$\underset{\text{payroll cost}}{\overset{\textbf{Daily fixed}}{}} + \underset{\text{payroll cost}}{\overset{\textbf{Daily variable}}{}} = \underset{\text{payroll cost}}{\overset{\textbf{Total daily}}{}}$$

The variable payroll cost is taken from the master schedule, which will be covered later in this chapter. Divide the total daily payroll cost by the anticipated sales for that day to get the estimated daily payroll percentage:

$$\underset{\text{payroll cost}}{\overset{\textbf{Total daily}}{}} \div \underset{\text{daily sales}}{\overset{\textbf{Anticipated}}{}} = \underset{\text{payroll cost percentage}}{\overset{\textbf{Estimated daily}}{}}$$

As an example, assume that the managers' combined salaries for a seven-day week are $1,400. The daily variable cost on Monday is $500, and the anticipated sales are $2,100 for that day. First, figure the daily fixed payroll cost:

$$\underset{\substack{\textbf{Weekly management}\\\textbf{salaries}}}{\$1,400} \div \underset{\textbf{Days open}}{7} = \underset{\substack{\textbf{Daily fixed}\\\textbf{payroll cost}}}{\$200}$$

Now, calculate the total daily payroll cost:

$$\underset{\substack{\textbf{Daily fixed}\\\textbf{payroll cost}}}{\$200} + \underset{\substack{\textbf{Daily variable}\\\textbf{payroll cost}}}{\$500} = \underset{\substack{\textbf{Total daily}\\\textbf{payroll cost}}}{\$700}$$

Finally, calculate the estimated daily payroll cost percentage:

$$\underset{\substack{\textbf{Total daily}\\\textbf{payroll cost}}}{\$700} \div \underset{\substack{\textbf{Anticipated}\\\textbf{daily sales}}}{\$2,100} = \underset{\substack{\textbf{Estimated daily}\\\textbf{payroll cost percentage}}}{33.3\%}$$

While the estimated daily payroll cost percentage is not as accurate as a weekly or monthly labor cost percentage, when compared to the operation's standard labor percentage it gives managers a picture of whether the operation is on budget for payroll cost. If the cost is out of line, they can take immediate action to correct the problem and help ensure that the weekly or monthly payroll is within budget. Without taking a daily reading on labor cost, managers could be unpleasantly surprised when the month-end report is prepared.

While the traditional labor cost percentage indicates to managers when costs are out of line, it does not provide any specific information. For example, a monthly income statement shows the payroll for the entire period as a single figure. This number includes wages from employees in all job categories: waitstaff, cooks, prep cooks, dish washers, and managers. It is not possible to determine from this which area of the operation may not be meeting standards. It also does not show during which meal period or day of the week the greatest variance occurred.

Another challenge with using only the traditional labor cost ratio to judge staff productivity is that the numbers are historical and after-the-fact. There is nothing managers can do about what has already happened. As much as possible, labor cost must be precontrolled, which requires cost figures to be calculated weekly, if not daily.

In addition to the issues that affect labor cost directly, there are several indirect factors that can cause an operation's labor cost to get out of line: quality standards and productivity standards. A **quality standard** is a level of excellence used to measure customer satisfaction, while a **productivity standard** is a level set by managers to measure the amount of work performed by an employee. The key word here is *standard*. Before managers can measure an employee's effectiveness, they must develop standards.

Quality standards are established with purchasing specifications and standardized recipes, and are measured using the steps outlined in chapter 7. Quality standards are particularly important since they affect not only labor cost but also the products that customers receive. The primary reason for establishing quality standards is to have a measure in place to ensure that customers receive the products they pay for. However, in an indirect way, quality standards also affect labor cost.

If an employee does not prepare a product that meets the standard, it must be redone. This costs money, not only in terms of wasted product that increases food cost, but also in terms of reduced productivity that increases labor cost. To track products in the back of the house that do not meet standards, a waste report is used. As explained in a previous chapter, the waste report gives managers a tool to track any potential problems with food-preparation standards.

Guests Served per Labor Hour

The two most widely used numbers for measuring restaurant or foodservice labor productivity are the guests served per labor hour and number of guests (covers) served per labor hour. The formula for calculating these numbers is simple, whether an operation uses a cash register, a POS (point-of-sale) system, or a cigar box. Since the guests served per labor hour formula does not include a dollar figure in it, managers may want to know the sales volume per each labor hour used. For this purpose, **sales per labor hour** is calculated by adding all the sales for a specific period (hour, day, week, etc.) and then dividing the total by the total number of labor hours used during the same time period, as shown in *Exhibit 9.5*.

In this example, the operation brought in $39,542 worth of revenue. It used 1,098 labor hours to generate that revenue. For every labor hour used, the operation brought in $36.01 in sales.

The guests served per labor hour is calculated the same way, but the total number of guests, or covers, is used rather than total sales dollars, as shown in *Exhibit 9.6*. In this formula, the operation served 2,297 people during the given time period. The operation expended 1,098 labor hours to service that number of guests. As a result, the operation served 2.09 guests for every hour expended.

Guests Served per Labor Dollar

Sometimes it is more helpful to look at productivity from a labor cost, rather than labor hour, perspective. This is because hourly wages are only one of the components of total labor cost. In other words, when a manager looks at labor hours, he or she does not distinguish between salaried and hourly employees. In addition, looking at labor hours does not offer any information about benefit costs. Therefore, using labor hours is useful for scheduling purposes, but labor dollars should be used when evaluating the profitability of operations.

The guests (covers) per labor dollar is calculated by substituting the total labor dollars for total labor hours, as shown in *Exhibit 9.7*.

In this example, the operation served 2,297 guests. It cost $12,176 in labor dollars to serve this number of guests. For every dollar of labor spent, the operation serviced 0.188 guest.

Exhibit 9.5

SALES PER LABOR HOUR

Time period: 7 days
Total sales: $39,542
Total labor hours worked for the week: 1,098

$39,542	÷	1,098	=	$36.01
Total sales		Total labor hours worked for the week		Sales per labor hour

---

Exhibit 9.6

COVERS PER LABOR HOUR

Time period: 7 days
Total number of covers served: 2,297
Total labor hours worked for the week: 1,098

2,297	÷	1,098	=	2.09
Total number of covers served		Total labor hours worked for the week		Covers per labor hour

---

Exhibit 9.7

COVERS PER LABOR DOLLAR

Time period: 7 days
Total number of covers served: 2,297
Total labor dollars for the week: $12,176

2,297	÷	$12,176	=	0.188
Total number of covers served		Total labor dollars for the week		Covers per labor dollar

Exhibit 9.8

LABOR COST PER COVER

Time period: 7 days
Total number of covers served: 2,297
Total labor dollars for the week: $12,176

$12,176	÷	2,297	=	$5.30
Total labor dollars for the week		Total number of covers served		Labor cost per cover

To calculate the labor cost per guest served, simply reverse the formula and divide the labor dollars by the number of guests as in *Exhibit 9.8*.

Using this final formula, the operation spent $12,176 in labor to serve 2,297 guests. Dividing the total costs by the number of guests reveals $5.30 per guest in labor costs. Labor cost per guest should be compared to operational standards. To do that, the manager needs to divide labor cost per guest by average check per guest. For example, if average check per guest for the period is $16.50, then the labor cost percentage would be 32.12 percent (5.30 divided by 16.50). If an establishment has a standard labor cost percentage of 30 percent, then the manager needs to reduce labor cost percentage by either controlling labor costs or increasing the average check per guest.

Calculating labor cost per guest per shift also enables managers to make adjustments for lunch and dinner shifts. In addition, labor cost per guest should be calculated for weekdays and weekends to make sure they manage labor expenses efficiently.

LABOR USAGE FORECASTS

Managers need to forecast the total labor usage budget. They do so by using the expected sales volume. Assume a given operation has a target labor cost percentage of 30 percent. Labor usage will be based on expected sales volume per shift and day. Managers will calculate the labor hours needed based on total labor budget for the respective period, but will allocate those hours according to the sales volume. More hours will be given to periods of higher sales volume (Friday and Saturday nights, for instance), and fewer hours to shifts with lower sales volumes. Once labor hours are estimated, then actual employee schedules should be prepared.

Exhibit 9.9 outlines the five basic steps to controlling labor costs:

1. The first step is to forecast the number of covers or revenues for each scheduled meal period.

2. The second step is to calculate what labor costs should be. The approved operating budget will give managers those data.

3. The third step requires managers to plan the number of labor hours to be used in each area, such as the kitchen, bar, or service.

4. The fourth step is to develop an employee schedule, also called the labor usage forecast.

5. The fifth and final step is to evaluate actual labor costs compared to budgeted labor expenses.

Exhibit 9.9

STEPS IN CONTROLLING LABOR COSTS

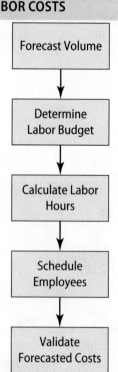

Forecast Volume
↓
Determine Labor Budget
↓
Calculate Labor Hours
↓
Schedule Employees
↓
Validate Forecasted Costs

Volume Forecasting

As noted, the first step in developing a schedule is to forecast the number of guests or revenue for the week. Based on historical guest counts or revenues, managers can make a "best guess" as to what might happen in the future. Again, managers should consider trends, future changes in the local economy, and special events such as sporting events, concerts, or holidays, all of which may affect business volumes (*Exhibit 9.10*). This is information that managers need in order to estimate guest counts and revenue for each day in the schedule period.

Exhibit 9.10

TRENDS AFFECT SALES

Both local trends, such as increased tourism or convention business, and national trends, such as the economy or unemployment rate, affect sales projections.

Determining the Labor Budget

A budget helps managers plan the financial activities related to their daily operations. A budget is a projection of sales, costs, and profit that is used to guide day-to-day operational decisions. It is also used to create the master schedule. Budgets are created based on historical figures and forecasts of what will happen in a specific period. These are projected on a monthly basis and totaled for a yearly figure.

The amount allocated for labor is dependent on several factors:

- Menu items
- Level of expertise needed to execute the menu items
- Method and amount of preparation needed
- Type of service
- Location
- Special events or holidays

In addition, managers must take into account any actions that may cause an increase in cost. For example, if the union contract that covers hourly employees will expire next year and must be renegotiated, managers would likely forecast an increase in the hourly rate paid to staff. This would cause the labor cost to increase in next year's budget. While budgets are basically an estimate, if carefully done, they can provide a guideline to assist the manager in achieving profitability. Budgets are normally generated in the form of a pro forma income statement, like the one in *Exhibit 9.11*. That is, they show sales, costs, and profit. Each line is shown in dollars as well as percentages.

Exhibit 9.11

LABOR COST PER GUEST OR COVER

Pro Forma Income Statement
Slippery Noodle Restaurant

Sales	$ 1,450,000	100%
Cost of food sold	− 493,000	34%
Gross profit	$ 957,000	66%
Labor expenses	$ 420,500	29%
Other controllable expenses	93,000	6%
Noncontrollable expenses	+ 330,000	23%
Total expenses	$ 843,500	58%
Profit	$ 113,500	8%

Note that for an operation to achieve its target profit, the sales projections listed in its budget must be met. Additionally, the operation's costs must be held to their standards, which is the budgeted dollar amount or percentage for each type of cost. Therefore, managers should make sure that payroll cost is in line with the budgeted standard. If the cost goes below the standard, the quality of food or service could suffer, resulting in lost sales. If the cost is above the standard, the profit will be reduced.

Calculating the Number of Labor Hours Needed

The third step in the process is to calculate the number of labor hours needed. Generally, the number of labor hours is translated into the number of **standard man-hours (SMH)**. SMH represent the number of employee work hours necessary in each job category to perform a given volume of forecasted production. For example, if it takes eight servers to serve 500 covers in a given three-hour lunch shift, the standard man-hours required would be calculated as follows:

$$8 \quad \times \quad 3 \quad = \quad 24$$

Number of servers	**Number of hours**	**Total man-hours of servers' work**

The 24 man-hours would become the standard for serving 500 covers over the lunch shift. Any extra hours scheduled would be a red flag for the manager. Of course, if fewer than the standard man-hours are scheduled, the manager should be concerned about the level of service being provided to customers.

Managers must decide what standards should be established for the different levels of sales volume. The number of standard man-hours required would not necessarily change in direct proportion with the volume of business. Twenty-four server hours for 500 covers works out to 20.83 covers per standard man-hour. At a lesser volume—300 covers, for instance—7 servers representing 21 standard man-hours may be necessary because of the accepted relative inefficiency at lower volume. At the lower volume, the number of covers per standard man-hour is 14.3 covers. So, based on the manager's service standards, 21 man-hours are required for 300 covers.

A table of SMH requirements used in conjunction with forecasts of sales volume is helpful in both forecasting labor usage and scheduling employees as efficiently as possible. There is no single industry standard that can be applied when calculating these numbers because each operation has unique variables. Kitchen design, dining-room layout, menu, and service style affect the efficiency of the system.

Creating Employee Schedules

The creation of a work schedule is the fourth step in forecasting labor usage. The schedule helps ensure that labor cost will meet the budgeted standard. After establishing the standard man-hour requirements and the minimum number of labor hours ("skeleton crew") that are necessary to operate, managers can begin to build a schedule. There are three main considerations when developing a work schedule:

- Labor cost
- Level of service
- Employee morale

The challenge is in achieving the appropriate balance in these three areas. Managers might be tempted to control labor cost by scheduling one or two fewer employees than necessary to handle the business volume. However, understaffing can significantly impact customer service.

An untrained or shorthanded staff will eventually result in higher product cost from waste, customers returning meals, or inaccurate portioning. On the other hand, overstaffing with the intent of improving customer service drives up labor cost. Having too many employees can even result in underperformance because employees may tend to stand around and lose focus on the guest.

Staffing requirements are unique to each operation. They can even vary from one location to the next within multiple-unit concepts, due to a difference in skill level of employees, hours of operation, layout of the establishment, and many other factors. Managers need to begin the process with a basic scheduling format. The ideal schedule for a particular operation will be influenced by customer counts, the flow of business, and the efficiency of the production system used to execute meal production and delivery.

When scheduling, it is important for managers to adopt the philosophy of a "customer-friendly schedule," which means to schedule employees to ensure that the last customer in the door receives the same level of service and quality of food as the first customer.

In addition to calculating the labor hours needed, managers must also determine the **payroll dollars**, which is the amount of money available for payroll for a scheduling period. Payroll dollars are calculated from anticipated labor costs, which can be complicated to calculate. Fortunately, there is a step-by-step process that managers can follow to forecast these costs for their operations.

Step 1. Determine total available labor dollars:

To determine the total available labor dollars for a period, the operation's standard labor cost percentage (discussed earlier in this chapter) is multiplied by the projected sales:

$$\begin{array}{ccc} \textbf{Standard labor} & \times & \textbf{Projected} & = & \textbf{Total available} \\ \textbf{cost percentage} & & \textbf{sales} & & \textbf{labor dollars} \end{array}$$

For example, if the standard labor cost percentage for the Tiki Hut is 28 percent, and the projected sales forecast for next week is $17,000, the amount of money available for labor that week is $4,760:

$$\begin{array}{ccc} \textbf{28\%} & \times & \textbf{\$17,000} & = & \textbf{\$4,760} \\ \textbf{Standard labor} & & \textbf{Projected sales} & & \textbf{Available labor} \\ \textbf{cost percentage} & & \textbf{forecast} & & \textbf{dollars} \end{array}$$

Step 2. Subtract costs of benefits and deductions:

Now that there is a forecasted amount of money available for labor, the next step is to subtract the cost of benefits and deductions. These amounts must be accounted for and subtracted from the total dollars available for labor.

Suppose the Tiki Hut expects to spend $1,748 on benefits and standard deductions during the upcoming one-week period. The dollars available for payroll would now look like this:

$$\begin{array}{ccc} \textbf{\$4,760} & - & \textbf{\$1,748} & = & \textbf{\$3,012} \\ \textbf{Amount available} & & \textbf{Benefits and} & & \textbf{Remaining} \\ \textbf{for labor} & & \textbf{deductions} & & \textbf{payroll available} \end{array}$$

Step 3. Subtract fixed labor costs:

Now that the dollar amount available for scheduling employees has been calculated, the next step is to figure how much of payroll is a fixed cost (management salaries) and how much is variable (hourly employees). This is important for creating a work schedule because, for the most part, only the variable-cost employees are listed.

To figure how many dollars are available for scheduling hourly employees, subtract the total of fixed-cost (management) salaries from the payroll dollars available. Assume that management salaries at the Tiki Hut total $1,350 per week. Then the labor dollars available for hourly employees are $1,662:

$3,012	−	$1,350	=	$1,662
Payroll dollars available		**Fixed-cost salaries**		**Dollars available for variable-cost employees**

Step 4. Convert budget costs into labor hours:

Steps 1 through 3 show the available budget that can be spent on labor hours. Now this figure must be converted into hours. Managers will need to do this for each labor area: kitchen, bar, and service staff (see *Exhibit 9.12*). Take the kitchen area as an example. Using the previous steps, a manager determines there is $6,678 for hourly employees, excluding benefits, for the first week of May. The operation is open for dinner only six days each week, and the employee schedule is planned on a weekly basis. The manager first determines how much can be spent on wages in an average day:

$6,678	÷	6	=	$1,113 (rounded)
Wage budget for week		**Work days in week**		**Average daily budgeted wages**

Exhibit 9.12

LABOR DOLLARS AND LABOR HOURS

Labor budget should be converted into labor hours for each labor area (*e.g.*, kitchen, bar, service staff).

If the average hourly wage (not including benefits) is $14, the manager can schedule no more than 80 labor hours in the kitchen (food production, ware washing and dish-washing employees) for an average day in May:

$1,113	÷	$14	=	80 (rounded)
Average daily wages		**Average hourly rate**		**Budgeted labor hours per day**

For the week, there should be no more than 480 average budgeted waged labor hours:

80	×	6	=	480
Average budgeted hours per day		**Days in week**		**Budgeted labor hours per week**

An average is used because there are days where more labor hours can be scheduled based on high business volume days, and these will be offset with fewer labor hours scheduled on lower business volume days to meet the average labor hours per day goal.

MASTER SCHEDULES

Creating a good work schedule for a restaurant or foodservice operation is difficult but not impossible. The right number of people with the right combination of experience and productivity levels must be available to work each shift. Managers often use a master schedule to simplify the preparation of weekly schedules. A **master schedule** is a template, usually a spreadsheet, showing the number of people needed in each position to run the restaurant or foodservice operation. There are no names listed on a master schedule, simply the positions and the number of employees in those positions. A master schedule is a useful tool for showing the staffing requirements for each day of the week. Managers should refer back to the master schedule to verify that the correct number of staff have been scheduled for each shift.

The master schedule should be divided into sections for each job department, such as waitstaff, bar staff, kitchen prep, line cooks, and so on. Alternatively, managers may decide to create a master schedule for the front of the house and one for the kitchen or back of the house. Having master schedules for these two areas is useful when more than one department manager is preparing schedules.

Once the total amount that can be spent on hourly employees is known, it must be broken down between the front-of-the-house and back-of-the-house positions. The reason for this is the difference in hourly wages paid to these employees. Servers generally receive tips and are therefore paid less by the operation than job classifications that do not receive tips.

Managers can determine the hourly staff needed in specific positions by using productivity standards. The most efficient method of scheduling the service staff is by using a productivity standard known as **covers per server**. This is the number of customer meals that a waitstaff member can serve in an hour. Each operation should have a standard figure for covers per server that is based on past customer counts and productivity levels. This standard is then measured against the sales forecast to determine the number of servers to schedule.

For example, the productivity standard at the Tiki Hut is 20 covers per server per hour. The forecast for a daily lunch rush (assuming a four-hour period) is 300 covers. Using this information, 3.75 servers must be scheduled:

$$\underset{\text{Covers}}{300} \quad \div \quad \underset{\text{Hours}}{4} \quad = \quad \underset{\text{Covers per hour}}{75}$$

$$\underset{\text{Covers per hour}}{75} \quad \div \quad \underset{\text{Covers per server}}{20} \quad = \quad \underset{\text{Servers}}{3.75}$$

THINK ABOUT IT . . .

Some people say that a server's tip is solely determined by the customer. Do you agree with this statement? In what ways might the server and other restaurant or foodservice personnel influence the tip?

The number of servers to schedule is rarely even. The question then becomes: round up or round down? There is no single answer, as it depends on the employees involved. If the staff is relatively new and not fully trained, it would be wise to round up and add another person. On the other hand, if the staff is experienced with a high productivity ratio, it would probably be best to drop a person.

The service schedule should then be further refined, as not all of the guests are going to arrive in an orderly fashion of 75 guests per hour. In the example shown in *Exhibit 9.13*, during the hour of 12:00 noon to 1:00 p.m., a spike of 90 covers is expected, which is 10 covers more than the standard for the 4 servers. During this period, the waitstaff will be working at a maximum rate with 4 servers. Consequently, the schedule may call for 1 server to open, and then more servers can be added as the customer count increases over the meal period. Given these patterns, the schedule would look similar to the one shown in *Exhibit 9.13*.

Exhibit 9.13

STANDARD SERVICE SCHEDULE FOR THE TIKI HUT

Position	10 a.m.	11 a.m.	12 p.m.	1 p.m.	2 p.m.	Total
Total covers	15	75	80	90	40	300
Server A						5 hours
Server B						4 hours
Server C						3 hours
Server D						3 hours
Total hours						15 hours

Once the servers are scheduled, the number of hours available for the rest of the positions must be determined. The remaining payroll dollars available are calculated using the following formula:

$$\begin{array}{ccccc} \text{Payroll} & & \text{Fixed} & & \text{Server} & & \text{Remaining} \\ \text{dollars} & - & \text{payroll} & - & \text{payroll} & = & \text{payroll dollars} \\ \text{available} & & \text{dollars} & & \text{dollars} & & \text{available} \end{array}$$

At the Tiki Hut, 4 servers have been scheduled for the time period of 10:00 a.m. to 2:00 p.m. The total hours for servers for that shift are 15. Assuming a rate of $2.13 per hour, the server payroll for the day is $31.95. Assuming the establishment is open six days, the server payroll for the week is $191.70. Therefore, the remaining payroll dollars available for the other hourly positions at the Tiki Hut would be:

$$\begin{array}{ccccc} \$3,012 & - & \$1,350 & - & \$192 & = & \$1,470 \\ \text{Payroll dollars} & & \text{Fixed payroll} & & \text{Server payroll} & & \text{Remaining payroll} \\ \text{available} & & \text{dollars} & & \text{dollars} & & \text{dollars available} \end{array}$$

At this point, the remaining payroll dollars available are divided by the average wage per hour to determine the number of hours available to schedule. Again, each operation should use a standard figure for its average wage per hour. Keep in mind that this standard is an average, and that some employees will make more than this and some will make less:

$$\begin{array}{ccc} \textbf{Remaining} & \textbf{Average} & \textbf{Number of hours available} \\ \textbf{payroll dollars} \;\div\; & \textbf{wage} \;=\; & \textbf{to schedule remaining} \\ \textbf{available} & \textbf{per hour} & \textbf{hourly employees} \end{array}$$

The resulting number gives the manager a good idea of how many hours are left to work with. Assuming the average hourly rate per hour at the Tiki Hut is $7.50, the number of hours remaining available to schedule hourly employees for the week can be determined:

$$\begin{array}{ccc} \$1,470 \;\div\; & \$7.50 \;=\; & \textbf{196 hours} \\ \textbf{Remaining} & \textbf{Average} & \textbf{Number of hours available} \\ \textbf{payroll dollars} & \textbf{wage} & \textbf{to schedule remaining} \\ \textbf{available} & \textbf{per hour} & \textbf{hourly employees} \end{array}$$

The rest of the necessary positions round out the master schedule. At the Tiki Hut, a host/cashier, a buser, a dish washer, two cooks, and a salad person must be added to the four servers already scheduled to work. The master schedule would then look like the one shown in *Exhibit 9.14*.

Exhibit 9.14

MASTER SCHEDULE FOR THE TIKI HUT

Time	8 a.m.	9 a.m.	10 a.m.	11 a.m.	12 p.m.	1 p.m.	2 p.m.	Total Hours	Rate	Total Payroll
Covers			15	75	80	90	40			
Position										
Server A			✗	✗	✗	✗	✗	5	$ 2.13	$ 10.65
Server B				✗	✗	✗	✗	4	2.13	8.52
Server C				✗	✗	✗		3	2.13	6.39
Server D				✗	✗	✗		3	2.13	6.39
Host/Cashier			✗	✗	✗	✗	✗	5	7.50	37.50
Buser				✗	✗	✗	✗	4	6.00	24.00
Dish washer				✗	✗	✗	✗	4	6.50	26.00
Cook 1	✗	✗	✗	✗	✗	✗		6	10.00	60.00
Cook 2		✗	✗	✗	✗	✗	✗	6	8.00	48.00
Salads	✗	✗	✗	✗	✗	✗		6	8.25	49.50
Total										$276.95

Based on this master schedule, the total variable payroll for one day at the Tiki Hut is $276.95. This total includes servers as well as all other hourly staff. To determine the total variable payroll for the week, multiply the daily number by the number of days an operation is open that week. In the Tiki Hut example this would be:

$$\underset{\substack{\text{Payroll} \\ \text{for a day}}}{\$276.95} \quad \times \quad \underset{\substack{\text{Days open} \\ \text{in the week}}}{6 \text{ days}} \quad = \quad \underset{\substack{\text{Dollars available for} \\ \text{variable-cost employees}}}{\$1661.70}$$

Validating Forecasted Labor Costs

The fifth and final step is to evaluate actual labor costs against the budgeted labor expenses. Once the master schedule is written, it needs to be validated to see if it meets the company standard. Managers perform this validation by adding the fixed payroll cost and the variable payroll cost to get total payroll cost. The employer's share of FICA and Medicare and the cost of employee benefits are added to total payroll cost to get the total labor cost:

$$\textbf{Fixed payroll} \; + \; \textbf{Variable payroll} \; = \; \textbf{Total payroll}$$

$$\underset{\substack{\text{Total} \\ \text{payroll}}}{} \; + \; \underset{\substack{\text{FICA/Medicare/} \\ \text{unemployment insurance} \\ \text{(employer's share only)}}}{} \; + \; \underset{\substack{\text{Employee} \\ \text{benefits}}}{} \; = \; \underset{\substack{\text{Total} \\ \text{forecasted} \\ \text{labor cost}}}{}$$

The total forecasted labor cost is divided by the forecasted sales. The result is the forecasted labor cost percentage.

$$\underset{\substack{\text{Total forecasted} \\ \text{labor cost}}}{} \; \div \; \underset{\substack{\text{Forecasted} \\ \text{sales}}}{} \; = \; \underset{\substack{\text{Forecasted labor} \\ \text{cost percentage}}}{}$$

Once the labor costs are validated according to this process, managers can then move on to creating the schedules that employees will actually see and refer to.

CREW SCHEDULES

Once the master schedule has been written, checked, and validated against the company standard, it can be used as the foundation for preparing both the management and crew schedules. A crew schedule is a chart that shows employees' names and the days and times that they are to work. A sample crew schedule is shown in *Exhibit 9.15* on the next page. Although the employee categories are different, there are common considerations for both groups. These include the following:

- Using all the elements of the master schedule as a source of information for the management and crew schedules

- Communicating well in advance and considering various events and business needs when developing the schedules

THINK ABOUT IT . . .

Have you ever been scheduled to work but really wanted the night off? What would have been the implications for the manager and other employees if you did not show up for your shift?

Exhibit 9.15

CREW SCHEDULE FOR THE TIKI HUT, WEEK OF JUNE 20

Schedule prepared by B. Hawk on June 10

Name	Position	Monday	Tuesday	Wednesday	Thursday	Friday	Saturday
Brenda	Server	10–3	10–3	10–3	10–3	10–3	10–3
Sung Lee	Server	11–3	11–3	11–3	11–3	11–3	11–3
James	Server	11–2	11–2	11–2	11–2	11–2	11–2
Tony	Server	11–2	11–2	11–2	11–2	11–2	11–2
Rubin	Host/Cashier	10–3	10–3	10–3	10–3	10–3	10–3
Wendy	Buser	11–3	11–3	11–3	11–3	11–3	11–3
Mike	Dish washer	11–3	11–3	11–3	11–3	11–3	11–3
Carlo	Cook 1	8–2	8–2	8–2	8–2	8–2	8–2
Judy	Cook 2	9–3	9–3	9–3	9–3	8–2	8–2
Tonya	Salads	8–2	8–2	8–2	8–2	8–2	8–2

- Keeping the schedule as balanced and equitable as possible
- Granting employees' scheduling requests whenever possible
- Building flexibility into the schedules
- Using sales projections to ensure that the right number of employees are scheduled

Keep in mind the legal constraints regarding scheduling minors. For example, minors cannot work after certain hours of the day. Also, when school is in session they may not be scheduled for more than three hours.

Crew schedules should clearly indicate the following:

- Dates and days of the week covered by the schedule
- Employees' names
- Scheduled days to work and to be off from work
- Scheduled start and stop times
- Date of schedule preparation and name of the manager preparing it

Crew schedules should be distributed approximately 7 to 10 days before the first day of the schedule period. Crew schedules can be distributed to employees in several different ways. In some properties they are posted on employee bulletin boards and in other central locations (*Exhibit 9.16*). They also can be included with paychecks. Increasingly, managers email schedules or make them available on the operation's intranet system. An intranet is a network of computers for a single organization that can be at the same or different locations.

Exhibit 9.16

It is almost impossible to build a schedule that will satisfy all employees. There will be some who are dissatisfied because they are scheduled for days and times that conflict with outside plans. Some may feel they did not get enough hours, whereas others will object to too many hours, and still others will resent not being scheduled for the "money shifts." It is recommended that the manager asks for schedule preferences from employees. This is particularly important when hiring part-time employees who may have other jobs, school, or other activities that limit their availability.

Factors that are unknown when the schedule is written can undermine even the most careful planning. An unforeseen winter storm can virtually close down a neighborhood establishment but stretch an interstate highway operation to beyond its capacity. A sudden thunderstorm will keep people inside, but a power outage caused by the storm will bring them out of their houses to get something to eat. Factors other than weather, such as earthquakes, crime sprees, and a national or international event on television, will also affect people's behavior.

Care must be taken when adjusting the schedule, however. Employees are dependent on the income provided by working their posted hours, and they also plan activities outside work based on the posted schedule. By frequently changing the schedule, a manager risks alienating some staff members and contributing to employee turnover.

Once a schedule has been written, calculate the projected labor cost. Compare the projected cost with the master schedule to see if the crew schedule meets budget expectations. If the budget target is not met, the gap between the budget target and actual performance is the variance. The manager should review all variances and should seriously investigate significant variances and make adjustments as necessary.

OPEN FOR BUSINESS

RESTAURANT TECHNOLOGY

There are literally hundreds of scheduling software solutions for restaurant and foodservice operations. Many of the POS systems offer labor scheduling tools. Most POS systems include time and attendance tracking, as well as a database of employee information. Schedule preferences, usually defined as employee availability, are maintained within the labor schedule modules. These types of programs help managers reduce the time it takes to build schedules and also serve as time clocks for employees.

There are also Web-based software solutions that can be accessed from any computer connected to the Internet. These time-clock management systems allow managers to post schedules online, providing access to employees and notifying employees of schedule changes.

MANAGING PAYROLL RECORDS

Another control in maintaining labor cost is tracking the time that employees work. There are three methods to do this—time sheet, timecard, and time-clock software. Regardless of which system is used, it is imperative that a manager or bookkeeper review the time recorded by the employee and compare it to the schedule. Some employees have a habit of coming to work before their shift begins, clocking in, and then spending some time visiting with other employees before actually beginning to work. The same thing can happen at the end of an employee's shift. It takes only a few of these occurrences to put labor cost out of line.

Time Sheet

Post a chart with all of the employees' names near the schedule. When the employee comes to work, he or she marks the time of arrival and initials the chart. When the employee leaves at the end of the shift, he or she marks the time of departure and initials the chart.

Timecard

In this system, each employee has a timecard placed in a timecard rack. When the employee reports to work, he or she inserts the timecard into a time clock. When the employee leaves at the end of the shift, he or she does the same thing and places the timecard back in the rack. In this way, the employee's arrival and departure times are recorded on the timecard.

Electronic Time Records

The electronic method includes time clocks, POS systems as shown in *Exhibit 9.17*, and personal computers with time-clock software. Upon arriving at work, the employee logs in using a preassigned password. The software records the time. When the employee leaves at the end of the shift, he or she logs out, again using the password with the time recorded. Many of these electronic systems have payroll software that will calculate the total hours worked during a payroll period, along with federal and state withholding, FICA, and other deductions like health insurance. The software will then calculate the employee's paycheck. In some chain operations, the system is tied into the accounting department in the home office.

Exhibit 9.17

OVERTIME

There are a few occasions when employees will be working outside the schedule. In most states, an employee must be paid for attending an employee meeting. They should clock in and out for these meetings, just as they would for a regular shift. In some states, when an employer requires that employees wear uniforms, they must allow the employee to change clothes on company time. In this case, a reasonable amount of time should be allocated for the employee to change. While under these circumstances the employee is working off the schedule, under no circumstances should employees be allowed to work off the clock. If employees are working, they should be clocked in and paid. Not only is this the ethical way to treat employees, it is also necessary for liability insurance.

But nothing can make a labor cost go over budget quicker than overtime. Federal law, as well as the laws of most states, requires that nonmanagement employees working **overtime**—any hours worked beyond 40 hours in a workweek—be compensated for overtime hours at a rate of at least 1.5 times the employee's regular rate of pay. At that rate, it does not take long to use up any available payroll dollars. Therefore, overtime should never be scheduled or planned. Only in an extreme circumstance should managers authorize employees to work overtime.

OPTIMIZING LABOR PRODUCTIVITY

It is important to balance benefits of employee productivity with expenses that need to be incurred to improve productivity. In other words, managers need to decide on the amount of training that improves employees' skills and knowledge to help them reach targeted productivity levels. In addition, controlling and reducing employee turnover is important for a restaurant or foodservice operation. However, managers need to carefully plan the employee labor budget and the rewards for performance because no organization has unlimited funds. Managers needs to be cognizant of the fact that there may be fewer returns on investment dollars after employees reach a targeted level of productivity. That is, disproportional spending on additional training, coaching, pay, or rewards may not further improve productivity.

Training

Training improves the skills and knowledge of employees. This in turn can increase productivity and lower labor costs. Offering training to improve skills and knowledge is a way to recognize and reward employees. Restaurant and foodservice operations that invest in employees through training programs generally have lower labor costs. Developing the capability of the people in an organization ultimately develops the capability of the organization. See chapter 8 for additional information on employee training.

Coaching

Some organizations, including certain chain establishments, use coaches. These professionals help engage employees and create focus on the company culture, which helps employees feel important, energized, and understood. Operations looking for improved employee retention may want to work with staff on a one-to-one basis, through coaching or in workshop groups, to help them develop or improve behavioral skills. Employees must know that there is a possibility to move from being the technical expert to leading a team, from kitchen manager to general manager, or from general manager to partner. Investing in talent development and management transitions not only helps the employee but also energizes the organization.

Labor Contracts

An organized labor contract can have a huge impact on an establishment's labor cost. A **labor contract** is an agreement between management and a union that represents the employees and deals with wages, employee benefits, hours, and working conditions. Unions in the hospitality industry are limited primarily to large metropolitan areas such as New York, Chicago, and Los Angeles, as well as entertainment destinations such as Las Vegas.

In an operation with a labor contract, the wages, employee benefits, and working conditions are all negotiated. Designated representatives from the union and management conduct the negotiations. However, it is important for the negotiations to be settled in a way that is acceptable to management and can keep labor costs within their controls.

For the most part, restaurant and foodservice operations that are under a labor contract will have a higher labor cost. This is due to higher wages and because more employee benefits are generally provided in union operations. In addition to wages and benefits, production output, layoff procedures, and disciplinary actions might also need to be negotiated. These actions also increase labor costs, since management may not be able to get higher productivity out of employees or lay employees off during a downturn in sales.

Reducing Employee Turnover

Employee turnover—the number of employees hired to fill one position in a year's time—is a factor that directly impacts labor cost. Unfortunately, it is a widespread problem in the restaurant and foodservice industry. While some turnover is normal, excessive turnover can be a major problem. Some restaurant chains have turnover rates of 300 percent. This means that for every position the restaurant has, three people have been hired during the past year to fill that position.

Many managers do not know how much turnover really costs. Others do not know how to reduce employee turnover. Yet others mistakenly believe that turnover is inevitable in the industry. Inevitable or not, turnover is expensive. One of the principal reasons that hourly workers quit is high management turnover, and many industry observers attribute high management turnover to situations created or aggravated by high turnover among hourly workers. Employees also mention unwillingness to increase pay, tendency to schedule impossibly long shifts, and generally poor recognition of good performance as common reasons for leaving.

Veteran industry trainers and consultants recommend that managers do the following to avoid high employee turnover rates:

Exhibit 9.18

- Recognize good employees for the work they do.
- Pay fair and competitive wages.
- Offer a fair bonus program.
- Offer competitive benefits and incentives.
- Conduct regular performance reviews so employees know where they stand and how to improve (*Exhibit 9.18*).
- Listen to employees' ideas and their goals.
- Find time to coach, not control.

CALCULATING EMPLOYEE TURNOVER RATES

To calculate the turnover rate, count the number of employees hired during the year and divide by the average number of employees needed. Multiply the result by 100 to convert the decimal into a percentage. The result is the turnover rate percentage:

Persons hired per year ÷ Average number of employees = Turnover

Turnover × 100 = Turnover rate percentage

For example, if an operation needed 50 employees to operate, and over a year it hired 150 people, its turnover rate would be 300 percent:

$$\underset{\text{Persons hired per year}}{\text{150 persons hired}} \quad \div \quad \underset{\substack{\text{Average number of} \\ \text{employees}}}{\text{50 employees needed}} \quad = \quad \underset{\text{Turnover}}{3}$$

$$\underset{\text{Turnover}}{3} \quad \times \quad 100 \quad = \quad \underset{\text{Turnover rate percentage}}{300\%}$$

A certain amount of turnover is normal and healthy. It takes new talent and ideas for an operation to keep its edge. The goal of a successful employee retention program is not a turnover rate of zero. A good retention program helps keep the achievers and the good workers. Ultimately the operation wants to cultivate and maintain a highly motivated professional staff.

Not all establishments have high turnover rates. Those that can control turnover have a better chance of making their payroll budget. This is because turnover is very costly. Consider these expenses associated with employee turnover:

- Cost of help-wanted advertisements, temp agencies, and employment agencies
- Lost management time for interviewing, holding orientation meetings, and training new employees
- Labor cost of the employee that the new hire "shadows"
- Unproductive time of the new employee on the payroll during training
- Accounting costs associated with new hires and employees who have left the company

While few companies track the exact cost of employee turnover, it can be expensive. Taking a conservative figure of $150 per hire, if an operation hires 25 new employees during the year, the cost is $3,750. If, as in the previous example, 150 employees are hired during the year, the cost of the new hires is $22,500. The cost for hiring comes directly out of profit.

Direct expenses notwithstanding, there are indirect costs of turnover to the operation as well. Two of the most prevalent indirect costs are loss of productivity and customer dissatisfaction due to the inefficiencies and mistakes of a new hire. It should be obvious that reducing employee turnover will improve the bottom line and also result in a smoother operation, ultimately resulting in customer satisfaction.

FACTORS AFFECTING EMPLOYEE TURNOVER

To reduce employee turnover, a manager should examine why employees leave in the first place. Some employees depart for other restaurant or foodservice operations, while some leave the industry altogether. Studies have shown that there are several common reasons for employee departures:

- **Lack of recognition or reward:** Employees should be rewarded and recognized when they display exemplary performance. Conscientious workers become disillusioned when exemplary performance is not rewarded.

- **Lack of teamwork:** The restaurant and foodservice industry is a team industry. Superstars or individuals who are interested only in advancing their own agenda damage the team. This sort of selfishness will kill the initiative of team players and drive them to other organizations.

- **Lack of control:** All employees must feel they have some input toward how their work environment operates.

- **Quality of life issues:** People work to make a living; they do not live to work.

- **Stress:** Workers who feel overwhelmed and out of control are not very productive, nor do they deliver quality, responsive service. There is a limit to how long anyone is willing to work in a high-stress environment.

- **Poor communication:** Employees must feel they are in the know. Proper communication impacts their level of personal job security and sense of importance to the company. Employees that are constantly left out of the communication loop become disenchanted and leave.

- **Poor recruiting:** Quality-motivated workers expect to work with other quality-motivated workers. Operations that fail to hire high-quality staff discourage their better workers. Operations that cannot fill vacancies and require employees to work short-handed will inevitably lose quality-motivated workers.

- **Lack of leadership:** Leaders provide a shared vision, inspire loyalty, and motivate their team to high levels of accomplishment. Leadership holds the team together and enables growth.

- **Lack of training:** Failure to invest in training undermines employees' personal sense of security and delivers a message that they are not valuable.

- **No opportunities for advancement:** High-achievers need to know that there are career opportunities that will allow them to grow in an organization.

- **Lack of benefits:** Health insurance continues to be an issue in many parts of the restaurant and foodservice industry. For workers with families, the lack of employer-supported health insurance can be the factor between staying and leaving.

- **Lack of standards:** Quality workers expect to work in an operation that will not tolerate poor sanitation practices, lack of commitment to guest services, sloppy personal appearance, and other failures of basic standards.

- **Working conditions:** Workers expect a safe, clean work environment.

Other reasons workers leave may include the following:

- Incompatible management style
- Pay versus effort
- Job inequities
- Boredom
- Lack of job security
- High turnover
- Lack of respect
- Lack of feedback
- Sexual harassment
- Racism
- Personal reasons

The financial costs of replacing employees are staggering. Managers should embrace practices aimed at not only reducing turnover, but increasing retention as well.

SUMMARY

1. **Explain how payroll cost, FICA, Medicare, and employee benefits make up labor cost.**

   Labor cost includes payroll cost, the employer's contribution to FICA and Medicare, workers' compensation insurance, and employee benefits. It is also important to distinguish that payroll cost is the gross (pay before taxes are deducted), not net, total of employee paychecks. Adding payroll costs, employer's FICA contribution, employer's Medicare contribution, and the costs associated with employee benefits gives managers the total labor cost.

2. **Explain the methods used to measure labor productivity.**

   Managers use several methods to track and measure labor productivity. The first method is to track labor cost percentage. This figure tracks the cost of labor in relations to sales. Some operations track these costs monthly, while others track payroll cost percentage on a daily or weekly basis. Managers also track indirect factors on productivity, such as performance against quality and productivity standards.

3. **Outline the steps involved in controlling labor costs.**

   Managers follow five steps in controlling labor costs. First, they calculate what the labor costs should be. Then, they forecast the sales volume, or the number of expected guests. Third, they plan the number of labor hours each department will use. They use this calculation to develop an employee schedule. Finally, managers compare and evaluate actual results against the plan to determine where changes or adjustments should be made.

4. **Describe the components and factors to consider in the development of a master schedule.**

   A master schedule is a template, usually a spreadsheet, showing the number of people needed in each position to run the restaurant or foodservice operation. Labor hours may be expressed as standard man-hours. The master schedule lists positions and the number of employees in those positions. To create the master schedule, the manager must forecast how many servers and other staff members will be needed to serve the expected customers. The master schedule should be divided into sections for each job department such as waitstaff, bar staff, kitchen prep, or line cooks. Having separate master schedules for the front of the house and the kitchen or back of the house helps when more than one department manager is preparing schedules. To estimate projected labor cost, multiply the number of hours scheduled for each job position times the average hourly rate for that job position. Add the results for each position to get a total cost. Actual cost will vary because not everyone makes the same hourly rate, but the numbers will provide a guideline for budgetary purposes.

5. **Describe the methods used for managing payroll records.**

   Operations use one of three systems to manage payroll records. Time sheets require employees to sign in and out when their shifts begin and end. Time-cards work similarly, except that each employee has a card he or she inserts into a time clock to register the start and end of shifts. Many operations now use electronic time records, which are often tied to an operation's POS system or to a personal computer. Some of these systems are tied directly to payroll records.

6. **Explain how managers can optimize labor productivity.**

   There are several steps managers can take to ensure high productivity. Training and coaching are often techniques that improve worker output and morale. Understanding how to work within labor contracts can also impact productivity and labor costs. Finally, reducing employee turnover is critical, and managers must understand the factors that cause employees to leave so that they can minimize the impact of these issues.

APPLICATION EXERCISE

Develop a server schedule using the following information.

Purpose: To prepare a three-day time schedule for variable employees based on the sales forecast. The operation is of a fast-food type located in a college town, with the variable employees able to interchange in the various positions. There are two full-time (Bob and Tammy) and eight part-time employees.

Scheduling Guidelines:

- No split shifts are allowed (e.g., lunch and dinner).
- Full-time employees always work 8 hours a day and are not given split shifts.
- Part-time employees should work at least 4 hours a day and no more than 8 hours a day.
- Part-time employees are limited to 20 hours total work for Friday, Saturday, and Sunday.
- The minimum number of employees allowed per shift is four; the maximum is five. Dinner shift on Sundays is the only exception to these rules.
- Dinner shifts on Friday and Saturday should always have two full-time employees on staff.

Employee Scheduling Constraints:

- Tammy needs to have Sundays off.
- Jamal cannot work after 7 p.m.
- Carl cannot work after 3 p.m. (except Saturdays).
- Lei cannot work after 3 p.m. on Fridays.
- Pete is not allowed to work after 7 p.m.
- Paloma is not available on Sundays.
- Jean is available for any shift on any day.
- Barb can work on Saturdays and Sundays only after 7 p.m.
- Miguel cannot work between 11 a.m. and 3 p.m. on Fridays and Saturdays.

Employee Pay Rates: The labor cost for full-time employees is $10 per hour. Part-time employees have a labor cost of $8 per hour.

Labor Budget Target: Labor cost percentage should be below 25 percent on a daily basis.

Sales Forecast: The sales forecast for Friday, Saturday, and Sunday is as follows:

	Hours: 11 a.m.–3 p.m.	Hours: 3 p.m.–7 p.m.	Hours: 7 p.m.–11 p.m.
Friday	$550	$ 900	$1,000
Saturday	550	850	1,100
Sunday	650	750	475

1. Prepare a labor schedule for Friday, Saturday, and Sunday.
   a. Show the schedule in table format.
   b. What is the total for labor hours for each day?
   c. How much is the total labor cost for each day?
2. What is the daily labor cost percentage for each day?
3. What is the average labor cost percentage for all three days?

REVIEW YOUR LEARNING

Select the best answer for each question.

1. **What is included in labor cost?**
   A. Both fixed and variable employee wages
   B. Salaries, taxes, and employees' hourly wages
   C. Only taxes and workers' compensation insurance
   D. All payroll costs, taxes, benefits, and insurance

2. **FICA is contributed to by**
   A. employer and employee.
   B. employer and union.
   C. federal and state governments.
   D. state and local governments.

3. **If an operation's sales are $48,000 per week and labor cost is $15,600 for the week, what is the labor cost percentage?**
   A. 0.286%
   B. 0.325%
   C. 0.312%
   D. 0.287%

4. **The most efficient way to determine the number of servers to schedule is**
   A. covers per labor hour.
   B. average wage per hour.
   C. sales per cover.
   D. weekly sales projections.

5. **Labor usage forecast is primarily based on**
   A. employee turnover.
   B. sales volume.
   C. food cost.
   D. benefit costs.

6. **What are budgets based on?**
   A. Projected profits
   B. Projected sales and costs
   C. Quality standards
   D. Standard benefits and payroll

7. **A manager is working to schedule cooks for her operation's lunch shifts in a given week. Each shift is three hours long, and the establishment is open Monday through Friday. She has budgeted $540 in labor costs for cooks, and her average hourly cost is $12 per hour. How many cooks can she schedule on average?**
   A. 1
   B. 2
   C. 3
   D. 4

8. **What are standard man-hours (SMH)?**
   A. Actual employees
   B. Numbers used to determine staffing needs
   C. Hours that can be calculated only by the week
   D. Number of productive hours

9. **Which method for managing payroll is most efficient to calculate labor cost?**
   A. Time sheet method
   B. Labor forecast method
   C. Electronic time record method
   D. Timecard method

10. **If an establishment needs 12 employees to operate and hires 50 employees during the year, what is its turnover rate?**
    A. 24%
    B. 41.7%
    C. 240%
    D. 417%

10

Protecting Revenue

INSIDE THIS CHAPTER

- The Importance of Revenue Control
- External Threats to Revenue Security
- Internal Threats to Revenue Security
- Enhancing Revenue Security
- The Four-Step Revenue Security System
- Cash Audits
- Managing Accounts Payable
- Verifying Receipt of Goods and Services

CHAPTER LEARNING OBJECTIVES

After completing this chapter, you should be able to:

- Identify and explain the three parts of a revenue collection system.

- List the external and internal threats to revenue security.

- Explain the basic control standards to safeguard cash and credit card information.

- Describe the four steps in the revenue security system.

- Explain several ways to discourage theft by employees.

- List two important areas affected by accounts payable.

- Describe the steps in verifying the receipt of goods and services.

KEY TERMS

accounts payable, p. 275

auditing, p. 274

card verification value (CVV), p. 264

collusion, p. 265

counterfeit currency, p. 263

extension, p. 261

fraud, p. 260

guest relations discounts, p. 272

merchant account, p. 271

merchant services provider, p. 274

open tab, p. 263

overcharging, p. 261

Payment Card Industry (PCI), p. 268

petty cash, p. 275

service charge, p. 262

undercharging, p. 261

CASE STUDY

For the last few years, the husband–wife owners of Haney's Irish Pub have been receiving notices from their bank and credit card issuers saying that they need to upgrade their POS software. Almost 97 percent of the annual sales of $600,000 come from credit card payments. While the volume of credit card sales is high, money is tight in an economic downturn, and like any small business owner, they have put off any nonessential expenses as long as they can. However, they are hearing about the new credit card payment security standards that reduce the possibility of identity theft. Recently, one of their competitor's establishments had an identity theft incident involving over 200 customers. Haney's Irish Pub has not faced any issues yet, but the owners need to decide if they can afford to postpone the upgrade another year.

1. Who might be able to help the owners understand the new payment security standards?

2. What might happen if they do not comply with the new payment security standards?

3. Would it be possible for a smart but dishonest employee to steal data from an older POS system? If so, what could they do with that type of information?

THE IMPORTANCE OF REVENUE CONTROL

All businesses, regardless of their size or industry, must guard against the potential for fraud and abuse. The restaurant and foodservice industry is no exception. **Fraud** is defined as an intentional deception to cause a person to give up property or some lawful right. Fraud includes employee theft and covers a broad spectrum of acts by all categories of personnel. According to National Restaurant Association studies, employee theft averages just under $220 per person each year. So, an operation with 20 employees would lose $4,400 per year. In an industry that employs more than 9 million each year, those losses can add up to almost $2 billion annually, and experts caution that this number is probably very conservative.

The reality is that a dishonest person is going to behave in a dishonest way. However, security systems and tight controls help keep some people honest by making them think they might get caught.

There are also dishonest guests who would attempt to defraud the operation by using counterfeit currency, personal checks with no matching funds, or stolen credit cards. Charging the guests and collecting payment is all part of the revenue collection system. Managers must be attentive when determining the correct amount owed on each guest check, collecting the funds, and safeguarding those funds until they have been deposited. Safeguarding includes securing and holding revenue on-site and making sure that credit card processing is handled correctly and securely.

The restaurant and foodservice industry is hard and demanding. Managers and their staff work very hard and often put in long hours to generate revenue. It is extremely important for managers to develop procedures, policies, and systems to safeguard the money generated by the operation until that money is safely deposited in the correct bank account.

Three Parts of a Revenue Collection System

Attracting customers who will make food and beverage purchases is of paramount significance to the success of an establishment. However, the process does not end there. Charging the guest and completing the sales transaction is only the first step of a revenue collection system. Next, revenue must actually be collected, and finally, collected cash assets need to be protected. Thus, this system consists of three parts:

- Charging the guest
- Collecting revenue
- Protecting the operation's cash assets

Not every operation will have the same systems or safeguards because of different operational needs and guidelines. However, there are basic controls that every operation should implement.

CHARGING THE GUEST

The first step in revenue control is to make sure the guest is being treated fairly and honestly in each transaction. Most restaurant and foodservice transactions are very straightforward; the menu price states the amount for each item. However, if the server charges less than the correct amount or does not collect at all, the operation receives less than the correct amount of revenue. **Undercharging** is the term used when not enough revenue is collected. Undercharging will affect the profits, budget numbers, food and labor costs, and cash flow.

Overcharging is the opposite of undercharging. **Overcharging** is the act of charging more than the amount that should have be charged and collected. The causes of overcharging may be an oversight by the server, a simple math mistake, or keying in incorrect numbers. Or, it may be an employee attempting to defraud the guest and the operation. Overcharging the guests is just as bad and harmful as undercharging.

These are some possible effects of overcharging:

- Guests feel cheated and tell their friends, which negatively affects future sales.

- Guests leave with the perception that the establishment is too expensive. This perception may result in fewer visits or sharing the lack of value with their friends, again affecting future sales.

- Employees may feel that they "got away with it" and begin to overcharge more guests as a way to increase their take-home revenue.

No matter the revenue control system an operation uses, there is basic information that should be included on all guest checks presented to the customer:

- The name of each item should be clearly and accurately recorded. Items should be printed legibly by a machine or the server. One copy of the guest check is given to the guest and one should be retained by the operation.

- The number of items purchased must be clearly indicated.

- The prices of each item purchased should be recorded. Prices should exactly match the prices listed on the menu or recited by the server.

- All items should be accurately totaled. The **extension**—the price of an item multiplied by the number of items being purchased—should be clearly indicated, and servers or cashiers should use a machine if possible to reduce the chance of error.

- Tips, gratuities, and service charges that are included should be clearly indicated. Many operations use the terms *tips* and *gratuities* interchangeably. Other operations use *gratuity* as a mandatory preset percentage—for example, 18 percent—and have a separate line item for additional tips. This is different from a **service charge**, which is a labor-related fee, added by management, to be paid by guests. For example, some managers may impose service charges of 18 percent for parties of six or more customers. Service charges are also often used in catering and banquet operations. Whichever term is used, the amount charged should be listed as a separate item.

Following these simple rules will help ensure that guest charges are correct. It should be noted that the form of payment used by the guest to settle the charges does not affect this process.

COLLECTING REVENUE

Step two of revenue control is collecting the revenue or getting paid. This is normally as simple as collecting the exact amount of money indicated on the guest check. The payment may be made in cash, by check, or with a credit or debit card. There are three simple but important steps to every revenue collection transaction:

- Identify the employee collecting the money.
- Collect the correct amount of money.
- Properly record the transaction.

These steps are vital to help managers account for overcharges or undercharges.

PROTECTING CASH ASSETS

The third component of effective revenue control is protecting cash assets once they have been collected. Managers are often surprised to learn that most theft or fraud happens after the collecting and recording process is over. This chapter will explore a number of processes and systems to help protect the operation's assets.

EXTERNAL THREATS TO REVENUE SECURITY

One of the primary external threats to an establishment's revenue security is its guests. Guests may leave without paying, use counterfeit money, use a fraudulent credit card, or try to pass a bad check. Sometimes, guests make purchases with no intention of paying for them. The guests may just get up and leave without paying. A skip, also called a walk or a dine-and-dash, is the act of ordering products in an establishment and then leaving without paying. Additional information on preventing skips can be found in chapter 8.

There are procedures that may help an operation limit the number of skips:

- Present guest checks promptly after the guests at the table have completed their meal.

- In the bar, obtain and hold a credit or debit card whenever an open tab is created. An **open tab** is a temporary guest charge account that allows guests to purchase and consume products before paying for them. Open tabs may be particularly useful when a single card is authorized for a large group of guests.

- Require servers to monitor guest checks.

- Always assume the guest will pay. If a guest leaves the table without paying but is still in the operation, approach him or her politely and remind the guest that the server still needs to collect.

- Cashiers should be stationed centrally to ensure maximum visibility of the dining area.

Counterfeit currency is money that is produced to resemble official legal currency closely enough that it may be confused for genuine currency. Counterfeiters have become more sophisticated with access to new technology, specifically high-resolution color printers. Despite the fact that a server or cashier took the bills in good faith, counterfeit money is the responsibility of the establishment. If a manager tries to deposit a counterfeit bill, the bank is obligated to remove it from circulation and not give the account credit for it. In other words, the operation simply loses the money.

There are millions of counterfeit bills in circulation. The "paper and print" detection system is sufficient for most operations to counteract counterfeit bills. This is a two-part system. First, the paper should feel crisp and substantial in a new bill and soft in a worn bill. It is illegal to reproduce the distinctive paper used in the manufacturing of United States currency. Genuine currency paper has tiny red and blue fibers embedded throughout. Often, counterfeiters try to simulate these fibers by printing tiny red and blue lines on their paper. Close inspection reveals, however, that on the counterfeit note the lines are printed on the surface, not embedded in the paper. Counterfeit bills will feel lighter and floppier than a genuine bill. Second, the print on a real bill is also raised in some areas. Most counterfeit money is flat in all areas. In addition, paper bills have watermarks that can be seen when held against light.

For large bills, employees should use a money-tester pen. This pen allows them to detect a counterfeit bill before they accept it. They simply mark anywhere on the bill and observe the temporary coloring of the marked spot. If the spot turns yellow or amber the bill is good; however, if it turns black or brown, the bill is a counterfeit. If cash sales account for a majority of total sales, an operation may elect to use a counterfeit detector that emits ultraviolet light (see *Exhibit 10.1*). Users place the bill in question on a surface. Under the surface there are bulbs that emit ultraviolet light. These bulbs highlight and show hidden watermarks using the ultraviolet light.

Manager's Memo

Accepting cash payments has its benefits, but these benefits may come at a cost. For example, one of the major benefits of accepting cash is that it can be immediately deposited to the company's bank account. This in turn helps pay for supplies and food to be used in operations immediately. The cost of cash payments is that they need to be carefully counted and safeguarded. In addition, staff should be prudent against counterfeits when receiving larger bills ($20 or higher) from customers.

Exhibit 10.1

Credit Cards

As society becomes more and more cashless, an increased number of guests use credit and debit cards to pay for restaurant and foodservice purchases. A credit card allows the consumer to make purchases based on an established line of credit from the card-issuing bank. A debit card allows the consumer to make a purchase based on funds available in his or her bank account. The increased use of this type of credit creates opportunities for dishonest people to fraudulently use these cards.

Guests may present a fraudulent credit card to pay their bill. The card may be stolen, or it may have been created through identity theft. Card issuers are working to create cards that can limit the chance of guest fraud. These include three-dimensional designs, magnetic strips, encoded numbers, smart chips, and other features. Today's preauthorization verification systems are fast, accurate, and designed to reduce the chance of loss. Each card-issuing company has security recommendations, and restaurant and foodservice operations are required to follow these specific procedures for processing the card payment. The fraudulent use of cards by guests can be significantly reduced by training employees in the following procedures:

- Examine the credit card. Compare the signature on the receipt to that on the back of the card.

- Compare the name and last four digits embossed on the card to the name and last four digits on the sales receipt. The terminal should be set up to print only the last four digits of a card number for security purposes.

- Verify the card's expiration date.

- Input the card security code that is known as the **card verification value (CVV)** to verify the card. This is the three-digit code on the back of most credit cards. For some other types of cards, the code is on the front of the card and has four digits. The CVV should be entered at the point of sale, and the cardholder's code is verified by the issuing bank when the credit card is processed. If the CVV does not match, the employee should call the manager to determine if the operation should decline the transaction (see *Exhibit 10.2*).

- If necessary, ask the guest for a driver's license or other form of picture identification to confirm that the person presenting the card is the person named on the card.

While it is important to run verifications, obtaining an approval code does not ensure that a transaction is legitimate. An approval code means only that the credit card is active and the funds are available.

Personal Checks

Very few operations still accept personal checks, though there are exceptions. Accepting personal checks increases the risk that an operation will not get paid. Typically it is not possible to call the bank to ensure that the person has

Exhibit 10.2

Employees should ensure that a credit card's CVV is verified by the issuing bank before accepting the credit card.

sufficient funds in the account. So, each check is a gamble that it will not be returned and declared to have nonsufficient funds (NSF). With the trend more toward credit and debit cards, most establishments no longer accept the risk of personal checks.

INTERNAL THREATS TO REVENUE SECURITY

If guests are the primary source of external revenue security threats, the primary source of internal threats are a restaurant or foodservice operation's employees. For example, an employee may commit credit or debit card fraud by ringing a charge in twice and then swapping the second credit card revenue for cash. Sadly, this is a standard way for dishonest servers to increase the cash in their pockets. Normally, it is weeks later that the credit card statement is mailed and the customer checks it. He or she will call the manager to complain, and get the extra charges reversed. In most cases, the manager absorbs the loss and never questions the server.

There is a lot of truth to the saying, "the only people who can steal from you are the ones you trust." In the restaurant and foodservice business, and particularly in a small-business environment, the people who are in a position to do the most damage are the manager, bookkeeper, partners, key suppliers, or employees. More than other types of businesses, restaurant and foodservice operations have a higher potential of fraud and abuse. They normally have food, alcoholic beverages, supplies, and cash that may all be vulnerable. Unfortunately, these assets are not always well managed. A study by an international accounting and audit firm reported that 75 percent of organizations experienced some type of fraud during the prior 12 months, with employees being the perpetrators the majority of the time.

Employees who will steal from the business will, if possible, also steal from the guests. On average, it takes 18 months for an employer to catch an employee who is stealing. Most employee theft comes to the attention of the employer either through another employee or by accident. **Collusion**, when two or more employees work together for dishonest purposes, may go undetected for long periods. It is recommended that managers set up a system whereby honest employees may report employee theft anonymously.

There is a principle that has long been accepted in fraud prevention circles called the 10-10-80 rule, which maintains that 10 percent of people are always honest no matter what, 10 percent of people are dishonest and will steal at any opportunity, and the other 80 percent of employees are much less likely to steal if they believe they will be caught. The purpose of internal controls in a business is to increase the chance of an employee getting caught if they attempt to steal. The perception that an employee may be caught is just as important as the actual chances when it comes to employee behavior.

THINK ABOUT IT . . .

Personal checks are viewed equivalent to cash and are accepted by many businesses in several industries such as retail, real estate, and health care. However, very few restaurant and foodservice establishments accept personal checks. Why?

Managers must develop systems and policies that are simple, measurable, and easily understood by employees. These systems must also be easy to follow up and must be applicable to the operation. Correct systems and policies will keep the honest people honest. A dishonest person is dishonest and there is not much managers can do, although appropriate systems can detect or minimize the damage. Internal theft is normally a result of a weakness that can be addressed in one of the following areas:

- Poor hiring practices or lack of training
  - Conduct a thorough background check and interview all job applicants.
  - Adopt a strict code of conduct, post it, and make sure all employees are aware of it.
  - Educate employees about all internal security measures such as surveillance, audits, and inventory checks.
  - Create a positive work environment, which has been shown to deter employee fraud and theft. Open lines of communication, positive employee recognition, and fair employee practices will help reduce fraud and theft.
- Ineffective or lack of internal controls
  - Be clear that the company has a zero tolerance for employee theft of any sort. This should include actions such as taking a long lunch break without approval, using sick leave when not sick, doing slow or sloppy work, or coming to work late and leaving early.
- Controls limited to one or two key employees
  - Make sure responsibility is spread out to create a system of checks and balances. For more information on this, refer to chapter 5.

ENHANCING REVENUE SECURITY

Operations focused on purchasing, preparation, and service may easily overlook revenue security. However, the business operations cycle of an establishment does not end with the customer purchase. The next step in the business is to safeguard on-premise cash during business hours and later safeguard cash deposits until they reach a bank. Cash revenue security is particularly important for businesses such as nightclubs, where cash purchases make up approximately 70 percent of total customer payments. With the increase in credit card purchases, protecting customer card information has become a very serious matter. Some experts point out that restaurant and foodservice establishments account for 40 percent of all credit card fraud cases in the United States. As a consequence, using the latest industry standards to protect customer credit card information is critical for an establishment's reputation and financial success.

Safeguarding On-Premise Cash

The number one rule in controlling employee cash theft is to make sure that anyone who receives cash is not also able to take a register reading. If servers, cashiers, or bartenders can calculate what they "owe the house," it makes it easy for them to skim excess cash from unrecorded sales. Only managers should have access to register readings. Cash-handling procedures are the activities that operations follow to ensure that all cash and charge transactions are accurate and accounted for. See chapter 8 for more information.

One part of the cash-handling process is the completion of a "checkout sheet" for operations that do not use a point-of-sale (POS) system that creates automatic reports of all server transactions. A checkout sheet is a summary of cash, credit card receipts, overrings, voids, discounts, coupons, paidouts, and so on. The amount each employee owes is determined by the checkout sheet. When managers observe the completion of a checkout sheet or review a server's sales report from the POS system, they can then become aware of a cash overage or shortage immediately. Checkout sheets should, if possible, be completed with the manager present. This makes it harder for an employee to attempt a coverup or an adjustment.

One of the most common ways for cashiers, servers, or bartenders to collect extra money on the side is to "build the till." In this process, all revenue is placed in the cash drawer. However, every small order of fries or fourth soft drink is not rung up, or a higher-priced item, like a premium drink, is rung up at a lower price. The guest is still charged full price for all items. This means more cash is collected and placed in the cash drawer than what was actually rung up for sales. The dishonest employee will have some type of counting scheme to keep track of how much unrecorded money has been placed in the drawer. When the opportunity is right and no one is looking, the employee removes the excess cash. To counter this practice, managers should perform surprise cash counts.

Most operations start each shift with a certain sum of money, called a beginning change bank, in each register. At the end of each shift, a manager counts the cash again. Cash overages indicate either unrecorded sales or customers being short-changed. Industry experts believe cashiers, servers, and bartenders should consistently be within $1 over or short. A variance of more than $1 either way is an indication that an employee needs additional training, cannot handle the position, or is trying to steal. However, when two or more people have access to the same cash drawer, it is not possible to hold an individual responsible for overages or shortages.

Managers should be the only people with the authority to void register overrings and mistakes. This prevents an employee from collecting the revenue and then voiding the transaction. However, there are extremely high-volume properties that cannot follow this procedure. So, they must pay

Manager's Memo

There are several procedures that can help increase the effectiveness of internal revenue control. The most common approach is bonding an employee. Bonding is an insurance agreement in which the insurer guarantees a payment to an establishment in the event of a financial loss caused by the action of a specific covered, or bonded, employee. Typically, employees who handle and deposit cash such as cashiers and bookkeepers should be bonded. Another helpful method is mandatory vacation policy for employees of trust. To detect potential fraud, bonded employees should be sent to a mandatory vacation before the end of the fiscal year. Thus, if an absent employee has committed fraud, the temporary staff member can identify the fraud and take corrective action.

close attention to the POS reports that show voids and overrings by server by the shift and week, looking for patterns. Typically, a large amount of voids or overrings by an employee usually means he or she is trying to steal.

Each transaction should generate a receipt that should be presented to each customer. Not giving a receipt makes it easier to hide unrecorded sales. There should be no exceptions to this policy. At the bar, the rule should be "No ticket, no drink." In most states, the liquor law requires the order to have been rung up before the drink can be presented.

Another important rule is to never let anyone who has access to the accounting records also handle cash. Many operations give the accounting department the daily receipts and Z-report, or the closing shift report. If the same department has access to the records and cash, it is very easy for a dishonest person to steal and cover up the theft in the books. Separation of duties is critical, and no employee should be responsible for both recording and processing a transaction.

Safeguarding Cash Deposits

First and foremost, all undeposited cash needs to be secured in a safe. Regardless of who makes the bank deposit, it should be a house rule that the cash is deposited in the bank every day or as frequently as possible (see *Exhibit 10.3*). Use a "for deposit only" stamp on all incoming checks to prevent an employee from cashing them. Review bank statements occasionally and compare deposit dates. Always verify that the cash is being deposited daily. If there is a time gap, there may be a problem.

Safeguarding Customer Payment Card Information

When customers offer their bank card at the point of sale, their card information is exposed, however briefly. Cardholders want assurance that their account information is safe. In recognition of the need for security control standards, in 2004, the credit card industry developed a program to protect consumer information. This evolved and became an industry standard known as the **Payment Card Industry (PCI)** data security standard.

The PCI standard is a series of technology requirements for retailers and companies that process credit cards. These requirements are designed to ensure the protection of cardholder data. This means all establishments that accept credit cards, particularly those that use a POS system to process the transaction, must be PCI-compliant. Many POS software programs store the tracking data embedded in the magnetic strip on the back of credit cards. That information can be sold on the black market and used illegally. Managers who want to securely run credit cards over their POS may need to purchase an expensive software and hardware upgrade or a new POS system. While part of PCI compliance concerns

Exhibit 10.3

Cash deposits should be deposited in the bank every day or as frequently as possible.

issues of network security, the majority of the requirements refer to the storage and handling of customer credit card data in day-to-day business activities. The objectives of PCI compliance are good for business in the long run.

THE FOUR-STEP REVENUE SECURITY SYSTEM

A revenue security system is a four-step process to track the amount of revenue that moves within a restaurant or foodservice operation. Revenue security starts with verifying product sales and ends with verification of bank deposits. The key benefit of developing a sequential revenue security system is that managers can uncover discrepancies at a certain step and make necessary corrections before proceeding to the next step. No matter the size of an operation, its revenue security system needs to satisfy the following equation:

$$\text{Product sales} = \text{Guest charges} = \text{Payments} = \text{Sales deposits}$$

Managers need to match all steps shown in *Exhibit 10.4* to make sure that generated sales equal actual bank sales deposits.

I. Verifying Product Sales

The first step of revenue security consists of verifying product sales. Verifying product sales is important not only for revenue purposes but also for product inventory and purchasing reasons. Verifying product sales has two components: kitchen issues and guest checks. In other words, this step matches production (kitchen issues) with sales (guest checks). The kitchen should never issue products without receiving a copy or electronic notification of guest checks.

KITCHEN ISSUES

Issued kitchen items fall under two basic headings: directs and stores. Directs are charged to food cost as they are received by the operation, on the assumption that these perishable items will be used immediately, most likely that day. Stores are considered part of the inventory until issued for use in an outlet. Stores are not included in food cost until they are issued. For this reason, it is necessary to establish policies and procedures for issuing items and tracking costs. The process starts with filling out a requisition, which is a form listing the items and quantities needed from stores. Each requisition should be reviewed and approved by either the chef or a manager. The requisition is then given to the storeroom, which fills the order and issues the product. See chapter 6 for additional information.

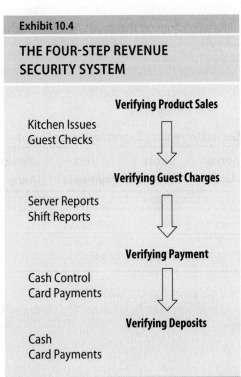

Exhibit 10.4

THE FOUR-STEP REVENUE SECURITY SYSTEM

Verifying Product Sales

Kitchen Issues
Guest Checks

Verifying Guest Charges

Server Reports
Shift Reports

Verifying Payment

Cash Control
Card Payments

Verifying Deposits

Cash
Card Payments

GUEST CHECKS

The duplicate guest-check system and the point-of-sale (POS) control system are the most widely used methods for verifying product sales in the restaurant and foodservice industry today. The duplicate guest-check system is a procedure that uses written records of what guests purchased and how much they were charged for the items. The POS control system uses a computer to ensure that what leaves the kitchen is billed to and paid for by customers. Although both processes are used to monitor, control, and ensure payment for food, the major difference is that in the POS system, technology takes the place of manually writing a guest check. As more establishments embrace technology, the POS system is rapidly replacing the manual check system. See chapter 8 for additional information.

II. Verifying Guest Charges

In the first step of the revenue security system, managers match kitchen issues with guest checks. The next step in the revenue security process is to match guest checks with actual guest charges. The verification of guest charges should be done by managers reviewing either server or shift reports, or both. When both reports are analyzed, if a discrepancy between guest checks and actual guest charges is found, managers can find out which server was responsible for the discrepancy and during which shift.

SERVER REPORTS

The cashier counts the drawer, sets aside the bank, totals the checks and the charges, and fills out a cash report or checkout sheet. If possible this should be completed in the manager's office with the manager watching. A cash report or checkout report form is filled out by the cashier to report all money, checks, and charge slips collected during the shift. See chapter 8 for additional information.

SHIFT REPORTS

The manager or bookkeeper completes a daily or shift sales report from the cash report and the register readings. A daily sales report is a form that shows sales, cash, and charges collected as well as any money overages or shortages for a shift. See chapter 8 for additional information.

MANAGER'S MATH

Detecting Guest Charge Errors

The manager at the Triple Crown Restaurant ran a dinner shift report. There was a total of $3,525.69 in guest charges, and a total of $3,523.46 in guest payments. Overall, guests were overcharged by $2.23. There were four servers working that evening. The manager prepares a discrepancy report that shows how much servers either overcharged or undercharged customers.

1. Calculate the discrepancies, if any, for each server.
2. Which discrepancies should be most concerning for the manager? Why?

Server Discrepancy Report for Dinner, Saturday, June 23

Server Code	Guest Charges	Guest Payments	Overcharge (Undercharge)
20	$892.52	$891.74	
25	784.25	784.25	
28	955.36	975.78	
30	893.56	871.69	

(Answers: Server 20, $0.78; server 25, $0.00; server 28, −$20.42; server 30, $21.87)

III. Verifying Payment

Exhibit 10.5

Verifying payment is as important a step as the sales transaction itself. Even if an establishment has done a great job in marketing its products, has excellent cooks, and excellent customer service standards, these attributes may not be sufficient to keep the operation in business. The manager needs to ensure that payments are made correctly and that cash, discount coupons, and credit card slips are stored securely and are accounted for (see *Exhibit 10.5*).

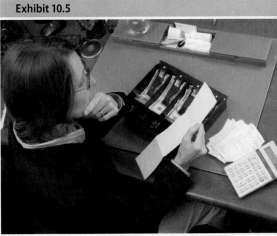

CASH CONTROL

At the start of each shift, an operation should count the cash in each register. At the end of each shift, the operation counts the cash again. Only managers should be able to void register overrings and mistakes, unless an operation is extremely high volume and cannot follow this guideline. Each transaction should generate a receipt that should be presented to each customer. Never let anyone who has access to the accounting records also handle cash. All undeposited cash should be secured in a safe. Cash needs to be deposited in the bank every day or as frequently as possible. Use a "for deposit only" stamp on all incoming checks to prevent any unauthorized person from cashing them. Managers should verify, through bank statements or other means, that the cash is being deposited daily.

CREDIT AND DEBIT CARD PAYMENTS

For a business to be able to accept payment by credit card, it needs to set up a **merchant account**, a designated account where funds from guest credit card payments can be sent. To accept credit cards or debit card transactions, the business needs three components: a credit card merchant account, a bank account, and a way to process payments. A merchant account allows credit card payments to be deposited. Transactions should be processed by the business within one to five days of the transaction. It is important to note that there are fees associated with establishing these types of accounts, plus monthly and per-transaction fees. In addition, organizations should establish a bank account where cash deposits and checks are deposited.

COUPONS AND OTHER PAYMENT FORMS

Coupons should be handled like cash. Each time a coupon is presented, the manager should write *void* across it, so it cannot be reused. It is recommended that coupons be accounted for in the same way as cash or credit cards. When running the server reports at the end of a shift, make sure there is a corresponding number of coupons stapled to the accompanying order tickets.

There is a certain amount of risk involved in selling gift certificates. Gift certificates are an easy target for color copiers, especially if the establishment leaves the payee's name blank. Managers should invest in custom-designed certificates that include the logo or other features that distinguish the certificates from the generic variety. It is also recommended that an operation's gift certificates include a statement such as "Only unused portion less than $5 can be refunded as cash." That way, someone can't use a $50 gift certificate to purchase a meal for $20 and attempt to cash out the remaining balance of $30. Managers should consider setting up a Gift Certificate Log and make sure all employees record the required information. Then establish a procedure to review the log each day to verify that all certificates have been accounted for.

Discount transactions are any price deductions of less than 100 percent. These are the normal categories:

- **Employee meal discounts:** Employees are often given a percentage discount when they purchase food or beverages.

- Guest relations discounts: Often managers may discount a meal because the guest was not satisfied with the quality of the food or services. A meal that is discounted 100 percent is called a *comp*, which is discussed in the following text; a discount requires the guest to pay something.

- **Marketing and promotional discounts:** These are any discounted food and beverage items sold to increase sales. This would include coupons, half-off specials, and early-bird specials.

- **Police, firefighter, senior citizen, or military meal discounts:** Establishments may offer uniformed public safety officers or active duty uniformed military personnel a discount.

Complimentary transactions, or comps, are food or beverage items given away without receiving anything in return. Even though no money changes hands, these transactions still must be recorded. These transactions may be grouped into the following categories:

- **Manager meal comps:** Many establishments allow owners and managers to eat for free. These orders should be transacted like any other order. Typically a guest check is presented and the manager signs the check, which is then placed in the cash drawer and included in the daily sales report.

- **Guest relations:** Sometimes comps are offered as giveaways at the discretion of the manager to make up for a poor dining experience.

- **Marketing and promotional comps:** These are similar to discounts, and typically apply to a specific item, such as an appetizer or drink that is given away with the purchase of other items. An example would be a "buy one, get one free" promotion.

There are two main ways to record and account for discount and comp transactions: the net sales method and the gross sales method. In the net sales method, none of the discount and comp sales are shown in the net sales P&L. However, the food cost still contains all of the food cost associated with the discounts and giveaways. This causes the food cost percentage to be higher than when using the gross sales method.

The gross sales method offers a better depiction of the food cost percentage because it includes discounts and comps and their respective costs. That is, all sales—regular, complimentary, and discount—are included in the P&L statement. In addition, food costs associated with all types of sales are reflected in the P&L. It is important for management to consider which of the two methods is being used when discussing actual and targeted food costs.

IV. Verifying Deposits

After guest payments are verified, the last step in the revenue security system is the verification of deposits. It is generally recommended that only the manager make the actual bank deposit of daily sales revenue. The bank deposit slip may be completed by the cashier or any other clerical assistant, but the manager should bear the sole responsibility for the actual deposit of sales.

CASH

The verification of cash deposits involves the actual verification of the contents of the deposit and the process of matching bank deposits with actual restaurant or foodservice sales. These two numbers obviously should be the same. That is, if a manager deposits Thursday's sales on Friday, the Friday deposit should match the sales amount of Thursday. If it does not, an establishment has experienced a loss of revenue that occurred after the cashier had matched sales receipts with guest charges.

Another issue that an operation may face is the falsification of bank deposits. To prevent this activity, the manager should take the following steps to protect an operation's deposits:

1. Make bank deposits daily if possible.
2. Ensure that the individual making the daily deposit is bonded.
3. Establish written policies for completing bank reconciliations, such as a comparison of monthly bank statements versus daily sales.
4. Review and approve bank statement reconciliations each month.
5. Employ an outside auditor to examine the accuracy of deposits on an annual basis.

Manager's Memo

The four-step revenue control system is critical for restaurant and foodservice operations. By implementing this system, managers have a way to identify any discrepancies or problems in real time. In other words, managers can detect any discrepancies between kitchen issues and guest checks well before the guest makes a payment. By the same token, an operation can detect any guest payment errors before funds for the sales transaction are received. This way, managers do not have to wait until the shift concludes to match the amount of sales with produced orders and payments made by guests.

PAYMENT WITH CREDIT CARDS AND DEBIT CARDS

An operation is able to reconcile payment card totals using the POS as part of the report generated when the machine is cleared at the end of each shift or day. If a restaurant or foodservice operation uses a credit card processing terminal, then the manager must manually match credit card slips with guest checks. Verifying transmission to the **merchant services provider**—the company that facilitates the transaction between an operation and the card issuer, or clearing—is usually completed within one day.

Confirming the deposit of payment card totals is vital for any operation, since credit card sales represent the major source of sales revenue in the restaurant and foodservice industry. Credit card sales reimbursements are normally received in one to five operating days, depending on the type of credit card. It should be noted that the amount received by an operation is not equal to actual credit card sales, due to the fees charged by card issuer companies.

CASH AUDITS

Auditing means a financial examination of an organization's accounts. A good internal revenue control system uses an audit trail that documents each transaction from the time that it was started. It should have an entry for each defined procedure and be recorded in the operation's general ledger. This allows managers to follow each transaction from start to finish to identify any errors.

Exhibit 10.6

Cashier and Server Banks

A bank consists of coins and bills sufficient to make change and is issued to each cashier, or in some operations, to a particular cash register or POS drawer that may be shared by multiple users. The size of the bank is determined by the number of anticipated transactions.

At the end of the shift, a register reading or daily sales report is taken by the manager. Register readings should never be taken by servers, cashiers, or bartenders. If a cash register is being used, the readings should be locked, with only the manager having a key. The readings are continuous. Thus, the reading from the current shift has to be subtracted from the previous shift to get the sales for the current shift. If the operation uses a POS system, the manager enters a code to obtain a reading.

The cashier counts the drawer, sets aside the bank, totals the checks and the charges, and fills out a cash report or checkout sheet to report all money, checks, and charge slips collected during the shift (*Exhibit 10.6*). The cashier should make sure there is a corresponding amount of coupons stapled to their accompanying order ticket. The manager or a bookkeeper completes a daily sales report from the cash report and the register readings. A daily sales report is a form that shows sales, cash, and charges collected as well as any money over or short for a shift. For more information, see chapter 8.

Petty Cash

Petty cash is a small fund established to handle minor cash disbursements. A petty cash fund should be established with a limited or specific amount of cash. Typically, it will be set up to handle from between one week's and one month's worth of transactions. Only one person should be accountable for controlling the petty cash fund. A receipt, invoice, voucher, or memorandum explaining the purpose of each disbursement should be included and they should all be marked as paid, so they cannot be reused. The manager should do random checks on the funds to make sure the amount of cash on hand, plus any documented disbursements, equals the limit of the fund. There should be no IOUs or postdated checks allowed. The fund is brought back to its limit by exchanging cash for receipts, invoices, or other disbursements.

MANAGING ACCOUNTS PAYABLE

Accounts payable represents the amount of money that an operation owes suppliers from which it has purchased goods, products, or services. The first step of the accounts payable process begins when an invoice is brought to the manager's office. Organizations should process invoices on a daily basis when transactions are still fresh and can easily be referred back to. Next, the manager needs to make sure that the invoice is addressed to the correct organization. Sometimes a supplier may deliver a similar item to a competitor's establishment and give them a wrong invoice. The manager needs to make sure that the invoice is signed by one of the operation's employees, indicating that item amounts are correct and contents are intact. In addition, delivery date, unit prices, and order amounts should be checked for accuracy. If everything is correct, the manager should stamp the invoice "Approved," which signifies that it should be paid. After the invoice is approved it needs to be coded. That is, if an invoice contains flour and vodka, the flour should be coded under food costs, and vodka should be coded under the beverage costs category.

Often, suppliers will allow a restaurant or foodservice establishment to buy products "on account," which means that payment is due within a certain period, such as 15 or 30 days. This flexibility enables operations to purchase products and sell them to customers before paying suppliers for these products. How the manager handles an operation's accounts payable affects two important areas: cash flow and supplier relationships. Sound accounts payable practices make a significant difference both in minimizing late-payment costs—such as interest charges, missed incentive bonuses for early payment, and late-payment penalties—and in establishing efficient operations. Operations that fail to make timely payments may have to be required to pay with cash on delivery of their orders. A smooth-running accounts payable department saves money by processing invoices with a minimum of staff and at a low cost of materials.

THINK ABOUT IT . . .

Some restaurant and foodservice operations elect to accumulate supplier invoices and process them on a weekly basis. What are some drawbacks pertaining to processing invoices weekly?

The manager should oversee accounts payable activities with these goals in mind:

- Pay invoices on a predetermined schedule established by the business, not the vendors.
- Make sure all invoices that are paid are accurate and authentic.
- Minimize the amount of time and expense in processing accounts payable paperwork.

How and when an operation pays its suppliers establishes and affects the trust between a company and its suppliers. Paying bills on time does more to build trust with suppliers than any other action the company could do. Failure to keep that basic original promise is the quickest way to tear it down. Remember, strong relationships with suppliers are important to every company. Suppliers provide needed product, but they also extend credit, expose an operation to new methods and products, and ultimately affect customer service.

VERIFYING RECEIPT OF GOODS AND SERVICES

A purchase order or requisition initiates supply and service agreements. A purchase order is a form that authorizes an approved supplier to deliver goods and services to the operation. The receiving report is then used to verify that the products received are as ordered and that the goods match up with the invoice. The accounting department should match the invoice with a copy of the original purchase requisition, a copy of the purchase order, and any related invoices. Accounting should then compare and verify all the relevant information. See chapter 5 for additional information.

Verifying Amount Due

In this process, a purchasing agent matches the purchase order with the purchase invoice to ensure that the invoiced amount is correct. If the amount is correct and the products have arrived, the agent will have to approve the invoice by signing off on it. If the amount invoiced exceeds a certain amount, for example, $5,000, set by the establishment, the invoice may require a supervisor's approval.

If there are any variances in the invoice due to incorrect pricing, goods not being delivered, spoiled or damaged products, or products not complying with purchase specifications, the purchasing agent should request a credit memo to account for these adjustments. If necessary, to verify the amount due, management may contact the supplier to confirm any adjustments or corrections to the invoice. Once the invoice is approved it is posted on the accounting system for payment processing.

Invoice Payment

Since most invoices are not due upon receipt of goods and services, the invoice amount needs to be recorded under accounts payable and also placed in the payment queue by the accounting department. When the internally predetermined invoice due date comes, accounting needs to issue payment to the supplier and record the payment in the vendor database and the restaurant or foodservice operation's purchase records.

SUMMARY

1. **Identify and explain the three parts of a revenue collection system.**

   Bringing customers to purchase food and beverages is of paramount significance to the success of an establishment. However, having a solid revenue collection system is of equal importance. This system begins with charging the guest and completing the sales transaction. Next, revenue must actually be collected, and finally, collected cash assets need to be protected.

2. **List the external and internal threats to revenue security.**

   External threats include guests that walk or skip without paying for their purchases, counterfeit currency, credit card fraud, and bad (NSF) personal checks. Internal threats include dishonest employees, including collusion between employees.

3. **Explain the basic control standards to safeguard cash and credit card information.**

   The number one rule in controlling cash is to make sure anyone who receives cash is not also able to take a register reading. A manager should be the only person able to void register overrings or mistakes. All transactions should generate a receipt that should be presented to the customer. The bookkeeper or accountant should never handle cash. If the same person has access to the records and cash, then it makes it very easy for a dishonest person to steal and cover up the theft in the books. Safeguarding credit card information requires being in compliance with the PCI (Payment Card Industry) data security standard, which sets standards pertaining to network security and the storage and handling of customer credit card data.

4. **Describe the four steps in the revenue security system.**

   A revenue security system tracks the amount of revenue that moves within a restaurant or foodservice operation. Revenue security starts with verifying product sales, moves on to verifying the amounts the guests were actually charged, then verifying that payment was actually made, and ends with verification of bank deposits. This is a sequential system where the manager matches the amount from the previous step and detects any possible discrepancies or errors.

5. **Explain several ways to discourage theft by employees.**

Follow best practices when it comes to hiring employees. Conduct a thorough background check and interview all job applicants. Test applicants for job skills. Create a positive work environment to help reduce fraud and theft. Implement internal controls to increase the actual, and the perceived, chance of an employee getting caught if they attempt to steal.

6. **List two important areas affected by accounts payable.**

How the manager handles the accounts payable affects two important areas: cash flow and supplier relationships. Timely payment to suppliers helps maintain good supplier relationships. In addition, paying invoices on time allows a restaurant or foodservice operation to benefit from supplier discounts and incentives that reduce food cost and increase operating cash flow.

7. **Describe the steps in verifying the receipt of goods and services.**

In this verification process, a purchasing agent first matches the purchase order with the purchase invoice to ensure that the invoiced amount is correct. If the amount is correct and the products have arrived, the agent approves the invoice by signing off on it. If there are any variances in the invoice, the purchasing agent should request a credit memo to account for these adjustments. Once the invoice is approved, it is posted on the accounting system for payment processing.

APPLICATION EXERCISE

The general manager of Tasty Grill is reviewing the revenue report for the Saturday night shift. The report is summarized in three sections (A, B, and C):

A. Guest Charges and Sales

Total amount for guest checks: $2,356.45

Total amount of food items charged to guests: $1,852.55

Total amount of food items issued by kitchen: $1,790.30

Total T-bone steak sales: $390.00

B. T-Bone Steaks Sold

Inventory

Beginning inventory for T-bone steaks: 63

Ending inventory for T-bone steaks: 38

Usage

Number of returned T-bone steaks by guests: 2

Number of burned/overcooked T-bone steaks: 2

Number of steaks sold: **?**

C. Credit Card Sales and Fees

Total credit card charges: $1,867.30

Credit card commission: 3%

Total deposit expected: **?**

Based on the previous information, answer the following questions:

1. How much is the discrepancy between food items charged to guests and food items issued by the kitchen?

2. How many T-bone steaks are sold to guests during the Saturday night shift?

3. Calculate the T-bone steak sales for the shift at $20 per steak.

4. Compare your T-bone steak sales figure with steak sales in section A. Report any discrepancies.

5. What percentage of total shift sales come from credit card sales?

6. How much is the total deposit expected from credit card charges?

REVIEW YOUR LEARNING

Select the best answer for each question.

1. **Which action can be considered fraud in restaurant and foodservice establishments?**

   A. Stamping the invoices

   B. Overcharging

   C. Checking the cash deposit during a shift

   D. Auditing the cash drawer by the supervisor

2. **What is a service charge?**

   A. Labor-related fee

   B. Charge added only to discounted guest checks

   C. Token of guest appreciation

   D. Cover charge

3. **What is safeguarding credit card information based on?**

   A. Amount of credit card transactions per day

   B. Availability of a POS system

   C. Established PCI standards

   D. Number of cashiers per shift

4. **What is the most basic method to detect counterfeit currency?**

   A. Tester pen

   B. Paper and print

   C. Ultraviolet light

   D. Incandescent light

5. **An internal revenue security system starts with**

   A. product delivery.

   B. kitchen issuance.

   C. invoice receipts.

   D. guest payment.

6. **"Building the till" is a technique used by**

   A. management trainees.

   B. dishonest employees.

   C. experienced managers.

   D. guests who skip.

7. **What is the first step in the revenue collection system?**

   A. Auditing the cash

   B. Controlling food cost

   C. Charging the guest

   D. Controlling labor cost

8. **Cash audits enable managers to**

   A. improve food cost.

   B. identify errors.

   C. track credit card sales.

   D. control labor cost.

9. **What is the benefit of managing accounts payable?**

   A. It helps safeguard cash deposits.

   B. It improves cash flow.

   C. It discourages employee theft.

   D. It improves revenue security systems.

10. **When there is a variance between the purchase order and the invoice amounts, the purchasing agent should request a(n)**

    A. requisition form.

    B. order variance form.

    C. order debit form.

    D. credit memo.

FIELD PROJECT

Divide into three groups. Select one of the major credit cards and research its benefits and services. For each credit card, look at its Web site and find the Merchants section. This section will help you learn more about the credit card's benefits and services.

In your group, prepare a sales pitch that you could use to persuade the manager to accept this credit card at your establishment. Present your pitch to the other groups.

After all the pitches are presented, answer the following questions:

1. How do the benefits of each company compare?

_____
_____
_____
_____
_____
_____

2. Which benefits do you think are most important to a restaurant or foodservice operation?

_____
_____
_____
_____
_____
_____

3. Which credit card(s) would you choose to accept at an establishment you managed?

_____
_____
_____
_____
_____
_____
_____

FIELD PROJECT

COST CONTROL THROUGHOUT THE FLOW OF FOOD

This field project will provide you with an opportunity to learn from practitioners in the restaurant and foodservice industry and find out how the concepts that have been covered in this book are used in actual practice. This project is designed to give you an in-depth look at how costs must be controlled throughout the many processes an operation must perform.

To begin, you must obtain a menu either from the place you work or from a local restaurant or foodservice establishment. Be sure to get the manager's permission first.

Part I

List all the menu items that indicate a specific portion size (e.g., six-ounce filet mignon). Create a table with this information, noting if an item is pre-portioned or portioned when it is plated. (You may need to talk with the manager about this if the menu does not make it clear.)

Part II

After you complete the table, select three menu items and trace how costs are controlled for each item as it passes through the various stages of the operation. Develop a set of questions for each stage that you can ask the manager or another staff member. Some sample questions are as follows:

1. **Purchasing and Receiving**
   - What is the as purchased (AP) price of the main ingredients in this menu item?
   - What is the yield percentage of the main ingredients in this menu item?
   - What is the edible portion (EP) cost?
   - What is the EP percentage?
   - How often do these items need to be purchased?

2. **Storing and Issuing**
   - How are the items stored?
   - What stock rotation method is used?
   - How is spoilage prevented?

3. **Production**
   - How many portions are prepared each day?
   - Is there a standardized recipe for each menu item?
   - How are wasted foods tracked?
   - How is each menu item portioned?

4. Service and Sales

- How was the selling price determined?
- What market forces affect the selling price for each menu item?
- How are sales tracked?
- What methods of payment are accepted?
- How is scheduling done?
- How does the manager forecast labor costs?
- What is the employee turnover rate?

Part III

Write a three- to five-page paper that summarizes your findings. Your report should start with the purchasing process and then move to production and service. Include in your report how costs are being controlled in this establishment. Also spend some time predicting what would happen if the costs were not controlled on these items at any point during the flow through the operation.

APPENDIX

Math skills are extremely important in restaurant and foodservice operations. Managers are expected to have a basic understanding of math and know how to apply mathematical principles to business situations. Math skills are also essential in the professional kitchen. Chefs and managers need to know how to determine recipe yields, convert recipes from customary to metric measure, and change the yields of recipes.

This appendix is a review of some basic math concepts.

MATHEMATICAL OPERATIONS

As you have learned in previous math classes, there are several operations performed on numbers, and each corresponds to a familiar symbol. Numbers can be added ($10 + 2 = 12$), subtracted ($10 - 2 = 8$), multiplied ($10 \times 2 = 20$), and divided ($10 \div 2 = 5$). They can also be expressed as fractions, which is the same as dividing them ($\frac{10}{2} = 10 \div 2 = 5$).

These four basic math functions are the basis upon which all other mathematical functions are performed. Knowing all four functions well will help you as you continue to learn about business math.

Addition

Numbers are added by lining them up in columns and then assigning each column of digits a value of 1, 10, 100, 1,000, and so on, beginning with the right-most column. In the number 372, for example, 2 is in the *ones* column, 7 is in the *tens* column, and 3 is in the *hundreds* column.

When adding a column, if the sum of a column contains two digits, then the right digit is written below the sum line, and the left digit is added to the next column as you move from right to left:

$$
\begin{array}{r}
1 \\
24 \\
+17 \\
\hline
41
\end{array}
$$

Subtraction

When subtracting large numbers, a technique known as borrowing is often used. If a digit in one column is too large to be subtracted from the digit above it, then 10 is borrowed from the column immediately to the left:

$$
\begin{array}{r}
7\,1 \\
82 \\
-17 \\
\hline
65
\end{array}
$$

To check your work on a subtraction problem, simply add the answer to the subtracted number. The result should be the first number:

$$
\begin{array}{r}
1 \\
65 \quad \text{(answer)} \\
+17 \quad \text{(subtracted number)} \\
\hline
82
\end{array}
$$

Multiplication

To multiply large numbers, the digit in the ones column of the second number is first multiplied by the digits above it, going from right to left.

For example, to solve 32×4:

1. Multiply 4 by 2; result is 8.

$$
\begin{array}{r}
32 \\
\times 4 \\
\hline
8
\end{array}
$$

2. Multiply 4 by 3; result is 12.

$$
\begin{array}{r}
32 \\
\times 4 \\
\hline
128
\end{array}
$$

The final result is 128.

Exhibit A1 will help you review multiplication for the numbers 1 through 12.

Exhibit A1

MULTIPLICATION TABLE

	1	2	3	4	5	6	7	8	9	10	11	12
1	1	2	3	4	5	6	7	8	9	10	11	12
2	2	4	6	8	10	12	14	16	18	20	22	24
3	3	6	9	12	15	18	21	24	27	30	33	36
4	4	8	12	16	20	24	28	32	36	40	44	48
5	5	10	15	20	25	30	35	40	45	50	55	60
6	6	12	18	24	30	36	42	48	54	60	66	72
7	7	14	21	28	35	42	49	56	63	70	77	84
8	8	16	24	32	40	48	56	64	72	80	88	96
9	9	18	27	36	45	54	63	72	81	90	99	108
10	10	20	30	40	50	60	70	80	90	100	110	120
11	11	22	33	44	55	66	77	88	99	110	121	132
12	12	24	36	48	60	72	84	96	108	120	132	144

Division

Larger numbers are divided using a combination of division and subtraction. The dividend is placed inside the long division sign, and the divisor is placed outside. For example, in the problem 728 ÷ 14, 728 is the dividend, and 14 is the divisor.

To solve 728 ÷ 14:

1. Divide 14 into 72; result is 5.
   14 × 5 = 70
   Subtract from 72.

$$
\begin{array}{r}
5 \\
14\overline{)728} \\
-70 \\
\hline
2
\end{array}
$$

2. Bring down 8.
   Divide 14 into 28; result is 2.
   14 × 2 = 28
   Subtract from 28.

$$
\begin{array}{r}
52 \\
14\overline{)728} \\
-70 \\
\hline
28 \\
-28 \\
\hline
0
\end{array}
$$

The final result is 52.

FRACTIONS, DECIMALS, AND PERCENTAGES

Fractions

In adding and subtracting fractions, the denominators, the lower portion of the fraction, must be the same (for example $\frac{1}{3} + \frac{1}{3} = \frac{2}{3}$). When the denominators are the same, the numerators, the upper portion of a fraction, are added and subtracted the same way as whole numbers.

If the denominators to be added or subtracted are different from each other, then you must first determine the lowest common denominator, which is the smallest whole number that is evenly divided by each denominator. The next step is to multiply each numerator by the number that its corresponding denominator was multiplied by in order to arrive at the lowest common denominator. For example, in the next problem, both the numerator and the denominator in $\frac{2}{3}$ are multiplied by 4, giving us the new, equivalent fraction $\frac{8}{12}$.

$$\frac{2}{3} + \frac{3}{4} =$$
$$\frac{8}{12} + \frac{9}{12} = \frac{17}{12}$$
$$\frac{17}{12} = 1\frac{5}{12}$$

Decimals

Fractions are often expressed as decimals. (See *Exhibit A2*.) All decimals are based on one-tenth, one-hundredth, one-thousandth, and so on. For example, 1.4 is 1 and 4-tenths, and 6.21 is 6 and 21-hundredths.

Exhibit A2

COMMON FRACTIONS AND THEIR DECIMAL EQUIVALENTS

$\frac{1}{8} = 0.125$	$\frac{3}{8} = 0.375$	$\frac{2}{3} = 0.6667$
$\frac{1}{6} = 0.1667$	$\frac{1}{2} = 0.50$	$\frac{3}{4} = 0.75$
$\frac{1}{4} = 0.25$	$\frac{5}{8} = 0.625$	$\frac{7}{8} = 0.875$

Decimals are added, subtracted, multiplied, and divided just like non-decimal numbers. When adding or subtracting decimals, the key is to line up the decimal points:

$$\begin{array}{r} 8.46 \\ +4.23 \\ \hline 12.69 \end{array} \qquad \begin{array}{r} 8.46 \\ -4.23 \\ \hline 4.23 \end{array}$$

When multiplying decimals, you must determine where to place the decimal point once you've calculated your final total answer. To do this, count the total number of digits to the right of all decimal points in the numbers that you are multiplying and then place the decimal point in your final answer by counting that many places from the right. For example, there are a total of four digits to the right of the decimal points in 8.46 and 4.23. Therefore, the decimal point goes four places from the right in the answer, 35.7858:

$$
\begin{array}{r}
8.46 \\
\times 4.23 \\
\hline
2538 \\
16920 \\
338400 \\
\hline
35.7858
\end{array}
$$

When dividing decimals, if the divisor is not a whole number, move the decimal point to the right to make the divisor a whole number. Also move the decimal point in the dividend the same number of places to the right. Divide as usual. In the answer, simply bring the decimal point up directly above the long division sign:

$$
4.23. \overline{) 8.46. }
$$

When a calculator or computer is used, numbers will often have more digits to the right of the decimal point than are practical or useful. In these cases, numbers are rounded to the nearest tenth, hundredth, or thousandth. Numbers are sometimes rounded to the nearest whole number in order to eliminate the decimal point.

In rounding, if the next digit to the right is less than 5, then the number is usually rounded down (5.12 is rounded to 5.1). If the number to the right is 5 or above, then the number is rounded up (5.19 is rounded to 5.2). The number 5.192635 can be rounded to the nearest thousandth (5.193), hundredth (5.19), tenth (5.2), or whole number (5).

THINK ABOUT IT . . .

The sports store at the mall is having a 25 percent discount sale on name-brand T-shirts. If the T-shirts usually sell for $15, what will the price be during the sale?

Percentages

One of the first mathematical operations you will come in contact with is percentages. Restaurant and foodservice managers and employees often express numbers as percentages, or parts per 100. If you are working with a fraction that you want to express as a percentage, the first step is to convert the fraction into a decimal. For example, to express $\frac{1}{2}$ as a decimal, the numerator (1) is divided by the denominator (2) for an answer of 0.5. Add a zero (0) in the hundredths place (0.50), and the two digits to the right of the decimal point are expressed as 50 percent, or 50%.

To determine a certain percentage of a given number, it is first expressed as a decimal and then multiplied. For instance, to find 20% of 60, multiply 60 by 0.20.

$$
\begin{array}{r}
60 \\
\times 0.20 \\
\hline
00 \\
1200 \\
\hline
12.00
\end{array}
$$

Then, place the decimal point as required, so that 1200 becomes 12.00. Thus, 20% of 60 is 12.

You can also determine the percentage of one number to another number. For instance, if 60 customers out of a total of 300 are ordering the house special, the percentage of customers ordering the special is found by dividing the portion (60) by the total (300).

$$
\frac{60}{300} = 0.20 = 20\%
$$

This equation shows that 60 customers out of the total 300 customers equals 0.20 or 20%. In other words, 20 percent of the customers are ordering the special.

REVIEW YOUR LEARNING

1. An establishment manager budgets 4 percent of her total $856,000 budget for marketing. What is her marketing budget? _____

2. In the number 3,897, the 9 occupies which of the following columns?

    A. Ones

    B. Tens

    C. Hundreds

    D. Thousands

3. Of 4,500 customers last month, 710 ordered items from the lighter menu selections. What percentage is this?_____

4. A vendor's invoice for purchases is shown. Calculate the amounts for each item on the invoice, the delivery charge, and the invoice total.

10 cases lettuce	at $35.76/case	$
12 cases tomatoes	at $25.00/case	$
6 cases radishes	at $14.28/case	$
4 cases strawberries	at $47.84/case	$
	Subtotal	**$**
Next-day delivery charge 7% of order subtotal		$
	Invoice total	**$**

5. After tabulating the results of a survey sent to frequent customers, an operation determines the following information about how customers rate the establishment's service:

Number of Customers	Rating
200	Excellent
250	Very good
330	Good
200	Fair
20	Poor

What percentage of customers rated the operation's service as very good or better? _____

GLOSSARY

Acceptable substitutions Substitutions previously agreed upon by both buyer and vendor.

Accounts payable The amount of money that an operation owes suppliers from which it has purchased goods, products, or services.

Actual price method A method that uses a product's cost that is listed on the closing inventory sheet.

As purchased (AP) method A method used to cost an ingredient at the purchase price prior to any trim or waste being taken into account.

Auditing A financial examination of an organization's accounts.

Averaged price method A method that uses a composite of all prices paid for an item during the inventory period to evaluate the inventory.

Baker's percentage A formula in which the weight of the flour equals 100 percent and all the other ingredients are calculated in proportion to the weight of the flour.

Bank An amount of money issued to each cashier that consists of coins and dollar bills sufficient to make change.

Blanket purchase order A purchase order that allows the buyer to purchase a certain amount of goods, usually indicated by a dollar amount, at the stated terms within a given time period.

Break-even point The minimum amount of sales an establishment must generate to cover all costs.

Budget A plan that indicates an operation's financial objectives or financial standards.

Budgeting process The way managers go about developing a budget, which is a process of both planning and control.

Butcher's yield test A method used to measure the amount of shrinkage that occurs during the trimming of a meat product.

Buyer The sole person responsible for purchasing particular goods.

Capital expenditure budget A budget that allows an establishment to plan for the replacement of high-cost equipment that wears out, and to purchase new types of equipment that may come on the market.

Card verification value (CVV) The three-digit code on the back of most credit cards.

Carry-over production Food that has been previously produced but not served to customers.

Cash-handling procedure An activity that operations follow to ensure that all cash and charge transactions are accurate and accounted for.

Cash report A form filled out by the cashier to report all money, checks, and charge slips collected during a shift.

Closing inventory The value of how much food product exists at the end of a given period.

Collusion The working together of two or more employees for dishonest purposes.

Composite (potential) food cost percentage The weighted average food cost percentage for all items sold, weighted by the quantity of each item sold.

Contribution margin (CM) The amount left over after the food cost of a menu item is subtracted from the menu selling price.

Contribution margin method (pricing) Adding the contribution margin (CM) figure to the cost of a menu item to determine that item's price.

Controllable cost A cost that a manager can directly control.

Controllable profit The profit amount that reflects only those line items over which a manager has any influence or control.

Controls A series of coordinated actions that help keep financial results within an acceptable target range.

Conversion factor When converting recipes, a multiplier used to adjust the quantity of ingredients on the existing recipe to the quantity needed to produce the desired yield.

Cooking loss test A way to measure the amount of product shrinkage during the cooking or roasting process.

Corrective action Steps that are taken to address a problem.

Cost of sales The cost of the food and beverage products to a given operation.

Cost structure The proportion or percentage of expense items to sales.

Counterfeit currency Money that is produced to resemble official legal currency closely enough that it may be confused for genuine currency.

Cover One meal served to a customer.

Covers per server The number of customer meals that a waitstaff member can serve in an hour.

Credit card A card that obligates the user to pay the credit card company for the products and services charged to the card.

Credit memo A document used to adjust information about product quantities or costs recorded on a delivery invoice; it specifies items to be deducted from the amount owed and explains the reason why the credit is being granted.

Credits to cost of sales A category of credits including such items as employee meals, complimentary meals served to guests, or grease sales sold to rendering companies.

Crew schedule A chart that shows employees' names and the days and times that they are to work.

Daily food cost An estimate of cost based on requisitions, transfers, and sales. To determine daily food cost, the daily requisitions for that unit are totaled. Transfers from that unit to another unit are subtracted and transfers into the unit are added to the requisition total to determine the daily food cost for that unit. This total number is divided by the unit's sales to determine a daily food cost percentage.

Daily sales report A form that shows sales, cash, and charges collected, as well as any money over or short for a shift.

Debit card A card used to pay for products and services in which the amount is immediately withdrawn from the cardholder's bank account.

Demand-driven pricing The theory that an operation can set pricing based on demand for the product or service.

Directs Items that are charged to food cost as they are received by the operation, on the assumption that these perishable items will be used immediately.

Duplicate guest-check system A procedure that uses written records of what guests purchased and how much they were charged for the items.

Edible portion (EP) cost A method used to cost an ingredient after it has been trimmed and waste has been removed so that only the usable portion of the item is reflected.

Employee turnover The number of employees hired to fill one position in a year's time.

Extending Multiplying the number of units of each item by the item's unit price.

Extension The price of an item multiplied by the number of items being purchased.

Factor method (pricing) A popular formula used to determine menu prices based on the standard food cost percentage, also called **simple markup** or **food cost percentage method**.

Federal Insurance Contributions Act (FICA) A program that sets aside money for Social Security payments, which is paid for by employers and employees through payroll deductions.

First in, first out (FIFO) A method commonly used to ensure that refrigerated, frozen, and dry products are properly rotated during storage.

Fixed budget A budget that is based on a certain level of sales revenue; expense estimates for food, labor, and other costs are then calculated based on that level of sales.

Fixed cost A cost that remains the same regardless of sales volume.

Flexible budget A budget that is based on several possible levels of sales activity, also known as a *variable budget*.

Food cost percentage method (pricing) A popular formula used to determine menu prices based on the standard food cost percentage. This method is also called **simple markup** or **factor method**.

Food-production chart A chart that provides the essential information a staff needs to know on exactly what and how much food to prepare.

Forecasting Making future predictions about the budget based on current situations and trends.

Fraud An intentional deception to cause a person to give up property or some lawful right.

Fringe benefits Benefits provided by an employer that have monetary value but do not affect an employee's basic wage rate, such as paid holidays or paid vacation.

Gross weight The combined weight of a food item and a plate.

Guest relations discount A discount on a meal offered by a manager because the guest was not satisfied with the quality of the food or service.

Ideal food cost The target cost an operation is aiming for.

Income statement A document that reports an operation's sales, expenses, and profits or losses for a period of time, such as month, a quarter, or a year.

Inventory An itemized list of goods and products, their on-hand quantity, and their dollar value.

Inventory breakdown A method of categorizing the operation's food and supplies.

Inventory turnover A measure of how quickly an item in storage is used.

Invoice A receipt for items delivered; it is a legal document that reinforces the terms of a purchase order.

Issuing Taking food or beverage products from storage.

Key drop delivery Delivery of food items and goods after hours when the establishment is closed for business.

Labor contract An agreement between management and a union that represents the employees and that deals with wages, employee benefits, hours, and working conditions.

Last in, first out (LIFO) An inventory method used when an establishment intends to use the most recently delivered product before using any part of that same product previously on hand.

Latest price method A method that uses the latest price paid for a product to value an inventory; this is the most widely used pricing method in the restaurant and foodservice industry.

Line item review The checking of every item on the budget against actual figures, and noting the difference, or variance.

Long-term budget A budget from one year to five years in the future.

Loss A situation that occurs when an operation's expenses are greater than its sales.

Market-driven pricing Pricing that is determined by the market, which is usually regional.

Market price A menu pricing strategy in which the price of a menu item changes based on the current market.

Markup The difference between the actual cost of producing an item and the price listed on the menu.

Markup differentiation Giving different markups to different categories of food, according to a range of expectations in the market.

Master schedule A template, usually a spreadsheet, showing the number of people needed in each position to run the restaurant or foodservice operation.

Medicare Contributions from payroll set aside for health benefits for people age 65 or older and for individuals with certain disabilities.

Menu engineering The process of analyzing the menu product mix, along with consideration of an item's contribution margin and its popularity.

Menu matrix The placement of menu items in different categories based on their popularity and profitability.

Menu product mix A detailed analysis that shows the quantities sold of each menu item, along with their selling prices and standard portion costs.

Menu training A list of all menu items with detailed descriptions, which teaches employees about the establishment's offerings.

Merchant account A designated account where funds from guest credit card payments can be sent.

Merchant services provider A company that facilitates the transaction between an operation and the card issuer, also known as *clearing*.

Noncontrollable cost A cost over which a manager has little or no control.

Nonperishable goods Products that have a relatively long shelf life.

Nonsufficient funds (NSF) A situation in which a check's bank account did not contain enough money to cover the amount written on the check.

Opening inventory The value of how much food product exists at the start of a given period.

Open tab A temporary guest charge account that allows guests to purchase and consume products before paying for them.

Operating budget A formal one-year operating plan to achieve the financial goals of an organization.

Operational standards The measures established for making comparisons and judgments about the degree of excellence in operations.

Order guide A form used as a tool for counting and tracking all the products an operation uses and must reorder.

Overcharging The act of charging more than the amount that should have been charged and collected.

Overtime Any hours worked by nonmanagement employees beyond 40 hours in a workweek, by law compensated at a rate of at least 1.5 times the employee's regular rate of pay.

Padding Inflating the inventory for the purpose of reducing the food cost.

Par levels The amount of stock necessary to get the kitchen through until the next order is delivered.

Payment Card Industry (PCI) A data security standard. A series of technology requirements for retailers and companies that process credit cards, which are designed to ensure the protection of cardholder data.

Payroll dollars The amount of money available for payroll for a scheduling period.

Percentage of sales method A method that involves estimating expenses for a future period as a percentage of the sales forecast.

Perishable goods Products that have a relatively short shelf life—usually one to three days.

Perpetual inventory A theoretical count based on goods received and issued, which exists on paper only.

Petty cash A small fund established to handle minor cash disbursements.

Physical inventory An actual physical count and valuation of all items on hand.

Plate cost The total sum of product costs included in a single meal, or plate, served to a guest.

Point-of-sale (POS) system A system for controlling the operation's cash generation, product usage, and inventory.

Popularity index The percentage share of a given menu item in its respective category (e.g., entrée), derived by dividing the number of portions sold by the total number of items in the same category that were sold.

Portion control The amount of food in a serving as determined by the standardized recipe or the company standard.

Portion control device A device that assists in the portioning of food items, including scoops, ladles, serving spoons, serving dishes, and portion scales.

Portion size The size of an item's individual serving, such as "six ounces of fish fillet."

Pour cost percentage The proportion of beverage cost to sales price.

Pre-portioned item A food item that is measured or weighed prior to going to the service line.

Price-per-person model Pricing determined by calculating the food cost for all the items included on a buffet and the backup inventory used to replenish the buffet during the service period.

Price–value relationship The connection between the selling price of an item and its worth to the customer.

Prime cost An operation's total food cost, beverage cost, and labor cost for a specific time period, usually a week or a month.

Prime cost method (pricing) A method that requires managers to determine the amount of direct labor spent in preparing an item; this number is added to the food cost to arrive at the prime cost.

Prime vendor A purchasing method that involves purchasing most, if not all, of an operation's goods from one supplier; also called the *one-stop shop*.

Productive Producing or capable of producing an effect or result.

Productivity The quality and quantity of output compared to the amount of input, such as labor hours, needed to generate it.

Productivity standard A level set by managers to measure the amount of work performed by an employee.

Product specifications Descriptions of the quality requirements of the products that are purchased.

Product usage report A report that details the number of items issued to the cook's line, the number returned to inventory, and the number sold to customers.

Profit The dollar amount that remains after all expenses are paid.

Purchase order (PO) A form issued by a buyer and sent to a vendor that indicates the items and quantities to be purchased.

Purchases The value of how much an operation spent on food products in a given period.

Q factor The quotient or cost of all other food items served with an entrée; the cost includes side dishes and garnishes as well as all complimentary items such as condiments, seasonings, coffee creamer, and sweetener.

Quality-control line check A system for ensuring product freshness and sufficient quantities, encompassing taste tests and checking standards.

Quality standard A standard that sets the degree of excellence of raw materials, finished products, and production standards for the employees.

Quantity standard A standard that refers to weight, count, or volume measure, such as portion sizes for menu foods and beverages, and employee production standards such as one cook per 50 covers.

Quote An offer made by a supplier.

Ratio pricing method A ratio derived by taking the sum of all nonfood costs (including labor costs, other controllable costs, and noncontrollable costs), adding it to the target profit, and dividing the resulting number by the cost of food sold in dollars.

Recipe conversion A method used to change the yield of a recipe from its original yield to a desired yield.

Recipe cost card A tool used to calculate the standard portion cost for a menu item, or the exact amount that one serving or portion of a food item should cost when prepared according to the item's standardized recipe.

Recipe yield The number of portions a standardized recipe produces.

Reduced oxygen packaged (ROP) bulk food Food contained in a package in which (a) oxygen has been removed, (b) oxygen has been displaced with another gas or combination of gases, or (c) something else has been done to reduce the oxygen content to a level below that which is normally found in air; also called *reduced oxygen packed bulk food*.

Requisition A form listing the items and quantities needed from the storeroom.

Return on investment (ROI) Profit resulting from specific investments made in an operation.

Sales The dollar amount the establishment has taken in for food and beverages.

Sales forecast The process of using historical information and knowledge of external factors to predict future sales.

Sales mix The percentage of sales volume each menu item contributes to total sales.

Sales per labor hour A number calculated by adding all the sales for a specific period (hour, day, week, etc.) and then dividing the total by the total number of labor hours used during the same time period.

Sales representative A supplier's salesperson who would be assigned to an operation.

Semivariable cost A cost that increases and decreases as sales increase and decrease, but not in direct proportion.

Service charge A labor-related fee, added by the manager, to be paid by guests.

Short-term budget A budget planned for a week, a month, or a quarter.

Short weight The amount a shipment actually weighs subtracted from the weight given on its label.

Shrinkage Decrease in the weight of purchased meat because of cooking or trimming.

Simple markup method A markup method based on expenses being increased by a predetermined amount, normally a percentage of the previous year's expense.

Slack-out seafood A type of fraud in which frozen seafood is thawed to appear fresh.

Specification A description of the desired product's name, intended use, grade, size, and other product characteristics; it can include general instructions regarding delivery, payment procedures, and other pertinent data.

Speed scratch Premade products that are nearly complete but lack finishing touches such as sauces and flavoring.

Standardized recipe A formalized, consistent guide to preparing menu items, which lists the ingredients and quantities needed for a menu item, the methods used to produce it, and its appropriate portion size.

Standardized recipe form A set of directions for preparing a food or beverage item, along with a list of ingredients.

Standard man-hours (SMH) The number of employee work hours necessary in each job category to perform a given volume of forecasted production.

Standard portion cost The exact amount that one serving or portion of a food item should cost when prepared according to the item's standardized recipe.

Standing order The replenishment of stock by a vendor made on a regular basis.

Stores Items that are considered part of the inventory until issued for use in an establishment and are not included in food cost until they are issued.

Suggestive selling Value-added suggestions from servers to increase the number or type of items customers purchase, often called *up-selling* or *add-on selling*.

Supplier A company that provides products purchased for use in restaurant and foodservice operations, also called a *vendor*.

Table management A process of managing customer preferences, seating capacity, and available staff.

Tare The difference between gross and net weight (e.g., the weight of the plate that the food is served on).

Taste test Tasting done by staff prior to the start of a meal period to determine if products meet the establishment's standards.

Temperature danger zone Food kept out at a temperature of 41°F to 135°F (5°C to 57°C) for a total of more than four hours is unsafe and must be discarded.

Time and temperature control Policies and procedures that monitor the amount of time and the ongoing temperature of food products in the flow of food.

Transfer A form used to track items going from one foodservice unit to another.

Undercharging The act of charging less than the amount that should have been charged and collected.

Uniform Commercial Code (UCC) Sets of guidelines established to harmonize business transactions law across states.

Utilization factor The percentage of an amount of a food item served to a guest.

Value perception A customer's opinion of a product's value to him or her.

Variable cost A cost that increases and decreases in direct proportion to sales.

Variance The difference between actual results (i.e., sales) and targeted or budgeted results.

Waste report A report that lists any item that had to be discarded and the reason why.

Yield test A test used to measure the amount of shrinkage that occurs during trimming and cutting products that are not cooked, such as produce.

INDEX

NOTES